JOSEPH LILLIS

(in association with JOAN SPIRO) presents

CHRISTY

book & lyrics by
BERNIE SPIRO

music by
LAWRENCE J. BLANK

a darlin' musical about a daring deed
based on John M. Synge's
PLAYBOY OF THE WESTERN WORLD

designed and directed by
PETER DAVID HETH

musical direction, vocal
arrangements and incidental music by
ROBERT BILLIG

BERT WHEELER THEATRE · 250 WEST 43RD STREET

DREAM ABOUT TOMORROW

Words by
BERNARD SPIRO

Music by
ESTHER STOLL

Slowly, with expression

DREAM A — BOUT TO — MOR — ROW IN ALL YOUR

DREAMS TO — DAY THERE'S A STAR JUST BE — YOND YOUR

DOOR — WAY THERE'S A WORLD FULL OF JOY THAT'S

HEAD — ING YOUR WAY DREAM A — BOUT TO — MOR — ROW

AND FATE WILL FOL — LOW THROUGH NO MAT — TER

FROM WHERE — BUT SOME — DAY SOME — WHERE YOU'LL SEE YOUR

DREAMS COME — TRUE. TRUE —

INTERLUDE

YOU'LL SEE YOUR DREAMS COME TRUE — YOU'LL FIND TH

Title song from our first show; music by Esther Stoller

OF RHYME AND REASON

My Lyrics and Other Loves

Bernard Spiro

Strawberry Hill Press

Strawberry Hill Press
Copyright © 1990 by Bernard Spiro
Strawberry Hill Press
2594 15th Avenue
San Francisco, California 94127

Proofread by Nancy F. Johnson

Cover art and design by Ku, Fu-sheng

Back cover photo courtesy of Morton Silk

Typeset and designed by Cragmont Publications, Oakland, California

Printed by Edwards Brothers, Inc., Lillington, North Carolina

Manufactured in the United States of America

Library of Congress Cataloging-in-Publication Data

Spiro, Bernard.
    Of rhyme and reason : my lyrics and other loves / by Bernard Spiro.
        p.   cm.
    Includes bibliographical references.
    ISBN 0-89407-103-3 : $9.95
    1. Spiro, Bernard. 2. Lyricists—United States—Biography.
I. Spiro, Bernard. Lyrics. Selections. II. Title.
ML 423.S755A3   1990
782.42164'092—dc20   90-36234
[B]   CIP
                                          MN

To Joan,

always in my heart.
I can be honest with you now.

Table of Contents

Mom and Dad at Rockaway Beach,
early '60's

Granddaughter Dana's 13th—1988

Joan, Teri, Bernie, and Jeri—1966

The last photo of Joan and me

INTRODUCTION

LYRICS CAN BE HARD TO READ when you're not familiar with the accompanying melody or rhythm. And since most of this book is to be a retrospective of lyrics I've written over the last forty-plus years, you may find it rough going if you're not a devotee of the musical theatre and the creative process as I am. I've therefore concluded I should be offering you something more than just the retrospective, in order to hold your attention beyond the lyrics in case they get too tiresome for you. My name is not exactly a household word in the lyric-writing world, not on a level with—naming a half-dozen of my own favorites for example—Oscar Hammerstein, Stephen Sondheim, Alan Jay Lerner, Yip Harburg, Johnny Mercer and Carolyn Leigh. I have imagined my readers wondering: "Who is this Bernard Spiro anyhow, and what has he written to deserve a retrospective?" Hence, on these pages, in addition to samples of almost fifty years of my rhyming of words and expressing ideas in song, you'll find some of the rhyme and reason of me as well. And as we proceed I hope that a fair share of the fun and excitement and blood, sweat, and tears of creating for the medium of the musical theatre will rub off on my readers, too.

My literary agent, Bertha Klausner, who, because I have never written a book before and who has till now represented me only on my theatrical endeavors since 1975, insists that books by lesser-known authors in this day and age don't have a chance of selling unless they're full of sex or violence. I can't promise much violence, unless I digress into momentary reflections on angry disagreements with collaborators or directors over the years which could have led to murder under less controlled conditions. But I'll include some observations and revelations on sexuality at various times within my rambling—so if that's your bag, hang in there.

When we've added it all up and we get to the end, what I hope we'll have is a representative selection of work by a lesser-known lyricist and some thoughts about being only an "also-ran" so far. What's wrong with that, anyway? The world is full of also-rans in every field, and some of us are perfectly respectable. I know I am. We can't all finish first. I also know we don't stand a chance of finishing first unless we've started climbing the ladder somewhere along the line and kept persevering. And so, regardless of my rating at this moment, I'm banking on my work and me being interesting enough as is to justify this book being published. And what I hope the end result will be is something to entertain as well as explain, and take its modest place among books about people involved in a creative process.

Why do I start with this (for me) new writing form at the age of sixty-five? First of all, I've been retired from my ad agency job now for over four years, so ostensibly I have lots of time on my hands for the first time in my life. The job, incidentally, is what paid the bills while I dabbled in theatre arts on an avocational level—dabbling for the last thirty-eight years which brought surprisingly formidable results: Five of the shows were produced!

DREAM ABOUT TOMORROW: Off Broadway—(1952)—lyricist
JOHNNY BELINDA: Canada—(1968)—contributor to book and lyrics
BORDELLO: London—(1974)—co-lyricist
CHRISTY: Off Broadway—(1975)—bookwriter and lyricist
THE SHOP ON MAIN STREET: Off Broadway—(1985)—bookwriter and lyricist.

There are also some thirty others in various stages of completion—not yet produced.

I'm supposed to have more time on my hands now that I'm retired. But there simply aren't enough hours in the day for all I have and want to do. Yet because I'd been feeling guilty about not writing anything at all in recent months, I have come up with the idea of doing this retrospective, and now that I've started expanding on it, I'm certain it's precisely the right project for me to be pursuing at this particular time of my life and career.

Evidently the spirit wasn't moving me to begin libretto and lyrics for another new musical. That's partly because for the last ten years or so it has been virtually impossible for anyone to get any new show financed and produced, even something wonderful, unless it comes from London or unless the author has a very big name. I do have an ambitious new one being circulated, but so far none of the important producers want to know from it or me. And even if I did have a better track record, how many new musicals have you heard of getting produced recently that were written by Jerry Herman, Jule Styne, Comden & Green, Sheldon Harnick, or Ebb & Kander, Martin Charnin, Charles Strouse or Cy Coleman?

So-o-o, while still showing around that one big completed project, which looks doubtful because of the economic climate in today's theatre but which I certainly haven't given up on, I have resorted to this review of my work to date, trusting that it will appease my creative juices for a while. Thus far it's doing just that, and is proving to be great fun, too, kind of like taking inventory, while riding out the famine in the veritable desert the musical theatre has become. It's also giving me a chance to renew old friendships with the projects the lyrics were written for, and to make more objective observations about them and the other people involved; and most important of all, it is permitting me the chance to cast off some ghosts and shadows that have been haunting me far too long.

Ghosts and shadows? I return to the question "Why suddenly a book at the age of sixty-five?" Actually, I've been experiencing a new phase in my life in other respects as well, so why not a new style in creativity, too? Just over four years ago I started thinking a good deal more about my mortality, since my wife's untimely death after her second bout with open heart surgery. When you spend six months going through the belongings of a partner of almost thirty-six years—papers, clothing, photos, jewelry, makeup, trinkets, mementos, everything—even if your own health is generally good (as mine is), you damn well better start thinking of your own mortality too, because the scenario has already been spelled out for you as to how someone may have to be doing the very same with the accumulation of your own belongings any one of these fine days.

Thus, in natural succession, when I was through with Joan's things, I started rummaging through my own. I began with—and stopped after—reviewing the accumulation of my writing over the years. My work had been sporadic, but the sheer volume of paper was enormous, for it was about fifty years' worth and I'd seldom deliberately thrown anything away. Sure, there's a record of my having been lyricist or lyricist/bookwriter over the years for the five musicals which played before live audiences either in New York, Canada, or London. Sure, the scripts of these shows are in binders that I'd be leaving behind when I die. And leaving behind several scores on professional LP records, and good demo tapes on several of the unproduced shows. Shouldn't that be enough immortality for me? Why not ditch all the rest?

All of the above projects do not come close to comprising the sum total of my work. What about the completed work that never did make it to live production or record or tape? What about all the work I myself rejected, some of which may have been better than what I settled for in the end? What about the warm-ups? Or the aborted ideas, or the projects explored ever-so-slightly then abandoned? Shouldn't I dump it all now? Or should I leave it for my two daughters to try to make heads or tails of after I'm gone? No, that would be selfish of me, for it would be so time-consuming for them, and to what end? What would they have to show for it after so arduous a job? God, there was a ton of paper! Some of the work perfectly awful. I should at least spare both the kids and my reputation the bad stuff. But then, some of it I'd forgotten about was promising enough, and some even pretty good. Yet with no one except my wife had I ever shared many of these lyrics and ideas. Throw them all away now indiscriminately? What else could be done with a mixed bag of chicken scratchings the likes of these?

Flash! Brilliant idea! How about publishing a collection of my lyrics? That'll preserve a large enough body of my work for posterity. And I'd have the opportunity of making the selections myself, retaining the best and discarding the garbage.

I casually ran the thought by dear agent Bertha Klausner, who'd never before pictured me as the author of a book. Predictably she responded, "No sex or violence? It'll never sell. Of course you'd have a better chance if your name were Oscar Hammerstein." For a few months I privately explored the idea, not of changing my name to Oscar Hammerstein, but of uniting the unlikely elements of lyric writing with sex or violence. What did one have to do with the other? I couldn't imagine anything lurid accompanying moon and June. Then came the inspiration for a possible circuitous route for me to take, and so I shrugged my shoulders and jumped into the water as I concluded to myself: "What the hell! Let this also be my 'coming out of the closet' book. That's how to make it sexy." And that's how the content and format for this book were determined.

"Coming out of the closet? You?"

"That's right. You read it right the first time." "Please, no! Not another story about a repressed gay!"

"Why not? Has there been one before with lyrics interspersed?"

"Well, no. But will it sell?"

"You never know until you try."

"OK. You win."

So here we are—trying.

Although this book with every good reason is dedicated to my late wife, Joan, there are two other people largely responsible for its existence. First is my kind, wise, gentle and witty friend Bill Narducci, a new friend since my "coming out," who happens to be blind and who also happens to be a playwright. I regard Bill, who was a performer in the theatre years ago, as the unknowing, inadvertent inspiration for this book. Inasmuch as he writes prolifically and is an extremely clever talent, it seems unjust to me that he has not yet met with much success professionally. But, taking his own disappointing career in stride, he has nevertheless been very supportive of others in the creative and performing arts—and by virtue of his sheer admiration for the success I have had with my work and my track record in getting produced, he has helped me to further appreciate my modest degree of achievement as a writer, refusing to accept my usual putting down of this career of mine to date as little more than an avocational lark. Through Bill I have discovered new pride in my own accomplishments in the musical theatre, enough pride to dare to now attempt a book on the subject. Well, good luck to you, too, Bill. I look forward to seeing your name in bigger print one day soon, and I hope to continue in every way possible to help you in your quest for professional recognition.

Secondly, a brief introduction to of all people, my father!—and to that part of my writing background that goes way, way back, over fifty years ago. It was then that the craft of rhyming to music first became a factor in my life. I have little in my conscious memory to thank my father for, except for my very life itself, and sustenance, and love. But oddly enough, never was there sufficient communication or real support from him—certainly not in the same sense in which we think of these elements of nourishment for children today. Dad was one of that generation of losers who, from a poor immigrant family of British Jews, had little self-image, no education, and no particular drive that I can recall. And no particular talents or skills, except one. Crude as it was, he wrote poetry. He wrote it to help celebrate people's birthdays and other special occasions. He wrote it to help entertain at the Fourth of July, and Labor Day end-of-summer, parties at the Rockaway Beach bungalow colony where our family had become summer fixtures. And since I had already started to write poetry in school by the age of ten, it was easy for me to imitate Dad when he invited help with his "Shweet Violets" verses from about my Bar Mitzvah age on—at which point I was finally old enough to dabble in those slightly risque rhymes without being thought of as a juvenile delinquent.

Dad's one creative talent must have impressed me enough to have stuck with me. I forgive him for never, to my recollection, having specifically told me he liked any creative work I did later on. I forgive him because I think he simply didn't know how to communicate approval. It must have embarrassed him, though it probably would have helped me immeasurably to achieve maturity and some sign of self-confidence much earlier on if only he had expressed his approval and confidence in me somewhere along the line. It was sad that he couldn't. But in retrospect, am I ever grateful to him nevertheless! His rhymes seldom rose much above the bathroom or sewer level, but they made his audiences laugh, and at that time that was good enough for me. In case my readers aren't familiar with the verses previously alluded to, my early training in lyric writing was little more than another type of toilet training. For instance:

My sister, she died in the bathtub.
She died of a terrible fit.
The drain from the toilet exploded,
And drowned her in six feet of . . .

Shweet Violets,
Sweeter than the roses,
Covered all over from head to toe,
Covered all over with Shhnow

Dear Dad:
Thanks. With these humble beginnings you helped start me on the writing career which is and has been one of the great pleasures of my life.

Your loving son,
Bernard

ONE

First things first—opening the closet door.
"Of rhyme and reason; of reason and rhyme."

I THINK THAT ALL BUT THE MOST HOMOPHOBIC OF US are willing to concede that everyone in the world is partly hetero- and partly homosexual. As I see it, it's the degree to which one is either or both that makes the difference in how one is labeled or viewed or how one feels about him or herself. Granting this certain basic similarity in all of us, it both appalls and amazes me that there is still so much prejudice against homosexuals that many are driven to remaining closeted until their dying day.

I've done very little reading about homosexuality, because till my wife died I dared not even keep books around lest they be discovered and I be confronted and questioned about my more than passing interest in the subject. But I always knew that I had strong homosexual tendencies, dating back to an age when I now hear it was normal to have them. Not understanding or knowing then that it was normal, I couldn't take the chance of even completely acknowledging my feelings. So I refrained from appearing too inquisitive; I denied, repressed, refuted and deluded myself into thinking my secret yearning was a minor quirk in my nature and I could keep it under control. They say most boys outgrow these urges and fantasies, and somehow I did manage to close the lid tightly on them through three years in the army in World War II in which I looked the other way whenever possible, even losing my heterosexual virginity to a female prostitute in India when I was nineteen because it was the thing all *male* young men were supposed to do, and I remained homosexual only in secret longings. But the forbidden lust surfaced again when I returned to college after the war was over and I found myself too admiring of several of my fraternity brothers and guys in the gym. If there appears to be an inconsistency in my attitude and behavior ("straight" while in the service but arousable by men again upon returning to school) one reason is that I was too scared to acknowledge the temptation in the army. Another is that the nice young Jewish men I was most attracted to were hardly visible in the army and overseas, while once back in the less worldly confines of Brooklyn College I saw them everywhere. I could no longer totally ignore the lust. I haven't been in touch with most of my frat brothers for well over forty years, but to this day the burning image of one of them occasionally comes back to haunt me. If it is possible to love someone intensely without ever in one's life telling him or touching him, I was in love then and I have loved him ever since, yet I have had no communication with him since 1947, and even then it was impersonal, and to this day I don't even know if he's still alive.

But there were others, too. I always had eyes for men. But only eyes. It was never verbalized, except to a psychologist I went to see for "help" during my last term in college. More about him later.

I figure so much is already published that I can't imagine *I'll* be saying anything new or revolutionary in my disclosure of my homosexuality and my coming out in print. Just as homosexuality dates as far back as mankind does, so, I presume, does coming out. For me at this time it seems to be a natural process and consequence.

Now that I'm doing it in print I can only tell you how things were for me before and how they are now. Whether I fit into one category of late bloomers or another doesn't matter at all. What does matter is that I want and need to talk about this now because it is providing a catharsis for me that is mind-blowing. Three-and-a-half years ago at the age of sixty-one-and-a-half I started experiencing a rebirth, feeling more like sixteen than sixty-one, and my true sexuality, deeply, deeply repressed all those years, became more and more intense every day at a time when in many men my age it would not uncommonly be waning.

Since I considered my father a "loser," it was hard for me to not think of myself that way as well. As was the career in which I worked for a living—as an ad agency production manager—a substitute for my real love, writing, my *chosen* sexuality was a substitute, too. I had loved my wife dearly, all the while also longing secretly for physical love with men. I performed well enough with Joan sexually, and she, the self-denying martyr she was, always allowed me to feel I was all macho man, and led me to believe she thrived on my physical prowess. Because of her reticence in verbalizing about sex, I did my thing and assumed that I was satisfying both of us. Odd that I should just recently have seen a made-for-cable British TV movie about AIDS, with Claire Bloom and Daniel Massey, called *Intimate Contact*, which gave me a new clue toward summing up my sexuality with my wife. A doctor in the movie, in explaining about one man's preference for another man as a sex partner, likened all men to animals with a certain physical sexual need. And when a partner of the opposite sex is unavailable, said he, a partner of the same sex will often do just as well. In my case I think the same was true, if you work it in reverse. To me *men* were unavailable, because I didn't go after them and they didn't go after me. For me, being actively homosexual early on would have been unthinkable and unspeakable. While I was growing up, and all the time I was conscious of being attracted to men, I simply could not face the attraction and do something about it with another guy, except once in an experimental touching session with a neighbor friend when we were about seventeen. At that time the thought or contemplation of it as an ongoing activity was evidently as abnormal to me as it was to society; and at various other times I was bamboozled enough by whatever segment of society I was exposed to at the moment to find myself rejecting the idea of it as queer, dirty, unnatural, and always very, very unspeakable. I had no one with whom I could share what was deep within my heart. I lived in morbid silence about it till seven months after my wife died, when suddenly the dam burst. So, in all the time prior to that, I permitted myself to enjoy a substitute as much as possible, which was the only sexuality I dared to be open about—in marriage. Loving my wife as a person as I did made the cover-up somewhat easier to carry off. For me there had been no alternative other than the straight and accepted way for a nice Jewish young man to behave in those days, and so in my case I was the animal who used the *available* partner and deluded myself into thinking that that's all there is.

As I heard about and could see new sexual mores developing around me in the 60's and 70's, it became obvious to me that I had been born a generation too early. Oh, would I have loved to have been one of the fearless newly outspoken minority of "gays" vocal enough to be standing up to discrimination by the world, proud of what and who they were! *I* had *had* to get married! Didn't all nice Jewish young men from good families have to get married? Didn't they *have* to date girls, to plant an awkward kiss as soon as possible, and cop a feel of the girl's breast if they dared and when permitted, and get laid—God, get laid!—if you were ever, ever lucky enough to hit bingo? And didn't they then have to have babies (never mind about readiness for the responsibility) like their fathers before them?

In the 60's and 70's, as I was drawn into acknowledging and occasionally guardedly discussing the gayness of a few theatre people my wife and I had met and several of my younger daughter's friends, I longed to be part of their scene. Till then what I hadn't seen or didn't know didn't hurt me. Now it was starting to hurt a lot, because I was facing the seductive situation of seeing *them* freely being themselves, while *I* still had to be completely secretive. I *had* to remain the duty-bound husband and father (even becoming a grandfather in 1975), thoroughly faithful from about this point on (except in my mind), even though I'd had a few brief and sleazy homosexual encounters up till then along the way, now as straight as an arrow, living in my own very private hell with my constant lie of omission to my wife, to the world at large, and oftentimes to myself as well. Not exactly a healthy atmosphere! Imagine the volcano of unexpressed emotion that was soon to erupt!

My wife's untimely passing in September, 1985, which I was not at all prepared for, and which to this day I still often cry about, nevertheless finally enabled me after a reasonable period of mourning to face my sexuality with new-found courage, without guilt. I hadn't consciously been planning to start exploring that hardly-ever-surfaced side of me, but it happened as if I had been born into it, as if my hand were slipping into a perfectly fitting glove.

I'd put on a lot of weight during the first seven months after Joan's death, during which time I'd obviously been doing more than my share of grieving, isolating and compulsive overeating to soothe the hurt. Once I started seeking help with my food problem, I simultaneously learned about a Gay Men's Group of O.A. (Overeaters Anonymous), and the idea intrigued me sufficiently for me to look into it promptly, thus aligning myself for the first time ever with a formally, openly gay-oriented activity. From this point on I started discreetly experimenting sexually, now as never before, without being concerned about cheating on Joan or somehow being discovered. I almost stopped caring about being discovered. I no longer needed to look both ways and in front of and behind me to see who might be watching as I stepped inside the Gay and Lesbian Community Center on West 13th Street, New York City. I felt instantly relieved from the fear of being found out, a fear I had grappled helplessly with during the years in which I occasionally furtively entered a gay porn movie house on my lunch hour for an hour's worth of surrender to my fantasies. I was soon being warmly accepted by new gay friends, as warmly as I accepted them. I started to participate in activities of two quite legitimate gay organizations that I'd never even known existed—SAGE (Senior Action in a Gay Environment) and Identity House (where I availed myself of some short-term counseling which the counselor and I both soon agreed I probably didn't need), as well as the aforementioned Gay Men's Group of O.A. I also visited meetings on a trial basis of several other gay groups which met at the Center which I thought I might find common ground with—Gay Fathers Forum, Gay Veterans, and the Gay Advertising Club. Here was a perfectly acceptable society I'd known nothing about, about which I was ravenously curious and with which I was immediately comfortable. I was feeling free and more relieved with each passing day and with every new meeting I attended. *I belonged.* Sexuality aside, the people were from all walks of life, from all backgrounds, and were for me a source of constant reaffirmation of my extreme pleasure in becoming one of them.

Yes, there were many other gay fathers, and many other gay professionals. Psychologists, psychiatrists, lawyers, artists, sculptors, chiropractors, Broadway producers, actors, teachers, principals, songwriters, musicians, playwrights, accountants, travel agents, computer experts, programmers, waiters, chefs, banquet managers, airline personnel, medics, nurses, salesmen—and at the risk of sounding prejudiced myself (and I mean this with good humor only and a passing wish that such stereotypes didn't exist)—there were of course hairdressers and decorators and designers, too. In this day and age they who still look quizzically at the gay scene, who still mock and jeer and hate, are more to be scorned themselves, for it is they, not we, who are committing a sin. We are simply following our hearts. They are practitioners of intolerance and hate. In no way except to choose to sleep and have intimacies with someone of the same sex have I become different now from the person I was before. In no way have others with backgrounds similar to mine changed any more than I have. I'm still the same father to my children, son to my mother, grieving husband to my beloved late wife (my love for her certainly hasn't lessened and never will). And I'm still the same friend to friends, cousin to cousins, and so forth. Fact of the matter is, I suspect I'm a lot better man now than when I was living the lie. I'm a lot less angry, a lot less volatile. No longer a constant nail biter. I'm a good deal warmer and more concerned with the welfare of others. As I now see it, Shakespeare can indeed once more be quoted with veracity: "To thine own self be true and . . . thou canst not then be false to any man."

Actually, as of just prior to writing this book, I still feel guilty about *continuing* to be false in one respect. Too many people from my former (married) background don't yet know about my new life-style and orientation, among them neighbors of almost 20 years, cousins, my mother, my sister-in-law and her family, the families of my sons-in-law, former bosses and business associates, all but one of my writing collaborators, and other associates in theatre projects and their families. In other words almost everyone from my former life still doesn't know. Well, they're sure gonna know soon enough now, aren't they? And with the coming out I've done till now feeling so very good and right and necessary and overdue, I can hardly wait to finally do it all the way.

Early on in my relatively short time so far as a gay man, I did come out to the two people in the world who were dearest to me, my daughters, and their kind and understanding husbands. In all modesty I must say it took courage. But down deep I knew in advance they would all be both accepting and understanding. I've always prided myself on the liberal bent of my political and social thinking, and I expected that some of that bent had rubbed off on my daughters, and I risked assuming that their spouses would be supportive, too. They were wonderful about it; incredulous, but wonderful! Teri, the older and more reserved of the two young women, found it harder to believe. She had not been exposed previously to as much of the gay "mystique" as younger Jeri had. But by and large I think they appreciated my honesty and were perhaps a little relieved that Daddy was at least not likely to be finding himself a new bride presently to replace their mother, one they'd probably have to publicly tolerate while privately resenting.

I had needed to tell them . . . to let them know that while I would always love Joan, I was no longer alone. I introduced them to Lonnie, the man with whom I'd entered into a tentative relationship. I wanted to reassure them that they needn't worry about my loneliness. Lord knows I'm occasionally still lonely in spite of that new relationship and other romantic liaisons I've had since I started opening the closet door. One cannot dismiss a 36-year marriage so easily. But life is simply no longer as dismal and bleak as it was during the first seven months I was alone. I needed to tell the kids in order to provide a connection between my present life and *someone* important from the past. Their knowing has enabled me to stay connected with the person I was in spite of having broken with a large part of the past and so many old faces in it.

My daughters and I agreed there was no need to tell my mother or granddaughter at that point. And so it has been. Till now.Beyond my agent, Bertha, and the several friends who know, and without going into minute detail over and over again with the hundreds of people in my acquaintance who haven't yet heard about the real me, I still feel so committed to the cause of taking pride and rejoicing in who and what I am, that I now indeed look forward to the day when I can say: "Read all about it. It's in my new book." In that way I'll be leaving behind the shadows and shackles of convention for whatever time I have left, and leaning back, taking a deep breath with a carefree smile on my face, and openly and optimistically facing the future and whatever it has to offer.

But now that I'm "coming out" in print, how do I deal with several important people from my old life whom I've always believed to be out-and-out and tried and true homophobics? One is Mama. She's 87 now, and at that age perhaps should be kept in the dark, just to make sure she doesn't get too upset and suffer a few extra heart palpitations. If I don't tell her maybe nobody else will either, and so maybe she won't ever know. But I can't really bank on that. So I've concluded that if she learns about it, so be it. I'm not going to stifle this book just to keep the news from Mom. At 65 I really shouldn't have to be troubled by what an 87-year-old woman would think of me anyhow, should I? At any rate if at 87 she's not easier to keep in the dark, perhaps we'll find out that for all we know she's easier to explore the light with than we expected—if I so choose. We'll see. Actually she may at one time have suspected that I was not "male" enough in my interests (another misguided premise!)—way, way back. After all, wasn't Mom likely the engineer behind that one very awkward attempt by my father to spend more time with me when I was about ten, by taking me out to an empty lot one Sunday morning and thereupon trying to teach me how to swing a bat at a ball? (To this day I still haven't bothered to master the skill.) Didn't they probably privately agree between the two of them that I wasn't masculine enough way back then?

And incidentally, if you are wondering what in hell would make an 87-year-old woman homophobic, and how do I know she is, good question! And the answer is simple.

She was a young married woman during the Depression years, and all through my childhood she had to go to work. For over thirty years she worked in a leading department store, and evidently came into contact with many effeminate young men on the store's staff. When she first started leering and jeering at them she was probably only taking a cue from some of the other homophobic "straight" people with whom they all worked. But leer and jeer she did. And so my father and I were frequent recipients of Mom's diatribes about the "fairy nice boys" she came into contact with. How often, unknowingly, she made *me* feel like shit! Though, on second thought, so many years have passed since then that perhaps I should give her the benefit of the doubt and conclude that maybe she wasn't truly homophobic after all—just misinformed.

The only other person I really care about confronting is cousin Ben, because he and his wife and Joan and I were so close and they mean so much to me still, and he is so intolerant. Well, let's put it this way . . . it's going to be *his* problem, isn't it? Maybe he'll find it in his heart to be a little softer in his judgment if he thinks back to that evening over three years ago when they visited me and he sat here and (I think) coincidentally and unwittingly roared through his tirade against the practice of homosexuality and all those who engage in it. I had to face him, here in my own home, and quietly take that crap from him while inwardly burning with anger at his intolerance and hate.

Tell me, Ben, is there the slightest chance you could be as disgusted with homos as you say you are because you're afraid to recognize and acknowledge that there may be a trace of it in you, too? Now, now . . . don't protest too loudly. You know what it means if you do that, don't you? We do have to be so-o-o careful about protecting that macho image, don't we? God forbid our vulnerability should be uncovered in front of all the world! Sorry to be airing our dirty laundry in public, friend and cousin, but as I said before, I remain firmly convinced that every hetero has at least the slightest bit of homo inside him, and so I'm finding some long overdue relief in challenging you on this issue in public because you have been so obnoxiously narrow-minded in private discussions about it. Nobody in the world can be all that straight! To wrap it up, really, Ben, there is nothing at all disgusting about giving affection to and receiving affection from another human being. The only real tragedy occurs when one is prevented from giving and receiving it by social pressures. I want desperately to advise: "Try it; maybe you'll like it." But that would be proselytizing, wouldn't it?

To answer the question of several of the straight people I've been close to who can't understand the attraction two men or women can have for each other . . . try to look at it this way: A) It's a very *personal* choice. B) We're a minority, but not *that* small a minority, and now (thank the Lord) no longer very silent, so you may now have to allow that there's something to gayness even though you can't imagine yourself in our shoes. (Or our beds.) C) We really can't help it. This is the way we are, and very likely the way we were born. Aren't we as entitled as everyone else to be what we are and not be ashamed of it? How awful it was for us that as children most of us were not even aware that such a choice existed!

It's funny, I could never understand why so many unenlightened and untraveled Americans to whom I've spoken about France seem to have very negative feelings about visiting there (more so than any other European country, I think) and are very suspicious of the French people. Evidently the untraveled American has heard mostly unfavorable comments about this foreign country with which he himself has no personal experience, so he trusts only what he's heard. What he doesn't know and evidently couldn't care less about is that Bernie Spiro and many other people Bernie knows have been to France and like it a whole lot. As with being gay, it's a personal choice and personal taste; and it's hard to accept that it's perfectly all right for some people who haven't been there to be making a judgment.

Earlier I mentioned that I'd seen a psychologist while in college. He tried to help me become "straight." According to him, my homosexual longings were due to my being a product of a domineering mother and a passive father, a reason that was fashionable then but is today, to my knowledge, no longer popularly supported. The psychologist and I tried to work hard on "curing" me. I permitted him to delude me and I deluded myself, presumably because of my intense desire to lose the "curse."

Soon after the six months with the shrink I proposed to Joan, whom I had known and dated on and off for two years. Nine months later we married. Ten months later—presto—a baby. But even while Joan was pregnant I found myself one morning on the way to work experiencing an unexpected exciting mutual rub job with a handsome Asian stranger on a very crowded subway car. And by a year or so later I was having constant enough feelings for men again (if indeed they ever left me), to act them out by buying a magazine now and then and bringing it into the office and keeping it well hidden but easily accessible for those occasional opportunities at a private few moments with them, a behavioral pattern I'd developed into an art form by now. Two years or so after that I had my first tantalizing out-and-out brief homosexual encounter after a pick-up in a movie house. And some 37 years later, baby, look at me now. Some cure! All the fighting it and denial of it in the world couldn't help and didn't help, although apparently I was a very good actor, developing whatever style and attitude I needed to pass as a straight family man for 36 years. To quote theatrical friend Joseph Lillis to whom I have come out, "Anybody, *any*body in the world, Bernie, but not *you*." I concealed it that well. But at last I am now very much what I truly think I should always have been.

Among the little reading I've done on homosexuality so far is a short book by Merle Miller called *On Being Different . . . What It Means To Be A Homosexual*. It was published 20 years ago, at about the time coming out first became fashionable (if it ever was.) In it Merle quotes a letter he received after the publishing of his coming out article in *The New York Times Magazine* in 1970. Part of that letter says: "Though, like you, Mr. Miller, I have found an adjustment to homosexuality, it is curious to speculate how much more might have been accomplished had the time spent on needless guilt and evasiveness been put to the service of self-fulfillment. The waste is one which is felt not only by myself . . . but by nearly every other homosexual, male or female, I have ever known."

From my own experience I add to the quoted "time spent in guilt and evasiveness" the pitiable waste in self-destructiveness I have permitted to pervade my life in years gone by, the fear and indecisiveness, the anger and torment, all of which perhaps worked in tandem toward preventing me from *truly* fulfilling myself professionally. Because I was afraid to make a choice other than the straight and narrow, I was limiting myself by recognizing only part of myself professionally. I was also, probably without knowing it, limiting myself in every other aspect of my life, too. To get to the crux of it, my failure to acknowledge the *real* me as a person evidently played its part in limiting me to becoming little more than the avocational lyricist and playwright I alluded to in the Introduction. This should be all the *reason* necessary for my *Of Rhyme and Reason* title.

Perhaps the future will hold greater recognition for me as a writer now that I'm "out," retired from advertising, and devoting as much time as I wish to my writing career. Perhaps not. No matter. At least I'm still in there pitching and enjoying every minute of it, and knowing that is more than half the battle. And that being the case, I think we can now be getting on with the rhyme.

TWO

The war- and post-war years.
Laying the groundwork
(for an avocational career as a lyricist).

"Tears are only souvenirs of laughter.
So I don't mind my crying over you."

MY ONLY RECOLLECTION OF RHYME-WRITING from age thirteen to sixteen other than the "Shweet Violets" already recorded on these pages is of my having been poetry editor of the high school yearbook in my senior year. (I started college before I was 16, which probably contributed to screwing up my head psychologically more than I care to consciously remember.) I no longer possess a copy of the yearbook, but I recall that my work in it consisted of a couple of full-page poems, mostly devoted to predicting what professional futures my fellow graduates would be facing, and celebrating senior class celebrities' specialties, all in silly rhyming couplets.

My only other recollection of rhyme-writing between my "Shweet Violets" and pre-army years (caught in the draft from age 18 to 21) involves a research assignment I was given by my college fraternity elders while I was a pledgee. In order to more advantageously compete with past entries (every pledge period in previous years included one such assignment), I chose to carry out mine in verse. The subject of the research and report involved the sex life of a remote South American tribe known as the Kaingang Indians. I achieved instant frat fame at 17—just prior to my being drafted at 18—when I used not only the boring research material in the library, but my imagination as well, successfully titillating the fraterhood sufficiently for me to be acclaimed the brightest new face to appear at the fraternity portals in years. The following re-quoting of the first four lines of the verse is from memory, for again no written record exists. But though this is now about 48 years later, I think my recall is as accurate as if they'd been etched in stone, for I often heard them repeated with glee and admiration by the D.G.R. membership en masse after having recited them myself the first time around to a large group of the fraters:

> The Kaingang Indians, unlike others
> Have intercourse with their own mothers.
> They do this frequently it seems
> In order to prevent wet dreams.

In my almost three years in the army I continued to do little toward laying the groundwork for a future career as a lyricist, unless we to count the composition of verses for the greeting cards I sent my family from overseas and a pompous epic poem called "The Liberators" which I wrote just after I and a bunch of other misplaced "replacements" straight out of Camp Shenango, Pennsylvania landed in North Africa. It was so pretentious, so God-awful, that I couldn't bear to inflict it on you. To think that I ever used the English language so badly! And to think, too, that back in 1943 I had the audacity to submit it to *YANK* (U. S. Army publication) for consideration for publication. They had the good sense and taste to turn it down! But let's at least make the allowance for me that I was only nineteen then, very impressionable, and very impressed by North Africa's cliffs, the Mediterranean, and being on my own for the first time in my life.

The greeting card verses referred to above were something else again. During my more than two years overseas I composed and crudely designed greeting cards for Mom and Dad for each birthday, anniversary, Mother's Day, Father's Day, Valentine's Day, etc. Unbeknownst to me, Mom saved them all, and later put them into a scrapbook with other memorabilia. Some of the verses were "cute" enough, though innocuously so. Some were saccharine (in the Mrs. Miniver tradition—after all, this *was* wartime, and families *were* separated). All the cards to my mother confirmed my rather abnormal and excessive crush on her and the failure on both our parts to have ever severed the umbilical cord (though the latter did finally happen a few years later when I saw that psychologist I wrote about previously, the one who was going to "cure" me of my "abnormal" fantasies and longings.)

I now share a few samples with you of these greeting cards, and by so doing unabashedly exhibit the nineteen- and twenty-year-old me in uniform, separated from home turf and apron strings for the first time in my life by—of all things—war!

I've selected the first sample because it involves a vestige of a bygone era which I thought might prove to be historically interesting to the reader. The greeting was written to Mom on V-Mail stationery. V-Mail was used to keep down the size and weight of the mail and thus lessen the massive tonnage of correspondence shipped daily from U.S. servicemen overseas back to the folks at home. The original V-Mail correspondence the G.I.'s wrote was then further reduced in size and delivered to the addressee as a fuzzy photostat. The illustration reproduced herein is the actual size V-Mail reproduction as it was delivered to my Mom by her postman. I shall first give you a separate rundown of the words, written January 20, 1944, in preparation for Valentine's Day, in case these same words are not legible on the illustration itself after the latter has gone through its velox-then-offset printing process.

Dear Mother:
 I may look around a corner.
 I may peek in any place.
 But whatever things I gaze upon
 I only see your face.
 That orta prove I love you
 And I think you're mighty fine.
 And I want you always as my best
 And lovin' VALENTINE.
        Bernard

Sample number two, for Father's Day 1945, celebrated Dad's girth, love for the beach, obsession with the Brooklyn Dodgers, and favorite food: Kosher deli.

To The Belly-Belly Best Ole Man:
 If I were king or power
 Getting richer by the hour
 I would give you every luxury desired.
 If I had the dough to buy land

I would buy you Coney Island
Where you'd always have a seabreeze when retired.

If I had half the moola
Of an Emporer or ruler
I would buy you food enough to feed an army.
And I'd fill your every closet
With a lifetime-long deposit
Of your fav'rite dinner, hot dogs and salami.

If I were lord of vassals
With a large array of castles
I would give you palaces befitting rajahs.
We would there install 4 bases
And an outfield and such places
And I'd gift you with a license for the Dodgers.

But alassy and alacky,
I am just a lad in khaki
And I own no land or home or food nutritious.
So this day I send you merely
My devotion and sincerely
Wish you all the very happiest of wishes.
HAPPY FATHER'S DAY / Love, Bernard

And last of the greeting card verse samples reproduced here—celebrating Mom's
birthday in August '45 (the month the war was over) and her most instantly recogniz-
able physical feature:

"When your hair has turned to silver,"
Thus the old song did exclaim
In its tender words and music . . .
"I will love you just the same."

But the song was not for us, Mom,
For your hair has silv'ry been
For as long as I remember you—
The silver had set in.

So I'll make some adaptations
And I'll add a bit of rhyme
Just to make the song more apropos
For us this birthday time.

When your hair has turned to golden
I will holler, shout and screech—
"I don't want to have a mother
Who is just another bleach."

And when you've become brunette, Mom,
I won't love you as before
For to me your head of silver
Is my everything and more.

Now it's time to toast your birthday

And your health and wealth and cheer
And that head of silver satin
That I'll see again this year.

"Through a garden filled with roses
Down that sunset trail we'll stray."
If your hair is still as silver
"I will love you as today."
HAPPY BIRTHDAY
Love and kisses, / Bernard

The war *was* over in August, but I did not quite make it back home before the end of the year as expected. There was such a back-up of personnel waiting to return to U.S. shores that I wasn't discharged till January, 1946, spending Christmas and New Year's so bored on shipboard that I resorted to—what else?—doing a bit of writing for the ship's newspaper.

After my discharge came completion of college for almost two years, formative years which included playing catch-up and inundating myself with exposure to Broadway and off-Broadway shows, seeing most of them with frat brothers who were also passionate enough about the theatre to travel with me to Westport or wherever. (I had learned to drive while overseas and was now enjoying the first car my family ever owned.) Homosexually I was still virtually as pure as the driven snow, and so some of my dates for going to the theatre were also with young women on my occasional efforts to bolster my "straight" image, and indeed my heterosexual pursuits.

Along with attending lots of theatrical events came seduction into the world of show biz, and I related particularly to the lyric writing I was being exposed to because I had already developed that certain "feeling" for rhyme from earlier on. So I was alternately and sometimes simultaneously moved and impressed and attracted and enchanted and inspired by Hammerstein and *Oklahoma* (catching up first to that particular oldie because it had opened and achieved fame while I was in the army—first out of New York, then out of the country—for almost three years). The wooing and love affair continued with Hammerstein again with *Carousel* and then *Allegro*; with Alan Jay Lerner and *Brigadoon* and *Paint Your Wagon* and *Love Life*; with Irving Berlin and *Annie Get Your Gun* and later *Miss Liberty*; with Yip Harburg and *Finian's Rainbow*; with Harold Rome and *Call Me Mister*; with Cole Porter and *Kiss Me Kate*, and with Frank Loesser and *Where's Charley?*

They don't write 'em like that anymore in thirty years, let alone three!

Somewhere around this time I reached a point with my frat brother, long since deceased Harold Stern (with whom I'd seen many of these shows), at which we said: "That looks like fun; let's write a musical together," paraphrasing the joyous exclamation of so many of the Judy Garland/Mickey Rooney films of the time: "That looks easy; let's put on a show."

Hal and I were both veterans. *Call Me Mister* had made a lot of sense to us. And we were evidently intuitive enough to know then what my agent Bertha confirmed later, that sex and violence sell. So while still in college we came up with book and lyrics for the first honest-to-goodness musical I ever worked on, *Free and Easy*. It was a "simple" little affair consisting of a mere 23 scenes, 40 characters *plus* chorus, which told the story of a paroled prisoner, Sam Fizz (note the similarity to the discharged veteran idea), whose mother, Daphne, was a hooker and whose girl friend,

Jean, had been unfaithful while Sam was in the pen for five years. If the description of the cast sounds to you like either collaborator Hal or I was a misogynist, you're right. Hal was. He may also have been a closeted homosexual (as I was). In any case, neither of us found out about the other, though we spent many long hours together collaborating. Nor would I have been interested in him in that way, not when there were so many more attractive hunks hanging around the frat at the time for me to silently admire and fantasize about.

I feel I must set down for posterity at least a couple of lyrics from that masterpiece of ineptitude, if only for the sake of this book serving as a complete enough historical document representing the work of an also-ran lyricist. But I'll take pity and spare you second choruses. After you've had a glance at this first show you should be sufficiently convinced that it was so dismal that everything that follows later *has to be* a vast improvement.

From *Free and Easy* Act I Scene II.

SCENE: The office of I.N. Carcerate, warden of a well known American prison.
AT RISE: Carcerate is sitting at his desk. Two guards enter with prisoner Sam Fizz between them.

WARDEN

(Reading.) Fizz, Sam? Prison Serial Number 32897787. Convicted of larceny. Sentence five years. (Puts down paper.) Well, Sam, it says here your time is up today. Now, as you know, I take a personal interest in all my boys. Listen carefully to this sound advice. (Sings: "Sound Advice")

My advice to you, you may well take heed:
Don't engage in crime when you are freed.
Now that you have paid the debt you owed
Always take the straight and narrow road.
Be fair, be just, and always trust your mother, Sam.
Don't steal, don't cheat, and never beat your mother, Sam,
Cause your mother's always good to you.

GUARDS

We hope you've learned the lesson taught.
If you're gonna steal, then don't get caught.

WARDEN

No vice is nice and shooting dice is sordid, Sam.
Don't bet roulette. It never yet rewarded, Sam,
And a gambler's life will never do.

GUARDS

Deal from the bottom with a smile.
If you gamble make it worth your while.

SAM

It's great to be out and I'm bubbling with glee.
No orders have I to respond to.
It's hard to believe that I'm finally free.

At last I can do what I want to.
So I'm going home to Mother.

ALL
He's going home, he's going home,
Sam's going home to Mother.

Act I Scene VIII

SAM
Jean!

JEAN
When did you get out?

SAM
Just a short time ago.

JEAN
Five years is a long time, Sam.

SAM
You're telling me.

JEAN
Now that you're back, why don't we get together?

SAM
I don't know, Jean.

JEAN (Singing)
Don't think that I've forgotten
Those thrilling times we shared.
Don't think that I've forgotten our love.
I never could forget you.
I guess I always cared.
I never could forget you, my love.

Just for old times sake let me feel you close to me.
Just for old times sake let's relive the memory
That we knew.
Then should you see me get affectionate,
There is no need for your objection. It
Would only be because of old times sake.

Oh, it's been so long since I gazed into your eyes,
Yes, it's been so long that I hardly realize
I loved you.
Don't ever think it reprehensible
If I imply you're indispensable.
Remember that it's just for old times sake.

Incidentally, we must have known the show was bad, because we never bothered
to try to find a composer for it, and never showed it to a soul. And now that the above

has been entered onto these pages I shall for all time destroy the only remaining typewritten copy of *Free and Easy*.

Upon completion of my Bachelor's Degree at Brooklyn College in August '47, and with my new Junior High School English License in tow, I embarked upon my one-year career as a substitute teacher. I am presently assured by several dedicated teachers who stuck with it longer than I that many new teachers feel like failures early on, and that it simply takes time to become expert at the profession. But as was true with just about everything I was involved in then in my young lifetime, I felt like a failure and didn't give myself a chance to succeed.

Before quitting teaching in mid-'48, I had enrolled in New York University's School of Education for my Master's degree. I now continued in the latter pursuit full-time for a while, then got my first job in advertising with a Long Island newspaper, and in general had my most active year of growth in several different directions simultaneously, including enrolling in a course sponsored by the Advertising Club of New York consisting of a series of lectures. I was doing a good deal of dating of young women during this time, too, and never then realized that one of the reasons why I left teaching after the first year may very well have been the subconscious one of feeling threatened by the "unwanted" sexual excitement I experienced in dealing with the young men in my classes. They had just crossed over into adolescence, and I must have been dazzled by rippling young muscles everywhere. I remember holding one particularly attractive but unruly young male by the upper arms and trying to shake him up a bit on several occasions in an attempt to discipline him. I also vaguely suspect having been somewhat aroused by the physical contact. I think now that the excitement I was feeling then must have frightened the hell out of me, and so I took the easy way out and quit.

At about this time I also met a pleasant composer of music by the name of Ken Hersey with whom I've long since lost contact. His work may not have terribly impressed me, but I think his looks must have a great deal. He was a bit older, I think, and very attractive. He had been exposed to my work as a lyric writer via the "graduation" show I co-authored for the Advertising & Selling Course, which we called *Dearth of a Salesman*, and which consisted of a series of short sketches and applicable parodies to pop Broadway-show melodies of the time, in the fashion of what was beginning to become a big industry: the "Industrial Show." When Ken saw the graduation entertainment I had co-authored, he liked my lyrics well enough to ask me to dabble in pop song writing with him, and he also hoped I would help with some special material for a church function he was involved in.

Till recently I had no record of the lyrics of the *Dearth* frolic, but an acquaintance out of the long-ago past, a man by the name of Jules Elphant, coincidentally phoned me several months ago and saved the day just before this final draft by telling me he'd heard my name at a meeting of a Gay & Bisexual Men's Social Group called Prime Timers we both belong to, and he wondered if I were the same Bernie Spiro who wrote the A&S Course graduation show in 1949. He remembered it well because he'd performed in it. And bless his heart, he had a carbon copy of the script he could lend me for duplicating, yellow with age, it's true, but then, aren't we all?

Credit Irving Berlin for the music, please. Here's a sample of material from *Dearth of a Salesman*.

MARY

Is it true what they say?

JULES

What do they say?

(MUSIC: "They Say That Falling in Love Is Wonderful")

MARY

They say the A&S Course is wonderful
It's wonderful, so they say.

JULES

Each lecture gets to the source. It's wonderful,
It's wonderful, as they tell you.

Last week I heard a lecture
On selling architecture,
And now I'm shaking millionaires by the hand . . .
(Removes bandaged hand from pocket and displays it.)
And . . .
The things you learn at the course are wonderful,
Wonderful, in every way, I should say.

* * * * * * *

BABS (to HAL)

There's one thing *I've* sure learned from this A&S Course.

HAL

What's that?

BABS

I'll never be happy with a husband out of the profession.

HAL

I decided I wanted a salesgirl for a wife, too.

(MUSIC: "The Girl That I Marry")

The girl that I marry will have to sell,
Or know merchandising and stock quite well.
The girl who gets my name
Must write copy B.B.D.& O. would acclaim.

BABS

The guy that I marry has got to know
The reason why layouts must be just so.
You'd be swell, beau,
If you could sell, beau . . .
And if you knew your ad from your elbow.

An A&S scholar the feller I foller must be.

HAL

In some such vocation my cohabitation must be.

* * * * * *

(Sound of cheering. Whole cast enters, Jules and Hal carrying Robin, labeled "Miss A&S", on their shoulders.)

ALL

Hooray for Miss A&S, 1949. Hip-hip-hooray!

JULES

How'd ya do it, Mabel?

BARBARA

Yeah, what have you got that I haven't got?

MARY

We're in A&S, too. We never make out as well as you.

MISS A&S (with Mae Westonian voice)

Put me down fellas. Gather round, everybody. Here's the inside dope. There's more to success than meets the eye. This A&S Course is all well and good in its place, but . . .

(MUSIC: "You Can't Get a Man with a Gun")

If I have ambition
To land a good position
It would take just a little while.
I look good in a sweater,
And a boss likes nothing better.
All you need for success is a smile.

If I met a prexy
And I did not look sexy
He would tell me to walk a mile.
But with men who are gallant
You don't need any talent.
All you need for success is a smile.

ALL

Just a smi-ile, just a smi-ile.
All you need for success is a smile.

MISS A&S

If I needed money,
I'd simply call him honey
And walk off with a great big pile.
But you don't need your learnin'
With bosses who are yearnin'.
If you're nice to your boss . . .
He'll of course come across.

ALL

All you need for success is a smile.

Sorry, there's no record of the church function lyrics for Ken Hersey's project, or for any but one of my pop song endeavors with him, but I do have that one in the form of a lead sheet (piano arrangement) from which I was able to transcribe the lyrics. It's perfectly dreadful, but it's of historically significant insignificance because it is actually my first lyric ever to an honest-to-goodness composer's "original" melody, so you're stuck with it. Lyrically it goes like this:

> I betcha if we turned down the light,
> I betcha if I should kiss you goodnight,
> I betcha I could getcha to confirm the delight
> In saying "I love you" to me.

> I betcha if you'd let down your hair,
> I betcha that you'd be devil-may-care.
> I betcha I could getcha to develop a flair
> For saying "I love you" to me.

> It's apparent that you've been missing
> The thrills that people find when they let themselves go.
> There's a past-time that's known as kissing,
> And it really packs a punch that gives you a glow.

> I betcha that you'll love what's in store.
> I betcha that love's a thing you'll adore.
> I betcha I could getcha to come cryin' for more
> If you say "I love you" to me.

Semi-professionally and socially, the mid-'48 to mid-'49 year was one of the high points of my life, as I operated full steam ahead as a macho hetero with a new feeling of self-confidence building up inside me with each new endeavor. If I had any secret doubts about my sexuality from time to time during those months, they surfaced, I recall, mostly when I became more and more intrigued by some of the scrawlings on the men's room walls at N.Y.U. in stalls where I spent occasional spare time still wondering what it would be like to engage in some of the forbidden activities these scrawlings described. But I stubbornly continued to be pure as the driven snow (with men, that is.)

Until Joan and I became engaged in April '49, about three years after we'd met, I'd been dating perhaps a half-dozen other girls on and off, and was just beginning to feel reasonably secure with my heterosexuality and with being moderately sexually aggressive. But even with this newly found self-confidence I wasn't yet making out too well as a Casanova.

At about the time of our engagement Joan made a professional match between her friend Esther Chiat and me. Esther was a brilliantly talented composer and who was truly a diamond in the rough. I find it hard to believe that she has failed through the years to find professional success on any but the most modest of levels. She and I did a number of "pop" songs together during this period, and I must admit in all honesty that Esther's talent far outshone my own. The following lyric samples give a good enough idea of the era they were from and the style of our work around that time. Unfortunately they won't give you a chance to hear Esther's enchanting melodies, which were rich, bouncy and original. Maybe some day, somehow. Keep plugging, Es, and I'll keep pulling for you, and doing everything I can to make up for my having kind of abandoned you in midstream somewhere around 1962 (after we'd done three shows together), for the greener pastures of New York collaborators (your

Jersey base was a real schlep!) and the wonderful professional doors that were to open up to me via Lehman Engel's B.M.I. Musical Theatre Workshop.

But back to the humble beginnings of song-writing with Esther and the likes of "Melody Canyon" in 1949, my first with Es, and also with lyric collaboration (only on this one) of our mutual good friend Leonard Koven. The subject matter for this number, by the way, was inspired by Western motifs being "in" at the time. We were obviously looking for a commercial blockbuster.

> Melody canyon
> Along the winding trail,
> Musical mountain
> Out of a fairy tale,
> Where I can dream all day,
> Yippee-ki-i-i-ay,
> I'll roam no more.

> Melody canyon
> Where just my horse and I
> Live in the open
> Beneath the Western sky
> Here in our hideaway,
> Yippee-ki-i-i-ay,
> I'll roam no more.

> Whistlin' across the canyon
> (Whistle)
> Hummin' a lazy lullabye.
> The echo is my companion.
> (Whistle)
> The hills and me . . . in harmony.

> Melody canyon,
> I've found my own frontier.
> I'll be contented
> To spend my life right here,
> Singin' the time away,
> Yippee-ki-i-i-ay,
> I'll roam no more.
> I'll roam . . . no . . . more.

Next: "Gosh What a Load Off My Mind"—written to express my relief at having proposed to Joan and having been accepted. This number was later also used as an entry on Jan Murray's "Songs for Sale" radio show before the latter was redeveloped for TV. Esther and I didn't win the competition, but at least it provided respectable showcase, although I still recall the experience with a bit of pain, inasmuch as my lyrics were criticized by a panelist as being sloppy with two particular sets of rhymes ("suit ya" with "future"—and "said it" with "wedded") singled out. Certainly I'm aware of their not being "perfect" rhymes; they weren't meant to be perfect. They *were* meant to be "cute."

Still later "Gosh" was also used in the first show Es and I did together, *Dream About Tomorrow*. Here's "Gosh."

Never let it be said of you
That you played the fool
By failing to impart
The feelings in your heart
Just to preserve the golden rule.

Wanted to tell ya I love ya,
Wanted to feel inclined.
Wanted to hold ya, and now that I've told ya,
Gosh, what a load off my mind.

Wanted to beckon you closer.
Wanted the love I'd find.
Wanted to suit ya and make you my future.
Gosh, what a load off my mind.

Though I had the feeling,
It wasn't easy to start.
It wasn't easy revealing
All that was here in my heart.

Wanted to hug ya and kiss ya.
Wanted the license signed.
Wanted us wedded, and now that I've said it,
Gosh, what a load off my mind.

Next to be recorded here for the annals of time, one of Joan's sentimental favorites, and inspired by my new state of fatherhood in September, 1950: "Who Puts the Light in the Bulb?"

Daddy, what makes the roses grow?
In summer what happens to the snow?
And Daddy, there's another thing I'd like to know:
Who puts the light in the bulb?

Daddy, why is the water wet?
Can I have a tiger for a pet?
And Daddy, there's another thing I don't know yet:
Who puts the light in the bulb?

What makes the hands of a clock go round and round,
And can I have a baby brother?
Why can't we walk in the sky like on the ground,
And don't tell me to go and ask my mother.

Daddy, why is an apple red?
And why do I have a pointed head?
And Daddy, if you'll tell me this I'll go bed:
Who puts the light in the bulb?

And last but not least of this group of "aspiring-to-be-pop" numbers with Esther that I hereby rescue from oblivion is the beautifully heartbreaking (musically) "I Can't Get Away From You," actually published later by Esther's late brother-in-law,

Matty Meyers, then a composer in his own right, too. But even the publishing was to no avail:

> I always find
> That you're on my mind
> While dancing with someone new,
> Darling, wherever I stray
> I can't get away from you.
>
> There's still a trace
> That time can't erase
> Of love that we both once knew.
> My darling, day after day
> I can't get away from you.
>
> Tried to forget you,
> But how could that be?
> Left me, but yet you
> Have not set me free.
> Just can't forget you,
> For now I can see
> That though you are gone,
> You'll go on and go on to be . . .
>
> Haunting me so,
> Wherever I go
> You're with me the whole day through.
> My darling, try as I may
> I can't get away from you.

And dozens of others with Es not to be set down here (these are just representative samples) . . . with scarcely an attempt to market any of them, mostly I guess because we were too busy with full-time occupations to take time out to pursue recording stars and publishers. What a waste!

During the above period and into 1953 I did explore an occasional "pop-geared" effort with several other would-be composers who I felt could help sell them better than Esther could. (Esther Chiat had become the suburban housewife, Esther Stoller, and a mother, and therefore somewhat less available for footwork, follow-up and presentation in the big city.) These other new compositions and composers included "Black Cloud, Son of Rain"—with music by now deceased singer/Yiddish entertainer Jan Bart who performed our song in his night club act. This kind of song was quite a departure for Jan, all right, but now, trying to look at it objectively, it seems to me quite on target for singer Frankie Laine, for whom it was originally intended. Frankie was doing a lot of this kind of dramatic narrative ballad at that time. Only trouble is . . . neither one of us (Jan nor I) had the balls or the know-how to get it to Frankie:

> There's an ancient Western legend
> That lives on in this refrain.
> It's the story of an Injun
> Called Black Cloud, Son of Rain.
>
> When the people of his village

Made him chief of their domain
It was then they chose a maiden
For Black Cloud, Son of Rain.

But along came bold intruders
On a raging war campaign.
With his bride to shield
He must take the field—
And the Injun king was slain.

Now a waterfall is flowing
Where his wounded form had lain,
Where her tears forever linger
For Black Cloud, Son of Rain.

The next non-Esther composition was "Tonight Must Live On," with music first by Sid Lubow, an art director in the office of the first ad agency I worked in; then with a second melody by musician Marty Gruen who was a neighbor; then still a third version by black musician and band leader Al Browne. I haven't the foggiest recollection of how I met Al, but he was a great guy and he even got us a record (45) out of our collaboration. Without total recall at this point, it beats the hell out of me as to why I thought three different, respectable (although unknown) composers would all be interested in this lyric as one they'd like to work on, but for whatever it's worth, it held some inexplicable fascination for them, so each of them wrote his own melody for it. Here's my contribution to the song:

Love me
As no one has ever loved me.
Let them know how much you love me
For tonight must live on.

Kiss me
As no one has ever kissed me
Tell them you could not resist me,
For tonight must live on, and on.

And thrill me
With a love that is tender and new
And fill me
With the will to surrender to you,

And blind me
So that if the world should find me
They will know someone has loved me,
For tonight must live on.

"Let's Give a Gift to Santa Claus" had music by Matty Meyers, Esther's brother-in-law, with Matty even going to the expense of publishing it himself because he had such great expectations for it. I think it's dreadful.

Let's give a gift to Santa Claus,
Give him our faith and good will.
Let's give him love and kindness

To pave the way for
The peace we pray for.

He does so much for everyone.
He fills our hearts to the brim.
If the joy of living
Truly lies in giving,
Let's give a gift to him.

"Tears Are Only Souvenirs of Laughter" and "After You've Called Me Sweetheart" both had music by now long deceased Sid Bass, an arranger, composer and bandleader. (I seem to have outlived so many collaborators long before I was 65.) Sid got a wonderful demo on the first of these two numbers, "Tears," and a single (45) I no longer have a copy of by a Spike-Jones-type combo I no longer remember the name of on a lesser-known label on the second number, "Sweetheart." In other words Sid was a hustler. Anyhow, the sassy latter lyric comes first, and the sentimental one will follow:

After you've called me sweetheart
How soon do you call others dear?
After you've told me you're under my spell
How soon does the spell disappear?

After you've made a promise
And filled it with phrases sincere,
After you've called me sweetheart, sweetheart,
How soon do you call others dear?

The lyric of the other with music by Bass (the sentimental one, "Tears Are Only Souvenirs of Laughter") was inspired by the content of one of the books of Kahlil Gibran, *Tears and Laughter*. Gibran was one of my wife's favorite writers. She had adopted his philosophy as her own, and though hardly new ("Every Cloud Must Have a Silver Lining," etc.) the doctrine of that book was so personal with Joan that for all time—here and now—in this book's quest for some degree of longevity and permanence I dedicate my "Tears," and all my love, still, to my beloved late wife and partner, Joan.

Tears are only souvenirs of laughter.
Rain must always follow skies of blue.
If we never had our share of trouble
How would we enjoy life as we do?

If there were no tears forever after
How could any smiles we smile be true?
Tears are only souvenirs of laughter
So I don't mind my crying over you.

Career-wise I'd spent Fall '47 to Fall '49 first as a teacher, then as an advertising space salesman for the *Long Island Star-Journal*, a Newhouse newspaper of somewhat lesser stature than its more prestigious sister paper, the *Long Island Press*. The latter job proved to be another dead end and another fiasco. But it did provide me with occasional time on my hands to drift into a movie matinee and check out the holes in the wall-dividers between the men's room stalls. I was still so closeted that I didn't even have enough nerve to stand up at a urinal and get a good glimpse at somebody else's business at the urinal next to mine, which I gather is the way it's done by most guys who are interested. I had to try to do it furtively, through a peephole. It never actually worked (I never got to see very much), but the activity itself was stimulating, and the homosexual fantasizing must have created enough relief for me to continue acting out my life as a heterosexual, for that is precisely what I continued doing.

The week I got married in November, 1949, I accepted the only ad agency job I'd had offered to me, though I was ill-suited for it. My rationale was that it wouldn't look good for me to go through with the wedding without having a job, and I thought that any ad agency job was better than the newspaper space sales job I'd been struggling with for a year, then quit in despair. But ad agency production was an area never covered by the A&S course I'd participated in, and my college degrees were in English and education and dramatic art, so I now seemed to be getting farther afield all the time. No matter, I thought, hadn't I *tried* (to no avail, albeit not too hard) to connect with a copywriting job—even at the trainee level—and run into nothing but a brick wall? Sure, I didn't know how to sell or package myself, nor was I at all adept at learning how to do so. So again I took the easy way out, accepted the production job, and deluded myself into thinking this was one way of getting to transfer into copywriting at a later time. That time never happened.

I now fully believe that my confusion over my sexuality must have been at least partially responsible for my mishandling of establishing the right career for myself, though in all modesty, in my now reviewing some of the material you've already read, I can't see how I wasn't grabbed for further grooming by an enterprising creative director of one of the large agencies to which I'd applied. But I wasn't. Of this I am now convinced—my best talents (in jingles, lyrics, parodies, etc.) must have by far exceeded those of ninety percent of the guys coming into the agency business during the 36 years I worked in it. Yet no one tapped those talents. (Just as my propensity for being a full-fledged homosexual remained untapped all these many years.) Why no decent job offer? I spoke well and made a nice appearance. And I'm too "butch" a gay man to fall into the stereotype of the "femme" so many "straights" find distasteful. Well, here's one other possible reason. I almost hate to bring it up at this late date, and I have no proof of this, mind you, but though my name didn't sound particularly Jewish, my background did (the Brooklyn College stigma, I think). And as recently as 1949 I believe most of the bigger ad agencies hired Jews new to the scene by quota only, though of course this was not written into their by-laws. It was probably unofficially "understood." For whatever it's worth at this late date, that could indeed have been a contributing factor in my being a bust in entering the competitive business world.

But what the hell, the fact is that with my advertising career going nowhere, I hung on tenaciously to my lyric-writing pursuits, trying to further develop whatever talent I had by writing rhymes for whatever the occasion, whenever I could. And so the creative process continued, with occasional lapses because there wasn't always enough time for it, since my first consideration had to be to continue working in advertising and support my family. But soon my avocational pursuit was to explode into lyric writing for the first honest-to-goodness show with full-fledged score that I had ever been involved in, *Dream About Tomorrow*, with music by Esther Stoller.

THREE

My first musical with real music: "Dream About Tomorrow," the
three public performances of it in 1952,
and my name in print in Variety for the first time.

"There's a star just beyond your doorway.
There's a world full of joy
That's heading your way."

ONCE YOU'VE BEEN BITTEN by seeing and hearing your work performed by a professional cast in a real, live honest-to-goodness theatre, you stay bitten. Thinking
back about this sporadic career of mine now, there is one more person to whom I owe
a deep debt of gratitude. His name is A. Arthur Altman, and back in '52 when Esther
and I were fiddling around with our 'pop' efforts, Arthur, who had also been bitten by
the theatre bug years before, newly inspired by some work he'd been doing with the
N.A.A.C.P. as I recall it, co-authored a libretto for an original musical with the idea
of seeking the participation of the N.A.A.C.P. in getting the show off the ground.
Having been friendly with both my wife and my collaborator, Esther, from years
before, he asked Esther and me to write the score.

As it turned out, the N.A.A.C.P. participation backfired, but Arthur's momentum
in creating and producing the show did not, and so he sank his own money into it in
order to provide a showcase for the talents of the performers and other artists who had
by that time dedicated months of hard work in preparation for an opening.

The show was another instance of "the best laid plans of mice and men" aft going
"agley." Back then it wasn't yet fashionable to be militantly opposed to racial stereotypes. But Arthur was liberal, and saw a more lofty purpose in this theatrical effort
than its simply serving as a showcase for theatrically talented people. He championed
and sought to participate in the "cause" of racial equality. But I think all he achieved
with the show was unintentional reinforcement of some of the very stereotypes he
was attempting to eradicate, by including among the characters he invented the
gorgeous young black prostitute, the crooked black politician, the black kids who
were emulating gangsters and bookies, etc. They were created to provide contrast, so
that the other, more well-intentioned characters wouldn't appear too unrealistically
perfect; but with Arthur's and his collaborator's failure to create a fresher approach,
according to criticisms we earned at the time, *Dream About Tomorrow* came off as
amateurish and hackneyed (with no small contribution to the latter result being in the
hands of the lyricist, me, although the content of the lyrics had more or less been
pre-prescribed by the already completed book).

Nevertheless, a production did come off . . . for three performances in December,
1952, at the lovely off-Broadway house on West 103rd Street then called the Master
Theatre, later to be far better known as Equity Library Theatre. And so the bug had a
chance to bite, all through rehearsals with a cast of 30 (count 'em!)—boy, we sure did

things on a big scale in those days! The cast included Joseph Lewis who had appeared in *Carmen Jones*, Lillian Hayman of the National Opera Guild (she later went on to co-star in several Broadway musicals), Richard Ward, who had played in *Detective Story*, and Wezlynn Tilden, who'd appeared in *Kiss Me Kate*. The show got the full treatment, including orchestra, sets, lighting, and costumes. Some of the accoutrements were a bit on the tacky side, (for instance, we used my wife's wedding gown for the scene in which the reformed prostitute gets married), but I was off and running as a bonafide "produced" though only avocational lyricist at the age of 28 while at the same time busy struggling to eke out a living in the advertising business in order to support my new family which already included two infant daughters.

The score for *Dream About Tomorrow* was lush, melodious, and far broader in scope than anything Esther had done previously. A couple of the numbers may have sounded a bit more like middle-class Jewish than ghetto black, but in every other way Esther was beginning to stretch, and on her it looked good. My own work as a lyricist may have shown promise, but as you'll see it was not yet polished because I was not yet sufficiently experienced. But, oh, did I try! I guess we were all responding with tremendous enthusiasm and energy to the sheer excitement of having an *opportunity* to create a musical—of weaving this story and shaping these characters and building this entertainment—fitting all the elements together with words and music. I'd always been reasonably good at matching lyrics to rhythms, but I began to be flexible enough to invent workable rhythm patterns of my own, and to not get locked in by existing rhythms when I had something to say that wouldn't fit them. Now what *Dream* was proving most about my work was that without yet studying the craft of lyric writing, I had an innate feeling for what I was doing, and with that coming naturally, the end result was usually pleasing to the ear. An example I remember is one which Arthur Altman himself complimented me on at the time. He had been exposed to one of my lyrics on paper and wasn't terribly impressed with it. Then, once he heard it sung, he realized that there was more to lyric-writing than the written word. The word must sound good when sung. The bland appearance on paper of the two-line rhyme:

"There's a star just beyond your doorway.
There's a world full of joy that's heading your way."

in the title song took on far more character for Arthur when performed. What he had not previously realized was that without putting the accent on "your," the lines would not appear to the eye to be particularly distinguished or interesting. What I had not previously realized about myself was that I was using precisely the right kind of sounds and rhymes for matching the corresponding notes—instinctively—thereby enhancing the sound and meaning of the entity. Anyhow, thanks again, Arthur, this time for helping me to appreciate the fact that I was doing things with words that the ordinary non-lyric-writing layman would not even have a clue to understanding.

And for the non-playwriting layman, what made this show important in the molding of my career and the channeling of my talents was the discipline needed and the collaboration required for helping to tell a story and shape characters in song. And now for some of the less painful lyrics from *Dream About Tomorrow*. First, "Let's Make Believe," the opening number sung and danced to by the neighborhood kids.

Let's make believe we are racketeers and gangsters
And we've decided to operate a gang.
But there's a cop who has trailed us to our hideout.

Don't shoot. Bang bang. Don't shoot. Bang bang.

Let's make believe we are bookies at the race track.
We fixed a race, but they pulled a double cross.
And from behind he came tearing down the homestretch.
Bang bang. Dead horse. Bang bang. Dead horse.

And maybe we could smoke a stogie,
And make like Bogie, and squeeze a gat.
And maybe we could spot a stoolie,
And act unruly: Rat-a-tat-tat! Bang!

Let's make believe we've been waitin' on the corner
To take a dame up to decorate our room.
The lights go out and we're ready for some action.
Bang bang. (Wolf whistle.) Boom boom.

Now to the mandatory number usually reserved for the opener, introducing most of the leading characters: "Where Is Tess?"

CHORUS
Where is Tess? Where is Tess?
Can't she see that we are in an awful mess?
Her assistance we can use.
Oh, we hope she won't refuse.
She's a grand lady, landlady Tess.

Where is Tess? Where is Tess?
When she's gone from here we feel so motherless.
How we need a helping hand
With the very special brand
Of that grand lady, landlady Tess.

None surpass 'er
As a friend.
She's a gasser,
The livingest end.

Where is Tess? Where is Tess?
We are grown up, but we own up nonetheless
To the simple fact that we
Need the tea and sympathy
Of that grand lady, landlady Tess.

DUKE (One of the boarders)
Where is Tess? Where is Tess?
Can't she hear our persevering S.O.S.?
There'll be trouble soon tonight.
We will need the guiding light
Of that grand lady, landlady Tess.

DOLLY (The hooker, running in)
There's some flatfoot, and he saw me
Just as I got some guy lined up for me.
Gotta hide, or confess.

Tell me, where oh where is Tess?

CHORUS (To TINY, another boarder)
Tiny's callin'.
Run, Tess, run.
Poor guy's fallin'
Away to a ton.

TINY
Where is Tess? Where is Tess?
I'm a guy who likes his food, I must confess.
Be it steak or be it stew,
Long as it ain't overdue.
Where is grand lady, landlady Tess?

REVEREND (Entering)
Where is Tess? Where is Tess?
There are rumors she must help us to suppress
All about the things you've done
In this dwelling that is run
By your landlady, grand lady Tess.

BILLY THE COP (Entering)
Where's Tess Miller? Gotta warn'er
'Bout that broad that I seen on the corner.
Ain't this here her address?
On the square, oh, where is Tess?

CHORUS (to the Cop)
Tess ain't here now,
Nor the dame.
But don't fear now.
We'll stake you a claim.

CHORUS
Where is Tess? Where is Tess?

TINY
I will have to eat alone tonight, I guess.
COP (leaving)
I'll be back to see this through.

REVEREND
You can tell her I will, too.

CHORUS (as they scatter & exit)
To see grand lady, landlady Tess.

Next, a torchy ballad for Duke, who loves Dolly, the hooker. Sung at a time when she has just stepped outside the boarding house to chat with a gentleman caller ... this song (which we unearthed from a previously crafted pop version followed by probable oblivion) seemed to fit smoothly into this spot in the show: "Good Thing."

What do I get ideas for?

Why am I acting strange
When I would give odds gladly
That you will never change?
Here I try acting nice and sweetly,
And you go off, goodbye . . .
With some guy.

Love can leave you lonely,
Even in a crowd;
Make the day seem gloomy
Though there may not be a cloud.
Good thing . . .
I ain't in love with you.

Love can leave you laughing,
Laughing through your tears;
Make a little second
Seem like half a million years.
Good thing . . .
I ain't in love with you.

Love is sweet, but it's sad.
Love is good, but it's bad.
Will I learn to leave it be
And not let love make a fool of me?—No . . .

I'll go right on living,
And I'll never learn.
I'll go right on giving
Getting nothing in return.
Good thing . . .
I know you can't be true.
Good thing . . .
I ain't in love with you.

Regarding the latter as a potential bluesy hit with the right artist recording it, we'd be very happy to hear from any interested party out there among our brethren in the music business. Why not?

Next, a syncopated, rhythmic, Gershwinesque beauty of a melody from Esther which was so good we re-used it for other projects later on. But this is the show it was written for, and the sound of the hand-clapping from the Master Theatre stage still rings in my ears today. "We Ain't."

REVEREND
Listen, my children, this I've heard today.
People are whispering you have gone astray.
Where are you going tonight?
Is your salvation in sight?
You will be judged by what you've got to say.

CHORUS
Though you've been hearing stories
All about how bad we are . . .

We ain't.
Though you've been hearing
How immoral and unclad we are . . .
We ain't.
Some of us do and some of us don't.
Some of us will and some of us won't.
You are the first to register your complaint.
(We should be insulted.)

Though you've been hearin' stories
All about how wild we are . . .
We ain't.
Any old time we'll gladly leave the door ajar.
Sometimes it's true we're right on the verge,
Right on the verge of getting the urge,
But nevertheless, the saint that we ain't . . .
We are.

REVEREND

Listen, my children, bear this well in mind.
Think of your future, leave your past behind.
Though you may wander tonight
Keep your salvation in sight.
Try to remain intact and act refined.

CHORUS

Though they're all spying,
Telling tales of how uncouth we are,
We ain't;
Even implying
We're corrupting all the youth, we are.
We ain't.
Maybe we're fast or maybe we're slow,
Slightly impure or pure as the snow.
You are the first to question our self-restraint . . .
But we're only human.

Though they're all saying
How improper and unkempt we are,
We ain't.
Any old time we'll gladly leave the door ajar.
Sometimes we feel that Adam was right,
Adam was right in taking a bite,
But nevertheless, the saint that we ain't . . .
We are.
But nevertheless, the saint that we ain't . . .
We are.

Here's our attempt at a "book" chorus number to establish conflict—with David, the crooked politician, being confronted by Tess. "Cast Your Vote for Me." It may seem much too obvious, but it performed like "The Name's LaGuardia" which followed it by a few years.

CHORUS

Look, everybody, here comes David. Hi, David, gonna make a speech? Yeah, tell us what you're gonna do for us.

DAVID

What am I gonna do for you? Why that's easy . . . (Sings.)

I'll build a subway to your doors
When you cast your vote for me.
Comfort and wealth will all be yours
And you have my guarantee.
I'll give you cars and big cigars.
You'll have a life of luxury
And this I promise—
I'll be another Santa Claus
When you cast your vote for me.

CHORUS

We all like cars and big cigars.
Such luxury we'd like to see . . .
And subways to our doors!
He'll be another Santa Claus
And we have his guarantee.

DAVID

I'll do away with city slums
When you cast your vote for me.
I'll do away with all the bums
And the girls who charge a fee.
And what is more, I'll run a store
Where you can get a drink for free—
Including chasers!
You'll see how grand the world becomes
When you cast your vote, you'll see.

CHORUS

He'll clean the slums and chase the bums
And all the girls who charge a fee,
And we will get it free!
We'll see how grand the world becomes.
When we cast our vote we'll see.

TESS

David, what's all this nonsense about?
David, things we've been doing without
Like bread to eat and clothes to keep us warm . . .
It's more the things like these that need reform.
David, let's get those feet on the ground;
David, let's end this fooling around.
They want to hear about the things they need.
Who needs cigars when they've children to feed?

CHORUS

Tell her she's wrong, David. Yeah, tell her we like the things you promise us. You know what's best for us. Right? Right, David?

DAVID

You want a man who knows you well,
And the man you want is me.
You want a man who you can tell
Is endowed with honesty.
And that is me, as you can see.
I'll give you wealth and luxury—
And television!
You will have chosen very well
When you cast your vote for me.

CHORUS

We know you well, and we can tell
That you're endowed with honesty,
And we will have TV!

DAVID

You will have chosen very well
When you cast your vote for me.

Next, the title song, as sung by the entire cast. In case one couplet seems familiar, you already read it a bit earlier on.

Dream about tomorrow
In all your dreams today.
There's a star just beyond your doorway.
There's a world full of joy
That's heading your way.
Dream about tomorrow
And keep your faith brand new.
With love beside you,
Someone to guide you,
You'll see your dreams come true . . .

You'll see your dreams come true,
You'll find the world brand new
And every passing breeze will echo with laughter,
The kind of laughter
You'll hear forever after.

Dream about tomorrow,
And Fate will follow through.
No matter from where,
But someday, somewhere
You'll see your dreams come true.

And to wrap up the sampling from *Dream About Tomorrow*—the big, dramatic monolog (with chorus) for Tess, our heroine, a sort of female "Old Man River"—in intention, anyhow: "Tess' Dream."

TESS

Day after day we work and toil,
Toil till we're numb in the brain.
Day after day we drain the soil,
Even too tired to complain.

CHORUS

We were poor when we were born and by and by,
We were poor when we were born and by and by
We will find one early mornin'
There ain't no new day a-dawnin'
Cause we'll still be poor the very day we die.

TESS

Die as we live in sweat and pain,
No one to care or to pray.
Not even death can break the chain.
Nowhere can we run away.

CHORUS

Run away up North.
You may find a future for you
Some day soon beneath the sun.
Your July the Fourth
May arrive tomorrow, and your sorrow
Will be over if you run, run, run.

Day after day we drain the soil.
This is the way it must be.
Day after day we work, we toil
Into Eternity.

TESS

The day has come, the day has come
For our equality.
We go to school and we're taught in school—
Equal and free are we.

FEMALE OFFSTAGE VOICE

We've got a place for a graduate.
Here is a future that's really great.
Just sign your name and fill in the date.
We've got lots of work for you.

MALE OFFSTAGE VOICE

Sorry, young fella, but in this shop
I've got a feeling you'd be a flop.
Course, if you're willing to grab a mop
Then I've got some work for you.

CHORUS

A doctor, a lawyer, a U.N. statesman.
A teacher, a general, they'll all be great men.

TESS
A future bright and new.
This is my dream come true.

CHORUS
The people, my people, will be respected
No matter how light or how dark complected . . .

TESS
The day when we will be
Completely, truly free . . .

ALL
Day after day we'll prove our worth,
Prove that it's right that we're free.
Day after day upon this earth,
Keeping in pace with our place in eternity.

We all have to start somewhere, don't we? Now onto bigger and better projects, though the polish still didn't start happening till the Workshop ten years later. For instance, it wasn't till then that I learned that one shouldn't be rhyming (as above) "free" with "eternity," even though not every lyricist is as much of a purist about it as I am now. But at least with *Dream About Tomorrow*, I did get my name in *Variety* for the first time. There's some small consolation to be found in any seemingly trivial early endeavor.

FOUR

The rest of the 50's including odds and ends like
the Bensack Follies, the Macy's Moth Square
Follies, a meager attempt at "Being Earnest,"
and continuing the quest for a pop hit.

"A man can't be a man without a woman
or a woman a woman without a man."

WHILE STILL AT THE FIRST AD AGENCY JOB I'd been working at during the pop single "Tonight Must Live On" with Sid Lubow and *Dream About Tomorrow*, immediately following the latter, a new copywriter on staff, Al Glass, and I made a brief attempt at collaborating on a musical version of Oscar Wilde's *The Importance of Being Earnest*, using Esther's already existing *Dream About Tomorrow* music. How far afield can one get—not knowing that you can't take music for a contemporary American black musical like *Dream About Tomorrow* and use it "as is" for a farcical

British comedy of manners of another period? Come on now, Spiro, that simply can't be done. But I didn't know it then, and so I tried.

Bookwise, Al Glass and I didn't get much beyond outline, and lyrically I fleshed out only a couple of ideas. Undistinguished as they are, and with apologies to the off-Broadway adaptation of *The Importance of Being Earnest* called *Ernest in Love*, by Pockriss and Croswell which came later, here are two lyrics from my early attempt at that project, my version. (Though they were written in my still-amateur days, I assure you I would be even more embarrassed to share with you my first chicken scratchings on *Pygmalion* if I could find them. Yes, I tried that one, too, before *My Fair Lady* came to be; fortunately, they've disappeared from my files.)

Here's the suggested Opener for *Earnest*—lyrics set to Esther's Opener music for *Dream About Tomorrow* ("Let's Make Believe" as recorded in the previous chapter), now entitled "It's Time for Tea."

When you're in Rome drinking wine's a sign of fashion,
And they are queer for their beer in Germany.
But every day when it's five o'clock in England
We all agree . . . it's time for tea.

In Mejico it's a shot of hot tequila.
For vodka each Russian lush in debt would be.
But every day when it's five o'clock in England
We all agree . . . it's time for tea.

And you will find in old Hawaii
They drink papaya, and ask for more.
And Inja's come upon a new juice—
It's called bamboo juice, sipped thru a straw. Pshaw!

While in the States people sigh for dry martinis
And in Brazil coffee's still compulsory,
It is the rule when it's five o'clock in England
It's time, high time for tea.

* * * * * *

Each afternoon while the Spanish have siesta
And Arab girls seek the Sheik of Araby,
What do we do when it's five o'clock in England?
We all agree . . . it's time for tea.

While Persian business is booming looming carpets
And Eskimos conquer snows to reach the sea,
On what pursuit when it's five o'clock in England
Do we agree? . . . it's time for tea.

In China girls emerge from paddies
To meet their daddies and then unite.
In Egypt men seek out the harem
And then they share 'em all thru the night. Quite!

And in the Arctic while folks are rubbing noses
And while the girls of Paree are saying "oui"
It is the rule when it's five o'clock in England

It's time . . . high time . . . for tea.

I see now that I must have been influenced by Cole Porter on that one. Or, to borrow a title from Irving Berlin—nice work if you can get it.

And now the existing record of the second number for *Earnest*—for which I simply ill-advisedly transformed the "We Ain't" of *Dream About Tomorrow* into "I'm Not" to be sung now in ever-so-much-more-refined and genteel a fashion by Algernon and Cecily.

CECILY

People are whispering you have gone astray.
People have called you Scoundrel! Cad! Rou!
How do I know they're not right?
Where are you going tonight?
You will be judged by what you've got to say.

ALGY

Though you've been hearing stories
All about how bad I am,
I'm not.
Though you've been hearing stories
All about the cad I am,
I'm not.
Maybe I do and maybe I don't.
Maybe I will and maybe I won't.
You are the first to put me in such a spot.
What? How can you accuse me?

Though you've been hearing stories
All about the wolf I am,
I'm not.
Haven't you found that I'm behaving like a lamb?
Sometimes it's true I'm right on the verge,
Right on the verge of getting the urge,
But nevertheless, the saint that I'm not . . .
I am.

(It lost its knee-slapping, hand-clapping fervor in the transition, that's for sure. And it could not have been more wrong for *Earnest* and we must have known it. So no wonder we called it quits on our own *Earnest* early on and waited for the Pockriss-Croswell version.)

My lyric writing efforts were at their most sporadic during the next perhaps half-dozen years, from about '53 to '59, when I had my hands full with job problems. There was turmoil in my paying career which included a couple of unexpected, traumatic and largely unjustified dismissals (firings)—that's done a lot in the ad business—and I had to give more intense attention to my earning a living and trying to better my status at it. Anyone who knows what stress advertising production can involve knows that taking that kind of job even more seriously than it's worth can leave one's nervous system in shreds. I learned to drink. I learned to be dishonest. And that was the period in which I finally learned how to escape from that private world of sexual fantasy that I had till now kept under wraps, and briefly act out the intense desire with a male partner for the first time. For real. And I liked it. So I did it again a short time later. But over the ensuing years and throughout the rest of my married life, brief homosexual encounters incredibly happened only three more times, though partly because, I must shamefully admit, on attempt number three I was severely beaten up by several "fag-bashers" and rendered scared shitless. Thus was I more than adequately motivated into cooling it in no uncertain terms.

Later on, when my wife's health started failing, there was no question but that I belonged at her side and nowhere else, ever. She was a most courageous woman who I truly believe knew she was going to die young. On occasion while we were married she would refresh the interest in palmistry she had developed during our college days, whereupon she insisted that her broken lifeline meant death at an early age.

Another reason for my almost rigid fidelity (in spite of its psychological toll on me) was that starting with about 1960, Joan had truly become a partner to me. Till then I had been unwittingly pressured into a position I was not ready to assume, that of being head of a family. From '60 on maturity finally set in, albeit late, but, I suppose, better late than never. Though I therefore suppressed and repressed overt feelings of homosexuality, I learned instead what many basically gay men never do, or never have a chance to—how to take control and take command, and little by little how to build self-confidence. Although this of course was a trade-off for me, I suppose it helped me succeed in deluding my wife, family and friends, and the world as to my true sexual preference. I was very much the "male" as the world perceived me, except *inside* me. But I now assume that all along it was mostly underlying weakness, with perhaps a pinch of compassion and conscience thrown in, that kept me married and faithful (the latter to a slightly imperfect degree, it's true). I never really had the courage to face up to my gayness, to break with tradition and what was expected of me, and to live my life honestly. Is it not a wonder that at 65 I finally can? Is it not a wonder I have finally earned to laugh a lot, and smile practically all the time, and respond with complete abandon to love and attention and affection from a reciprocating partner, and think of writing a book for the first time in my life, and appreciate Spring and music and humor and friendship and warmth as I never have before in my life?

The Bensack Follies of 1956, or "Sacky Get Your Gun" (with apologies again to Irving Berlin), was a short Christmas office party entertainment presented at the lavish home of my then boss, Ben Sackheim, on December 30, 1955. The lyrics (of which I have no copies) were all "in" lyrics, the music was Berlin's (*Annie Get Your Gun* again), a lovely young Latin-looking production department assistant named Beverly Sweedler co-wrote the script with me, the "saga of a young woman bent on an ad career, who starts at the bottom and finds hard work, heartbreak and love at the Bensack agency," and the songs were a big hit. I see from the program (of which I *do* have a copy) that they included "It's Wonderful" and "The Girl That I Marry" with special lyrics, and "Working for this Agency" to "Doin' What Comes Nacherally," "We're in the Agency Too" to "I'm an Indian Too" and "All You Need for Success is a Smile" to "You Can't Get a Man with a Gun."

My next fling at an "industrial"-style project was called "The Moth Square Follies." When I mentioned before that my mother had worked in a leading department store, I didn't say which. Now I realize I have to, in order to include these lyrics: The store was Macy's. For a few years running, Mom elected me to write the entertainment for the end-of-season or holiday season party or dinner that her "Moth Square" invariably celebrated. To brief you on the "Moth Square" before including these few more ditties—it was the section in Macy's Basement where Mom and her group physically displayed their merchandise and made their sales, dedicating themselves to peddling anything the customers asked for, but pushing the products of a company called Reefer-Galler, which manufactured a line of moth preventatives and evidently had a special deal going with Macy's.

Here are some of the lyrics I wrote for the stars of the "Moth Square" to sing over those few years, again with apologies to the ubiquitous Irving Berlin—and Hammerstein, and Frank Loesser, and whomsoever.

(To the tune of "You're Just in Love," with a woman customer singing the first chorus and a salesman singing the second.)

> CUSTOMER
> I need mothballs, I have moths around.
> I need mothballs. May I have a pound?
> Moth balls really are the best I've found.
> When springtime calls I need moth balls.
> I have closets where the moths have been
> There's no pocket they did not get in.
> Clothes that once were each a precious gem
> Now all have holes in them. I need mothballs.

> SALESMAN
> You don't need mothballs, Madam.
> You would not once have had 'em
> If you used what we call Mothine.
> We sell spray, we sell crystals.
> They kill moths just like pistols
> And keep clothes oh so nice and clean.
> And that great Mothine Refill
> Doesn't make insects gleeful,
> And you'll find after what you've seen
> There is nothing better than,
> That can do the same as can—
> Better than our grand Mothine.

*****

And to "There is Nothing Like a Dame"

> We get customers with wrinkles,
> And we get them in their teens
> Who complain of all their insects
> In Manhattan, Bronx or Queens,
> And to all these different customers
> Who come upon the scene . . .
> What do we sell? We sell Mothine.
>
> Do you carry it in crystals?
> Yes, in nuggets pure as gold.
> Do you carry it in liquid?
> That is how it's often sold.

Is it strong enough for closets
If you follow what I mean?
What could you mean? You mean Mothine.

It surpasses every product you've been buyin'
And it's also strong enough to kill a lion.

There is nothing like Mothine,
Nothing in the world.
Every moth will leave the scene
When you've sprinkled it with Mothine.
It's the best you've ever seen,
Best in all the world;
Makes your closets fresh and clean
When you saturate with Mothine.

There is absolutely nothing like a can of Mothine.

Can I purchase it at Gimbels?
Will it really kill the bugs?
Is it safe to use on fabrics?
Is it wise to use on rugs?
Can I use it in the bedroom
And the kitchen and latrine?
Wrap up a can. I'll take Mothine.

There are no sprays like Mothine
And nothing stays like Mothine
Or is as strong as Mothine
Or lasts as long as Mothine,
And nothing sells like Mothine,
Or smells like Mothine.
There ain't a bug alive or any moth here
That can't be killed by putting him near
A can or cake or great big bag of Mothine.

* * * * * * * *

From "Guys and Gallers" or "The Saga of Mothine"

Experienced salesperson, Mrs. S., is coaching a trainee, Miss J. (To "Daisy, Daisy" or "A Bicycle Built for Two")

MRS. S.
Mothine, Mothine . . . that is what you must sell.

MISS J.
Will I ever get used to the awful smell?

MRS. S.
There's nothing you'll find can beat it.

MISS J.
I'll sleep it, drink it, eat it.

MRS. S.
Yes, it will kill—as none else will—
When a customer buys Mothine.

Later, at the Square, Miss J. gets her first customer (To: "The Daring Young
Man on the Flying Trapeze")

CUSTOMER
My clothes are infested, I've nothing to wear.
A family of moths made their headquarters there.
I've cross ventilation in my underwear
Where I never had it before.

I have hired a private detective,
And a doctor I also have seen
But they've given me no satisfaction at all.
Tell me, what is this thing called Mothine.

MISS J.
Ohh-h . . .
Detectives and doctors from what we have found
Would not know a moth from a hole in the ground,
But here we have experts and they've been around
And they'll kill off your moths evermore.

Etc., and into the grand finale to the tune of "M is for the Million Things She
Gave Me"

M is for the Moth Square down in Macy's.
O is for our Orders from the Chief.
T is for the Tired Feet we stand on.
H is for the Hours of Relief.
I is for Insecticidal Incomes.
N is Notwithstanding the above
E we'll Ever pledge our lives to Mothine,
The product we all truly love.

I recall it all being as much fun as it sounds, particularly in rehearsal and performance, and every bit of it good experience for me for what was to be created later
when the more serious projects came along. But now onto a few samples of the
continuation of the pop quest in the 50's. Basically they're not much different from
pop attempts of earlier years, though I suspect that they show a bit more maturity and
polish.

In the romantic vein, "Just Right"

She's not too pretty, not too plain—
Just right, just right.
She's not too modest, not too vain—
Just right, just right.
She ain't no super being,
No goddess from above.
She ain't no saint, but though she ain't

Wow, how that gal can love.

She's not too salty, not too sweet—
Just right, just right.
She's not as dumb as some girls come
And not as bright,
But if she said she'd marry me
I'd run but one-two-three
To be at the side of the blushing bride
Who's oh-oh-oh just right for me.

Another entry far too "straight" to come from the typewriter of a gay man. Part of the cover-up? Could be. "A Man Can't Be a Man Without a Woman"

Since I left the farm and strayed from sunny Texas
It's amazing what peculiar sights I see.
The city folks, they pay no mind to sexes,
Though somehow it has always seemed to me . . . that . . .

A man can't be a man without a woman
Or a woman a woman without a man.
Way back where roads are muddy
There ain't no buddy-buddy
And boy-meets-girl is still the basic plan.

And I still think with women it's more human.
They thrill me like no other people can.
Oh, a man can't be a man without a woman
And a woman a woman without a man.

Next, a ballad, "You Touched Me"

You touched me, and all at once
My heart began to sing.
Winter turned to Spring.
Love was everything.
You smiled and there was all
I'd ever dreamed or planned
Suddenly at my command.

You touched me, and swayed my life
And made my life your own.
Thrills I'd never known
Now were mine alone.
You kissed a pair of eyes
That never saw the dawn.
You touched me,
And my darling, I was born.

My one tribute to my home town, "The Flatlands of Brooklyn"

You've heard of the hills of Montana,
And the plains of the old Cherokee,
And all the other places
Where all the open space is,

But there's only one prairie for me.

The Flatlands of Brooklyn, the prairie I roam,
The wild, woolly country I know as my home,
The marsh and the meadow across Sheepshead Bay
Are calling me back and I'll get there some day.

The Flatlands of Brooklyn, the goats in the corn,
The strongest aroma that ever was born—
The boats at Canarsie, the shore and the sea
Are calling me back, and that's where I should be.

For I've roped the steers out yonder
Till I loaded ten corrals
Till there ain't a thing that's left for me to learn,
And a man can't rightly wander
With so many purty gals
Back home in Brooklyn waiting his return.

So keep Oklahoma and Idaho too
And then give Sioux City straight back to the Sioux.
For me it's God's Country to feather my nest—
The Flatlands of Brooklyn, the land I love best.

Another lighthearted romantic entry, "Simple Mathematics"

In school I was told
On failing a quiz
That I'd never be
An arithmetic whiz.
But teacher was wrong.
It's easy to do
When a fella like me
Meets a girl like you . . .

It's simple mathematics
When I propose to you.
Take one boy.
Add one girl.
One plus one is two.

It's simple mathematics.
Without you life is done.
Take a pair.
Then subtract.
Two less one is one.

Honey, that's why I think I'd die
If you make the wrong decision.
It's no mistake to give a guy a break.
That's provable by long division.

It's simple mathematics:
We'll raise a family.
Start with two.

Multiply.
You end up with three.
There's nothing to it
When you do it . . . mathematically.

And several slightly more serious pop attempts, "The Curtain Rises"

All of life is like a play
With every player in it
Acting out his own important part.
Soon we'll see the play—the lights
Will dim in just a minute.
This is how it always has to start.

The curtain rises,
And girl meets boy
And soon we know
They'll end the show in love.

He sends her roses.
She feels the joy
And wears the glow
Of being so on love.

But in the second act he meets another.
Her heart is broken far beyond repair.
To think that he would ever love another!
He doesn't care! But don't despair.

A few surprises
Before we're done.
One lonely night
He sees the light and calls.
He realizes
That she's the one
And runs to find her
As the curtain falls.

And the wistful "Ladies' Man"

Some men are born clever,
Some men are born wealthy,
And riches and brains have their place
But no woman ever
Whose ego is healthy
Would fall for a man without seeing his face.
Features and form in their beaux
Are what they're all after, I know.

Ladies' man, oh to be a ladies' man,
Oh to have my choice of mate
Await my beck and call.
Dapper Dan, to be a Dapper Dan . . .
The happiest and best to be of all.

If I were handsome
Instead of talented and rich
I'd have too many belles to ring
To even tell which belle is which.

(Just imagine playing switch.)
Ding a ling a ding dong!

Ro-me-o, to be a Romeo—
To be their leave-them-ashen
Passion. Yes, I can.
The best I own I'd gladly trade
Or give for free to make the grade
To be a gosh-to-goodness ladies' man.

None of them is a world-beater, but I didn't want to discard this group of lyrics entirely without saving some few for posterity—so there they are, even though I realize that the last half-dozen were never set to anybody's music. Nevertheless, they're valid enough samples of what I used to do to keep my hand busy—while convincing myself that my talent and desire weren't drying up—during the years in which I was concentrating more on my paying career than on my avocation. And now it's time to get back to show lyrics—for me they're infinitely more interesting. And so we now enter the next decade, the 60's . . . with the start of my second musical-with-music, *Sylvester*.

FIVE

"Sylvester" tries to be to "Cyrano" what "Kiss Me Kate" was to
"Taming of the Shrew."

"The twilight years / Are the sweetest years
When you have someone to love."

ONE OF THE DEEPEST SATISFACTIONS I've experienced during my career as a writer has been in achieving the goal of completed musical adaptations (book and lyrics) of three of the plays I was most impressed with as a young playgoer. They were *Cyrano de Bergerac*, *The Playboy of the Western World* and *Johnny Belinda* (I'm one of the three people I know still alive, although surely there must be many others, who saw the original production on Broadway of the last of the three named—with Helen Craig as the deaf mute. The other two survivors I know of are my mother and friend Lonnie—curiously one of the things that attracted me to Lon in the first place when I learned soon after meeting him that we had shared that entertainment experience 38 or so years before. Interestingly enough, two of the above plays deal with a person with a physical handicap or deformity; the other, *Playboy*, at the very least deals with a person with a moral deformity. What does that mean, if anything? Are we to find out along the way? Perhaps I identified because of my own moral or emotional "deformity." Who knows?

By the time I got around to them (later in my career) I couldn't see any advantage to extensively changing *Playboy* and *Belinda*. But *Cyrano* I thought too flowery for popular consumption as a musical "as is," so I eliminated a good deal of the floweriness by eliminating a good deal of the play, converting my version, *Sylvester*, into a play within a play, about actors performing *Cyrano*, borrowing shamelessly from the idea used in *Kiss Me Kate* and certainly others before it ("a troupe of strolling players are we; not stars like L.B. Mayer's are we"), and making the umbrella story contemporary. This format enabled me to retain the core and heart of *Cyrano* while discarding many of its embellishments. Unofficially my wife helped me with the outline of the book of *Sylvester*, though I certainly can't blame her for it turning out juvenile, excessively romantic, even saccharine. After all, isn't the original *Cyrano* all of that, too?

In addition to influences upon me and *Sylvester* by the Spewack show, many other influences abound, including ye olde Mickey-Judy movies rearing their heads again. And there is a Roz Russell type (conveniently named Roz) who is the wise and wise-cracking mature theatrical producer lady at the helm, and who not accidentally is also Roxie's (Roxane's) mother. And there is an amiable Paul Ford type, Horace, who not accidentally is father to Sylvester (Cyrano), the young aspiring actor with a long, long nose, who wants nothing more than to play the part of Cyrano. And there is also the handsome but stupid and somewhat slimy Steve—imitating Cyrano's rival, Christian. (I secretly had movie actor Steve Cochran in mind for that one. As a matter of fact, I occasionally had Steve Cochran secretly in mind for other things, too. Wouldn't you if you were in the closet?)

The libretto of *Sylvester* was and still is a mish-mash, but at least part of the score by Esther was delightful, and some of my lyrics were finally bordering on being funny and touching and appropriate for the material.

Sad to say we never did anything with *Sylvester* either. Oh, many years later when the previously mentioned Arthur Altman was prosperous enough to dabble in theatre ownership and producing on a more professional scale than with *Dream About Tomorrow*, he briefly considered doing a showcase or at least a reading of *Sylvester*. That never materialized, and so *Sylvester* remains one of the many projects I originated which is still lying around in a file drawer collecting dust.

Until recently we didn't even have a decent demo tape of the score, so we were never even able to use any material from it as a showcase for our talents. A couple of years ago, however, Esther and her husband and I were so impressed with Steve Martin's free adaptation of *Cyrano* in his film *Roxanne* that we discussed the possibility of making that long overdue demo of our score, hoping then to present it and ourselves to Steve Martin, along with the idea of merging all our talents and material, with an eye toward an eventual stage production of a merged version of "Sylvester/Roxanne." The entire concept and plan was so highly speculative that it was probably poor judgment to spend even a cent on the recording, were it not for the fact that the Steve Martin angle provided the incentive necessary for us to finally commit to a tape, for whatever might come of it—with or without Mr. Martin.

The result? Steve said no. We do indeed have the demo, and it's a reasonably good showcase of about a third of the score. My book is still the weakest link, and being displeased with it, I have given some thought to one of these days trying to rewrite it with a new twist—that of Sylvester/Cyrano being uncertain of his sexual orientation. (Where could I have gotten that idea from?) I may be trading old book headaches for new ones, but no doubt I could have great fun with it—when and if I'm ready—reshaping the story and characters as necessary and yet making sure I keep the score intact. As I often say to myself when I'm about to address a new challenge—"Good luck, Bernie."

There doesn't seem to be much more to write about *Sylvester* in any other context at the moment, and so I'll save further comments till they come up preceding or following the lyric samples from the show which follow.

The mandatory ensemble show-opener . . . this one with an office full of aspirants waiting around to see theatrical producer Roz Gilbert in "Broadway Has Ups and Downs," was probably inspired by "There's No Business Like Show Business" and numbers of that ilk.

> Broadway has ups and downs,
> Blue jeans and evening gowns,
> Hopes riding handsome,
> Dreams gone astray.
> Magic successes,
> Horrible messes.
> Broadway has highs and lows.
> Nobody ever knows.
> Pray Lady Luck is making her rounds
> And then wait for the curtain,
> Doubtful but certain.
> Broadway has ups and downs.
>
> First night's come and gone.
> The pattern never fails.
> Sit around and wait
> For that review and chew your nails.
> Stewing in martinis
> Till you're ready for the worst.
> Dreaming, hoping, praying
> That the bubble doesn't burst,
> Tears and sweat and sorrow
> And the laughs and goofs and dough . . .
> All these things were lavished
>
> On your infant of a show.
> Shape it, feed it, nurse it—
> Will it ever turn out right?
> Dress it up with bows,
> Silk and satin clothes,
> Love it, paint it, shine it,
> Wrap it up for op'nin' night.
>
> Broadway has ups and downs,
> Broadway has smiles and frowns,

Lights burning brightly,
Lights dark and cold,
Big biz or no biz—
Oh well, that's show biz.
Broadway has highs and lows.
Nobody ever knows.
Pray Lady Luck is making her rounds
And then wait for the curtain,
Doubtful but certain.
Broadway has ups and downs.

Now for the first song actually based on *Cyrano*. Though in its existing form I know it was one of the show's mistakes—lyrically and musically—it is important enough to include here, as is—even though considerably less than on target. "The Ballad of the Duel" (sung by Cyrano and the Male Ensemble)

SYLVESTER (holding up his hand)
Wait! I am choosing my rhymes . . . There . . . I am ready . . .
(Sylvester struts forward and sings, suiting action to the words, and dueling with Steve. The musical number is performed in mock genteel fashion as if Cyrano and the Viscount were dancing a minuet rather than fighting for their lives.)

CYRANO
My fine felt hat I toss away
And never harm the plume.
My cloak I gently cast aside
To give me lunging room.
I draw upon thee, faithful sword,
In never ending trust
And warn you, Viscount, as I end
Each new refrain, I thrust!

MALE ENSEMBLE (while swordplay is taking place)
Thrust home. Thrust home.
With blood and gore galore, thrust home.

CYRANO
A favor you'd have done yourself
To turn about and leave.
Where shall I lard thee, turkey—
In the side below your sleeve?
The heart, the ribs, the neck, the breast?
My point collects no dust.
Beware thy belly as I end
This new refrain, I thrust.

MALE ENSEMBLE (with swordplay)
Thrust home. Thrust home.
With blood and gore galore, thrust home.

CYRANO
I need another word, it seems,

To rhyme with "cowardly."
You break off white as chalk, my friend,
Yet you would aim at me.
I open wide; I block it up.
Perhaps I'm too robust.
May I remind you as I end
Each new refrain, I thrust.

MALE ENSEMBLE (with swordplay)
Thrust home. Thrust home.
With blood and gore galore, thrust home.

CYRANO
Prince, ask the Lord to pardon you.
I guard; I flash my sword.
Prepare to have your armor pierced,
And finish finely gored.
I lunge, I cut. Ha! There we go!
You knew it was a must
That as I end the last refrain
I thrust, I thrust, I thrust!

MALE ENSEMBLE (as swordplay ends in the Viscount being finished off)
Thrust home! Thrust home!
With blood and gore galore . . . thrust home!

Back to the contemporary story again . . . a bit of motherly advice from Roz to Roxie, because young Roxie is pining because Steve won't give her a tumble. Mama thinks maybe Steve would care more if Roxie took up with Sylvester and flaunted it in Steve's face. "Make Him Jealous"

ROZ
Make him jealous, make him jealous
Make him jealous, jealous, jealous
Till he's fuming, fuming, fuming seeing red.
Make him worry, make him worry,
Make him worry, worry, worry
Till there's gray in every hair upon his head.
Keep him guessing, keep him guessing,
Keep him guessing, guessing, guessing
Wond'ring how and where and why there's someone new.
Make him jealous, jealous, jealous
Till his glands are over-zealous
And he'll come running after you.

Think how wee ol' Cleopat prompted Antony's
Well documented penchant for seeing red.
As she whipped Marc up some hot Lobster Cantonese
Then served it to Caesar instead.
She set Marc wild—that nasty child!
The smell drove him out of his mind.

ROXIE

I get it.
> Make him jealous, make him jealous,
> Make him jealous, jealous, jealous,
> Till he's steaming like a lobster fricasee.
> Make him itchy, make him itchy,
> Be as teasing and as bitchy
> As a tantalizing temptress on a spree.

ROZ

Right!
> Think how busy Isabella rocked Ferdinand's
> Composure—with only the slightest push.
> As she kissed poor Chris and whispered "A bird in hand's
> Worth two Ferdinands in the bush."
> She could demean, that nasty queen.
> She drove Ferdie out of his mind.

BOTH

> Make him hustle, make him bustle,
> Thinking someone else'll muscle in
> As soon as he has gone and been untrue.
> Make him jealous, make him jealous,
> Tell him he can go to hell-us
> And he'll come running after you.

ROZ

And moreover—
> Think of breasty Desdemona's revealingly
> Historic example of "get his guts."
> She played hanky-pank with Iago so feelingly
> Othello went stark raving nuts!
> What did she do, that nasty shrew?
> She drove the Moor out of his mind.
> Drive him crazy, drive him crazy,
> Drive him crazy, crazy, crazy
> Till he's ready for that cottage with a view.
> Make him jealous, make him jealous,
> So the muses always tell us
> And he'll come running after you.

BOTH

And he'll come running after you.

Now for some meat and potatoes. I have seen *Cyrano* in a few forms since I wrote *Sylvester* . . . as a revival of the play, in Ferrer's film, in two different musical stage versions including the more renowned Plummer production, and most recently in Steve Martin's free adaptation. With reasonable due modesty I judge that the following two numbers, when enhancing or replacing the original text from which they were inspired, serve to convert their respective scenes in my version into quintessentially the most entertaining of the lot. The only difficulty in recognizing them as such lies in the other versions having been produced while mine was not. So this may very well be another case of "what might have been." Sour grapes? Perhaps, but no matter—because for me these two numbers work so well that they were always there when I was creating future projects, as if helping cheer me on from the sidelines, saying: "You can do it, Spiro. You can do it, cause you've done it before." First: "Two Heads Are Better Than One"

CHRISTIAN

Roxane expects a letter tonight. Alas, I am so stupid. I am one of those who are unable to talk of love. I need eloquence.

CYRANO

I will lend it to you. You lend me your conquering physical charms and together let us make a hero of romance. Could you repeat the things I would teach you each day? Are you willing to let your lips cooperate with my phrases—and soon her heart shall be on fire? I will be your wit, you shall be my beauty.
(They sing.)

CYRANO

Two heads are better than one.

CHRISTIAN

Two heads are better than one?

CYRANO

Together we'd make quite a man

CHRISTIAN

To woo and win the fair Roxane

BOTH

For two heads are better than one.

CYRANO

Few heads speak better than mine.

CHRISTIAN

Few heads look better than mine.

CYRANO

I have the wit and it is keen.

CHRISTIAN

I have the face and manly mien—

BOTH

So two heads should surely combine.

CYRANO

To get ahead in this age of competition
One must borrow someone else's classic looks.

CHRISTIAN

To get ahead one would need but one condition:
The grace of words as found in classic books.

CYRANO
Oh, two heads are better, it's true.

CHRISTIAN
Two heads are better, it's true.

CYRANO
It's evident eugenically
And even schizophrenically
That one head just simply won't do.

CHRISTIAN
You've got to . . .

BOTH
You've got to have two.

* * * * * * * * *

CYRANO
Few heads are plainer than mine.

CHRISTIAN
And few heads inaner than mine.

BOTH
Though we lack uniformity
The plan has such enormity
That two heads should surely combine.

CHRISTIAN
To get ahead leads me only to frustration
For whenever I'm ahead I feel behind.

CYRANO
To get ahead might imply decapitation
But mine is not the head I have in mind.

I merely mean that—

Two heads are better, tis true.

CHRISTIAN
Two heads are better, tis true.

CYRANO
So if we're going wooingly . . .

CHRISTIAN
We ought to do it twoingly

BOTH
For one head just simply won't do.

CHRISTIAN
You've got to . . .

CYRANO
You've got to . . .

BOTH
Have two!

The second of my two favorites from *Sylvester* includes ground-breaking efforts by Esther and me, for it is written for three singers, two of whom are vocalizing in an overlapping round. Neither Esther nor I had ever done that before, but we tried it and it worked. And it couldn't have been more right for the situation, which was the famous balcony scene following the previous number. The title: "Eloquent Words"

CHRISTIAN
Cyrano, help me. I shall die if I cannot get back in her good graces, this very instant. Look there! Her window!

CYRANO
It is a dark night. I think we can chance the deception. Stand there in front of her balcony. I will take my place underneath and will whisper your words to you. Throw some pebbles up there. Then call her. Now.

CHRISTIAN (throwing the pebbles, then calling)
Roxane!

ROXANE (opening her window a little way)
Who is calling me?

CHRISTIAN
I am.

ROXANE
When we met last week your speech was too awkward. Go away.

CHRISTIAN
Forgive me.

ROXANE
No. You no longer love me.

CHRISTIAN (to whom Cyrano first whispers what he is to say)
Accuse me, righteous heavens, of loving you no longer when I love you so much more?

ROXANE (stopping just as she was about to close her window)
Ah, that is better. Say more. Say more.

(MUSIC . . . during which Cyrano remains hidden under the balcony while singing softly to Christian)

CYRANO
To bring thee eloquent words,
To bring thee eloquent words of love
Your lips must free this child in me
And meet me in one delicate kiss.

CHRISTIAN (repeating to Roxane)
To bring thee eloquent words,
To bring thee eloquent words of love
Your lips must free this child in me
And meet me in one delicate kiss.

ROXANE
I hear in the air . . . passions roar.
But why did you ne'er . . . speak before?
Were you not aware . . . I'd adore
And tenderly care . . . evermore?

CYRANO to CHRISTIAN and CHRISTIAN to ROXANE:
I bring thee eloquent words.
I bring thee eloquent words of love.
My heart now sings. My lips have wings
And leap to take one delicate kiss.

ROXANE
Oh, Christian!

CHRISTIAN
One kiss, my love. May I come now?

ROXANE
First tell me how much you want my kiss. Tell me in beautiful flowing phrases.

CHRISTIAN
Cyrano, help me.

CYRANO: I bring thee eloquent words.

CYRANO: I bring thee eloquent words of love.
CHRISTIAN: I bring thee eloquent words.

CYRANO: My lips may speak, but still they're weak
CHRISTIAN: I bring thee eloquent words of love.

CYRANO: From hung'ring for your delicate kiss.
CHRISTIAN: My lips may speak, but still they're weak

CYRANO: I bring thee passionate thoughts;
CHRISTIAN: From hung'ring for your delicate kiss.
CYRANO: I bring thee passionate thoughts of bliss.
CHRISTIAN: I bring thee passionate thoughts;

CYRANO: My thirst for you would drain the dew
CHRISTIAN: I bring thee passionate thoughts of bliss.

CYRANO: From rosebuds in each delicate kiss.
CHRISTIAN: My thirst for you would drain the dew

CHRISTIAN: From rosebuds in each delicate kiss.
ROXANE:

How sweetly you say . . . your appeal.
I know that it may . . . be a spiel.
But since you convey . . . how you feel,
I'll give you your way . . . it's a deal.

CYRANO: I bring thee eloquent words.

CYRANO: I bring thee eloquent words of love.
CHRISTIAN: I bring thee eloquent words.

CYRANO: My heart now sings, my lips have wings
CHRISTIAN: I bring thee eloquent words of love.

CYRANO: And leap to take one delicate kiss.
CHRISTIAN: My heart now sings, my lips have wings

CHRISTIAN: And leap to take one delicate kiss.

ROXANE
Oh, Christian!

CHRISTIAN
My love . . . may I come now?

ROXANE
Soon, soon. But first tell me how long you would wait for me, or how hard you would fight for me. Tell me in beautiful, flowing phrases.

CHRISTIAN
Help me, Cyrano, help me!

CYRANO: I bring thee bottomless wells

CYRANO: Of patience never ever known before.
CHRISTIANf: I bring thee bottomless wells

CYRANO: I'd wait for thee eternally,
CHRISTIAN: Of patience never ever known before.

CYRANO: Beyond all time—forever and more.
CHRISTIAN: I'd wait for thee eternally,

CYRANO: I bring thee infinite heights
CHRISTIAN: Beyond all time—forever and more.
CYRANO: Of courage set to get your heart aflame.
CHRISTIAN: I bring thee infinite heights

CYRANO: I'd fight to death with my last breath
CHRISTIAN: Of courage set to get your heart aflame.

CYRANO: The scoundrel who's untrue to your name.
CHRISTIAN: I'd fight to death with my last breath

CHRISTIAN: The scoundrel who's untrue to your name.

ROXANE: How bold is your deed . . . lover mine.
How far you exceed . . . my design.

That you'd even bleed . . . is divine!
I'll have to concede . . . you'll do fine.

CYRANO: I bring thee eloquent words.

CYRANO: I bring thee eloquent words of love.
CHRISTIAN: I bring thee eloquent words.

CYRANO: My heart now sings, my lips have wings
CHRISTIAN: I bring thee eloquent words of love.

CYRANO: And leap to take one delicate kiss.
CHRISTIAN: My heart now sings, my lips have wings
CHRISTIAN: And leap to take one delicate kiss.

(As he ends the song, Christian leaps onto the balcony and takes his one delicate kiss.)

"The Trace of a Tear" which follows was sung by Roxane to the motionless form of Christian after he has been killed in battle.

ROXANE

Your last letter, and upon the pages your last tear. Oh, Christian, brave Christian! You knew you were going to die, and wrote to tell me we would never meet again. You had only to send me a blank piece of paper. (Sings)

The trace of a tear on your letter,
The letter you wrote me last night
Says much more to me—more eloquently
Than all of the words you could write.
For if loving and losing is better
Than to never have loved as we do,
Then the trace of your tear
Makes it even more clear
That you loved me as I love you.

Next came our bid for a "pop standard" to extract from the *Sylvester* score—with the two senior cast members singing this very simple ballad, "The Twilight Years"

The twilight years
Are the sweetest years
When you have someone to love.
To share in your dreams about yesterday,
To care about plans for tomorrow.
The twilight smiles
Are the wisest smiles,
The tears are the tenderest tears,
And the highlight of love
Will be my light of love
In the twilight years.

"The Twilight Years" as a song was reprised several times. As a philosophy it was a goal Joan and I shared, a period of life we were looking forward to together. Granted, when I wrote it I was thinking more about our parents than about us, but we were all sentimental enough to have made it "our song" when the show was completed—since *Sylvester* wasn't going anywhere in particular, and no one outside the immediate family or friends had ever heard what it sounded like.

The last lyric of *Sylvester* reprinted is a number that has more than a passing reference in it to my more than passing interest in male anatomy, but in this context the interest was perfectly justifiable, and I must admit I had lots of secret fun in committing the subterfuge. Near the end of the musical Sylvester has run off to a local brothel to try to establish his manliness. We catch up to him being pawed by not one but by two women of the evening in the Tangerine Room of Kozy Korner Klub, half-drunk. The song number: "Long, Long Nose." Lyrically it's rather undisciplined, but I think it's fun nevertheless.

SYLVESTER

Heaven! This is sheer, incomparable heaven. Two women at one time. I'm yours, Charlotte. You come next, Violet. Get on your mark, get set . . . (They paw him and sing)

Is it true, is it true
What they say about a man
With a long, long nose?
If it's true, if it's true
Then I'm gonna find a man
With a nose that shows.
By the way, I hear it say
If he really sets his sights
Goodness knows, his passion grows
To the most fantastic heights
Like the Eiffel Tower and Statue of Liberty
He can tame the most inhibity
Blushing rose
With his long, long nose.

Cyrano, nay thou art Romeo—
Juliet is hung'ring for your touch.
Come to me, my handsome Romeo.
No one ever thrilled me half so much.
Isn't he . . . the most earth-shakeable
Living doll, when all is said and done?
Come to us, for we are takeable.
Come and take us, lover, one by one.
I'd give my all,
Each piece and bit o' me—
And all because
You're the epitome.
Come twitter me.

Cyrano, our loving Romeo,
Here at last is man enough for me! . . .
You send me sprawling with that enthralling nose,
Send me reeling with that appealing nose;
Your anatomy sure can shatter me, gee.

I'm all ecstatic from that emphatic nose,
All chaotic from that erotic nose,
Rendered Gallic by that so phallic marquee . . .

Is it true, is it true
What they say about a man
With a long, long nose?
If it's true, if it's true,
I am gonna find a man
With a nose that shows.
By the way, I hear it say
If he really sets his sights
Goodness knows, his passion grows
To the most fantastic heights,
Like the Eiffel Tower and Statue of Liberty
He can tame the most inhibity
Blushing rose—
With his long long,
I said long, long,
With his long, long nose.

There were more songs in *Sylvester* but it was never my intention to include them all here. Among others was a mandatory (for me) number between Sylvester and his analyst. I had spent six months or so a couple of years before with a second analyst—this time as an outgrowth of my having had the only real trouble I'd ever experienced in my relationship with Joan (during the period of job hardships and temptations into the lurid world of those few sleazy sexual experiences). I was now through with the sleaze for the time being, and the job troubles, and problem of lack of communication with Joan, and was obviously starting to transfer some of my conflicts onto the typewritten page again, with *Sylvester* the first major writing project I'd gotten involved with in perhaps eight years. So in a sense *Sylvester* was a ground breaker, and if it has served no other purpose over the years, it brought me a measure of fulfillment then that I'd not experienced in some time.

I was very lonely the summer I got *Sylvester* going. Joan was away at a summer camp with the children—it was the first of many summers in which she worked as head counselor to help pay for the children's summer as campers. But while she was working I spent much of my time on weekends writing lyrics in longhand while out on a rowboat on the lake at Camp, and simultaneously distancing myself sufficiently from the hustle and bustle and distraction of camp activity (to say nothing of the distraction created by lots of rippling young male muscles).

And though it wasn't technically good enough to use as a demo recording, one of my fondest memories from *Sylvester* is a home-made taping Esther and I did—in which Joan performs the Roxane part in "Eloquent Words." Hearing it always brings a big smile to my face. And the same tape at the very end also includes Esther's children and mine—all very young—singing a reprise of "The Twilight Years." A recording like this, though played infrequently as it is, is some of the stuff of which lifetimes are made, and provides some of the memories death cannot take away. Even with my new life-style having become the center of my present life, the memories of the old that are the fondest, like *Sylvester* and all it involved, are only enhanced with the passage of time.

SIX

"Kazoo."
"From the top of the mountain, see the rainbow
And the big overflowing pot of gold—

Popularity unceasing and your royalties increasing
When you're famous and your memoirs have been sold."

THE WORD "KAZOO" is my affectionate, abbreviated title for the next writing project of any importance in which I was involved, *The Golden Kazoo*. Before it became my writing project, "Kazoo" was first a satirical novel by John G. Schneider, published in 1956 by Rinehart. As conceived, it was a fantasy, taking place four years into the future. (The adaptation done by my collaborators and me advanced the time slot to twenty years ahead; thus we thought we were allowing ourselves more than ample time to get the show produced. Ha!)

The novel concerned itself with an ad agency's handling of a presidential election campaign. In 1956, politics and advertising weren't yet being mixed on an intimate basis, or if they were, the fusion had not yet been well publicized. But as if John Schneider had been a fortune teller with eerie psychic powers, many of the predictions in his book proved later on to be more than accurate.

Some months after I'd finished *Sylvester* with Esther in 1960, my dear Joan, always encouraging me, thought it was about time I started working on something new. Getting into the act herself in her impatience to see me embark upon a new project on my own, she began by industriously scanning newspaper columns in search of a subject which appealed to her, which she hoped would then appeal to me. Thus it was Joan who came up with the idea for my next musical adaptation, "The Golden Kazoo," after she'd read the book on the sly, and after she'd noticed a fanciful comment in somebody or other's newspaper column that *they* thought *The Golden Kazoo* would make a good musical. What I evidently didn't make clear enough to Joan was that that subject had to appeal enough to me, too, since it was I who was going to be doing the writing. In this one instance I let the selection be influenced and in fact be oversold to me by Joan, more out of regard for her interest in it than my own. But I shouldn't have. I was no more the right writer for a musical version of *The Golden Kazoo* than she was, and obviously she certainly was not, for in the almost 36 years we were married she barely ever even wrote a letter, much less a musical.

Be that as it may, I permitted myself to be swayed by her confidence in me . . . "Aw, come on, Bernie, you can do it, you know you can," etc.—I suppose in part because I had absorbed some feeling for the advertising business by this time, and the new project dealt entertainingly with that subject. In retrospect I see that if "Kazoo" were ever going to be done as a musical at all, it would have needed a lot more sophistication and expertise than I thought I was capable of at that relatively early period in my career. We were talking about brittle and nasty social satire, and I don't believe I viewed myself as quite up to the task. Nor was I sufficiently knowledgeable about the ins and outs of politics. In the end I needed John Schneider, the original author of "Kazoo," to feed me a lot of basic background about the political scene that wasn't in his book. But asking him to do so rather made me feel more like a student to his teacher than author to author. My less than confident approach to the material first had to be reckoned with when, after making the initial inquiry about the rights, I was suddenly stymied in preparing a suitable draft of an outline of the prosposed libretto to show Mr. Schneider before we proceeded.

The rights to "Kazoo"? I don't remember who, (possibly Joan again), but someone suggested I get in touch with Schneider through his publisher. I was evidently a good enough letter writer even then, because my letter sold him, and before you know it Schneider and I were batting out weekly or twice-weekly correspondence to each other, just getting to know each other, and tossing around ideas. He was amenable to our (Esther's and my) working on a projected musical stage adaptation at no advance fee to him providing that we agreed to make a presentation to him after about three months worth of early exploration and planning. A retired ad exec himself, he was full of suggestions about the project, but very agreeable to giving us our own creative space.

I'd further "sold" him early on, on the strength of several "sample" lyrics I sent him, and he waited patiently for the three month deadline to arrive. About halfway along toward that date I despairingly had to admit to him that I didn't think I was yet a resourceful enough librettist to overcome the various obstacles I saw developing in the musical's book. I explained that my fort till then had been with lyrics, and that—if he didn't mind—I needed to bring in still another collaborator, this one a copywriter I'd been working with at the ad agency that was then paying my weekly salary, the Zlowe Company. The copywriter's name was Don Sheerin. Don had no track record as a librettist, but he was a howl of a laugh getter in conversation, and a writer of clever commercials. Schneider again agreed. Evidently no big shots with multi-bucks were knocking at John's door for the rights to "Kazoo," so he was willing to give us the extra time we needed to get more comfortable with the project.

After a few weeks' extension on the three month deadline (typical enough for the ad business) Don and I (with spouses at our sides) made our way by auto early one Saturday morn to Westerly, Rhode Island, where the Schneiders lived in retirement, set to present to Mr. and Mrs. Schneider the fruits of our labor up to that point. The Schneiders had no piano, so we uncomplicated our visit by a third by leaving Esther and her spouse at home, and bringing in their stead a reel-to-reel tape recorder (I don't think the smaller cassette kind had yet been invented or popularized)—along with a heartfelt though hardly professional demo recording of Esther and my singing all the roles in whatever part of the score had already been completed (a good half-dozen numbers, I suspect). The day proved to be a roaring success, partly due to camaraderie being achieved instantly—along with the arrival of the martinis John and/or Jane generously poured. Don and I were already well indoctrinated into the drinking pattern, since we worked in the ad business where almost every deal or social contact was consummated while martinis were being consumed. Our wives were not yet well trained as drinking buddies, but on this occasion they joined in as moderate social drinkers, and enjoyed the afterglow along with the rest of us. We all became famous friends automatically, not really well equipped for tackling the creative task at hand with clarity, but deluding ourselves into thinking we were doing just that. Our wives' semi-sobriety was at least going to get us home safely, after a suitable interval of drying out along with our dining out.

"Kazoo" was going to be a daring show. It dealt with a mature couple who were living together but not married (the ad agency president and his talk-show host mistress). In the early 60's that shocking theme simply wasn't being explored in the musical theatre, with the one notable exception being *Pal Joey*, which was a flop the first time around and thought to be "ahead of its time." One of my difficulties in getting the libretto of "Kazoo" off the ground was that I simply didn't know how to get around that kind of "deviate" behavior.

The story also dealt with adultery (by the wife of the presidential candidate yet!) and lots of double dealing in both the political and advertising scenes. For an innocent babe-in-the-woods like me—no way! Wrong, wrong, wrong! Even with a sophisticated collaborator like Don Sheerin steering the way, we were having our troubles. But we tried, oh, how we tried!

John Schneider had a connection with theatrical producer Kermit Bloomgarden, who was indeed a name to be reckoned with in those days. And so as soon as we had complete script and score—we presented the first live presentation I was ever involved in—to a producer! One qualification: The score was still being performed not live, but via tape recorder, this time on a studio-recorded tape for which we used a professional enough musical director (Esther was not qualified in that department), one semi-pro male singer, and Esther's good voice and my own passable one.

Fine quality though the Wollensak was, using it proved both a schlep and a detriment to our overall effectiveness in trying to sell our show. But out of inexperience we had settled for taped rather than live performance of the songs, none of us fully realizing in advance how uncomfortable it feels for a group of people to be sitting around in a circle, trying not to stare at each other, listening to tape-recorded material that part of the group is trying to sell to the other part. I mean—where is everybody supposed to fix their eyes?

Well, we didn't yet have the know-how to simplify the arrangements for grouping the people together "live" and thus making a completely live presentation, even though with all the know-how in the world, that grouping would have been a tough nut to crack. Why? Because Esther was a mother and had small children at home; Pat Conti, the male singer, and I had full-time jobs that we had to rush back to; Angelo, the pianist, had his own responsibilities elsewhere in teaching, arranging and studio administration; John Schneider would be traveling in from out of town; and the Bloomgarden people themselves naturally weren't able to give us all the time in the world or any schedule that would fit all our needs best. So we didn't even try, and we settled for using the recording. But imagine how awkward it was for there to be three Bloomgarden people listening to John providing occasional live comments and to me reading live narration between each song, as they watched me fumblingly turn the reel-to-reel machine on an off at appointed times within the narration, and as John and I tried inconspicuously to read their minds from their vacant stares, *we* all the while certain *they* were feeling like a captive audience.

As a matter of fact I have always thought—ever since this very first "audition" of material to producers in their office till practically the very last one I was involved in some twenty-five years later—even when performed all live, this type of theatrical ritual has to be just about the hardest thing in the world to carry off. Performing by writers for prospective producers (usually in a stiff and stilted or nervous and jerky manner) of an abbreviated version of a score along with a brief narration of the story line leading up to each song, almost invariably has to take place at one point or another during the course of trying to engage producers' interest in writers' work. But while that performance is physically going on, the performing authors somehow have to rise above the deep-gut feeling that their small professional audience (sometimes just one producer alone) is bored stiff, and resentful of being asked to overlook the imperfect quality of the authors' presentation, concentrate on what is supposed to be happening to whom (instead of the lousy performance), and wind up being sufficiently impressed with the material and presentation to drop everything he has on the drawing board for the next several seasons and go-go-go with this one.

Especially with the producer(s) scarcely cracking a smile through the entire hour or hour-and-a-half in which the presentation is being made, the authors must either be gluttons for punishment or incurable optimists not to lose all hope that there's a chance for their new work after all. Even with all the performing training and skill in the world, and even if the material is brilliant, writers are still fighting too many obstacles at the same time to come off with much more than a handful of hope, and then perhaps only if their name is Jerry Herman.

I use the latter name specifically because of a story I once heard and which I often wonder about in which Jerry Herman was supposed to have sat down at David Merrick's piano, brightly run through five representative numbers from *Hello Dolly* and been immediately lauded by a grinning Merrick with a congratulatory handshake and a boisterous "Sold!" Does it ever *really* happen like that? Has it *ever* happened like that to virtual unknowns? Forget it.

Although our presentation to Bloomgarden and associates wasn't exactly a fiasco, it got us nowhere. John Schneider and I did manage a marvelous correspondence with each other for a year or so afterward, during which time he lost faith in Don Sheerin's book and Esther's score, but never either in my lyrics, my ability, or my perseverance. We kicked around other ideas, such as his re-writing the libretto himself, and my coming up with an alternate set of lyrics which would therefore free me from any ties I had with Esther on previous work on the project. Unfortunately I didn't save that correspondence. It in itself would have made a fascinating book, for John was a stylish writer, and he also brought out the best in me.

However, just as we were about to give up the entire effort and relationship, he got word that a nephew of Kermit's, Hank Bloomgarden, who had achieved sudden fame as a contestant and winner on the TV quiz show "The $64,000 Question," was interested in latching onto "Kazoo" as a property, and so John suggested that I come up with a recording in a hurry of a few new alternate songs with music by a name composer, in order to present them to Hank. The best I could do was to write a few new lyrics for the new "Kazoo" and have them set to the music of a wonderful Tin Pan Alley tunesmith by the name of Al Frisch, who was somewhat better-known than Esther, and with whom I'd started working sporadically but concurrently on one or two new projected show ideas. (I'll be spending more time with and about Al Frisch later.) The aim was to see Hank Bloomgarden as soon as possible with what Schneider and I had re-done libretto-wise and what I had re-done on the score with Al Frisch. But all to no avail.

For the first time in my life I learned to drink martinis before lunchtime, because on appointed days when I was to meet John in town for occasional late morning confabs and I took an early lunch hour, his suggested favorite meeting spot for me to find him was at the bar of the hotel where he'd stayed overnight. But soon after these confabs and a few meetings with Hank Bloomgarden, Hank gave up, John gave up and obviously so did I. Our correspondence thinned out, then came to a halt.

A couple of years later I read that John died. I sent a note of condolence to Jane, then read that she'd returned to her hometown and died soon afterward herself. It had almost seemed as if my Joan's latching on to John's last baby, "Kazoo," briefly gave him the lift he'd needed from the alcoholic doldrums he'd been stewing in since retirement and very probably since long before, and that once the scenario for that fairy tale of a sudden successful musical was over, so was his will to live. But that was and still is only conjecture on my part. Despite all the wonderful correspondence we had with each other, and the martini mornings, I never actually got to know the inner man well enough, and that's too bad.

What I did know, and what therefore had to suffice, was that he was a kind man, a gentle man, a wise and very funny man, and although his world and mine were many worlds apart, there were ties and bonds between us that inevitably happen when two people are working on a project together, and are spending lots of quality time together, either in person, or, as in our case, largely by mail. I grew very fond of him, admired and respected him, and in the end was proud that he had allowed me to tamper with his most successful book, *The Golden Kazoo*. Beyond that I was sad in the end in having let him down, in not having helped him sufficiently to start that new life he sought through our adaptation of his "Kazoo."

Now for some "Kazoo" lyrics, with dialog leading into or asides about some of them as we move along.

First, computer analyst Schmucker's assessment of early results of the presidential polls, as being reported to Pete Fowler, Chairman of the Republican Party National Committee: "Percentagewise" from "Kazoo" Number I, with sprightly music to match by Esther Stoller.

> Percentagewise, the Democrats are in.
> The popular vote's almost seventy-thirty
> Against us; the midwest is doing us dirty;
> The farm vote is slipping a little bit more each week.
> It's bleak.
> Percentagewise we're up the creek.
> (Up the creek, getting weak, so to speak.)
>
> Percentagewise, we'll take it on the chin.
> Electoral college's spread as I figger
> Is sixty to forty against, growin' bigger.
> New England is swinging to Jonas' camp en masse.
> I pass.
> Percentagewise we're out of gas.
> (Alack, alas!)
>
> With her colored lights illuminated brightly
> For the most important job she's ever had,
> My computer has been churnin' day and nightly,
> But the only news she ever views is bad, bad, bad!
>
> Percentagewise, we're heading for a spin.
> We're losing the Negroes and Jews and the Vatican

Seventy-two twenty-eight Democratic an'
Slowly but surely the athiest vote as well.
Oh, hell!
Percentagewise, we're S. O. L.

* * * * * *

When I saw the first results I called the doctor
Who examined my computer's every tick.
He dismantled, tested, oiled her up and clocked 'er
And his findings were, it's us, not her,
That's sick, sick, sick!

Percentagewise we're never gonna win.
Our contact in space, though at present adrift, he
Is sure that up there we're at best fifty-fifty.
Who cares about voting when daringly floating on high?
Oh, my!
Percentagewise, percentagewise
We'd better kiss our boy goodbye!

Next was a throwback for Esther and me to a bygone era . . . that of "We Ain'"
which you may remember I had later re-written for another project as "I'm Not." Here
it goes once again, for a third time, in "Kazoo." (This time it's for the male lead,
Blade, and the female lead, Flaire, singing an explanation of and disavowing any
sinful aspect to their relationship.) Once again, this material worked better in its
originally intended form as the hand-clapping Gershwinesque gospel type number it
was first conceived as, for *Dream About Tomorrow*, but Es and I weren't yet learning
that lesson well enough. In this instance it's called "We're Not"

> BLADE
> Though they're all saying
> What a hot romantic pair we are,
>
> BOTH
> We're not.
>
> BLADE
> Even conveying
> In the midst of an affair we are
>
> BOTH
> We're not.
>
> FLAIRE
> Wish all their tales were torridly true.
> Wish I had time for no one but you,
> But as we are love constantly goes to pot.
>
> BLADE
> Shot.
>
> FLAIRE
> Flying out the window.

– 74 –

BLADE
Though they're all saying
Just as close as man and wife we are,

BOTH
We're not.
Any affair we share is strictly from afar.

BLADE
Some day for kicks while right on the verge
Let's take the time to yield to the urge
And prove to the world the lovers we're not we are.

Because I was successful in finally using the same subject matter and at last changing the framework for it, when the time came to re-write the project as "Kazoo II" with Al Frisch as composer, the following was my effort at creating a whole brand new number in place of "We're Not"—given the same basic text ideas in Schneider's novel to follow for situation. This is called "I Love You But"

FLAIRE
(Singing on the phone to Blade, expressing her disappointment in his not having shown up the night before)

I love you but
Seems like I'm in love
By myself, all alone.
Can't you see
There's a time in love
When women need more
Than love on the phone?

I love you but
In the game of love
Heads you win, tails I lose.
Take my hand
In the name of love
And carry me off
With rice and old shoes.

My satisfaction
Won't come from words.
I need some action,
The kind you find in bees and birds.

I love you but
It takes two in love.
Drop that phone. Take that fling.
I hear tell
Things they do in love
Can bring you a thrill
Like nothing on earth can bring.
Come on and try the real, real thing.

BLADE

Don't start playing the housewife.
Don't make formal demands.
Ask me not for valentines
And hours of holding hands.

Don't start playing the housewife.
Don't sit home by the fire.
Ask me not for valentines
To fill your heart's desire.

I crave the action,
But if you please . . .
Let's save the action
Till we are free as birds and bees.

Don't start playing the housewife.
Build no cottage for two.
Ask me not for valentines
To prove my love is true,
And I will not ask you.

Besides having a bouncy, rhythmic Al Frisch melody, the above new version of exploring Blade and Flaire's romantic predicament had the added attraction of being composed as a two-part song in which each part could be sung both separately and against the other. It was the first time either Al or I had tried our hands at that device, and it worked well, and we had a winner in it. But as I've already explained, "Kazoo II" also went down the drain, and so "I Love You But" did, too. Now to return to "Kazoo I."

Early on in the show cornfed Republican presidential nominee Henry Clay Adams and his equally cornfed wife Zelpha, speculate on their new future personalities as they become victims of ad agency hype. "I'll Give 'Em Me"

HENRY

I'll give 'em me, I'll give 'em me
And all my personality.
If they're bent on entertainment
A la Jolson and Astaire
I'll holler "Mammy" from my knees
And spring into the air.
And I'll protect the little man
As only movie he-men can.
With the "Yup" of Gary Cooper
And the "Myaah" of Edward G.
I'll give 'em something for nothing and me.

ZELPHA

I'll give 'em me, I'll give 'em me
And all my personality.
With the lilt of Judy Garland
I'll deliver loud and clear
The only singing recipe

They'll ever likely hear.
I'll be the vamp and ingenue,
And even Lassie's mother, too.
With a burst of versatility
Recalling Sarah B.
I'll give 'em something for nothing and me.

HENRY
I'll be dash-dash-dashing for the ladies.

ZELPHA
I'll be sec-sec-sexy for the guys.

HENRY
I'll be two-two fisted for the young 'uns
As I route that ruthless ring of spies.

ZELPHA
In the Ei-Ei-Eisenhower story
Sure it's May-May-Maymie I'll portray.

BOTH
They'll get some-some-something
All for noth-noth-nothing
If they cast their votes our way.

HENRY
I'll give 'em me, I'll give 'em me
And all my personality.
With a hint of Valentino
And a trace of Francis X.,
I'll be the inspiration for
A new rebirth of sex.

ZELPHA
I'll be their nurse and confidante
As I fulfill their every want.
With the mystery of Garbo
And the heart of Helen Hayes . . .

HENRY
With the spunk of Wyatt Earp
A-settin' Western trails ablaze

BOTH
I'll unlock my inner being
And I'll throw away the key,
And give them something for nothing
And me-me-me . . .
And give them something for nothing and me.

Though John Schneider wrote "Kazoo" several years before the Kennedy era, it was amusing, though in the long run sad, that some of his predictions about future presidencies had validity in the JFK years. (Fact is, for me everything about that era is sad now, for I loved that president so. Can this country ever return to the threshold of Camelot?)

Here we have the agency wunderkind, Blade Reade, laying it on for the aspiring first lady, Zelpha Adams, in "Top of the Mountain"

BLADE

From the top of the mountain, see the rainbow
And the big, overflowing pot of gold.
Popularity unceasing,
And your royalties increasing
When you're famous and your memoirs have been sold.

From the top of the mountain see the stardust.
Catch the glitter, touch the glamour, feel the glow.
Just command when you are high up
And have Frank Sinatra fly up
To the White House for your own exclusive show.

You'll love to dine at eight in . . .
Buckingham Palace,
Marvel at the Taj Mahal.
They'll have you dedicatin' . . .
Oil wells in Dallas;
There'll even be a Zelpha Adams doll

(Who wets her panties.)

From the top of the mountain see adventure
At a thrill-packed and overwhelming pace.
Was there ever more beautiful a place?

ZELPHA

But I read that it's expensive
Entertaining so extensively
And all first ladies work around the clock
Planning parties by the scores
For all those State Department bores,
And then for each affair I need a brand new frock.
If this is true, I'll never last.
I'm just as frail as I can be-e.

BLADE

Your cloudy view will soon have passed.
Come over here and take a look with me.

From the top of the mountain see assistance.
Fifty servants are at your beck and call.
When you feel like making merry,
Call your social secretary
And your staff will work while Zelpha has a ball.

From the top of the mountain, see Aladdin.
Rub his lamp and the fashion world is yours
For there soon appears a genie

With a vision by Cassini.
You will never need to shop again in stores.

And when you're all alone and . . .
Missing your kin folks
There's a simple remedy.
Pick up the telephone, and . . .
"How've ya been, folks?
Come on and spend a month or two with me.

(There's so much room here.)

From the top of the mountain see the grandeur!
Why, it's almost too wonderful to face.
Was there ever more glorious a—
Ever more marvelous a—
Ever more beau-ti-ful—a place!

A favorite of mine which was cut from the final script, but which happens to be one of the few cornball patriotic lyrics I ever wrote, and for that reason alone deserves to be reprinted here, has our Republican candidate, in a reflective mood, singing "I Cut My Teeth on Kansas"

Think of all the chances I've missed
Being Kansas bred and Kansas born.
I've settled for a lot less,
But my career was spotless
In the midst of all that corn.
Think of all the chances I've missed
Being honest as a new born lamb.
I haven't got a bank full
But still and all I'm thankful.
Kansas made me what I am.
Kansas made me what I am . . . for . . .

I cut my teeth on Kansas.
She made me strong and true.
She's sprawling with wheat fields,
With corn fields and beet fields.
Why, even the dung heap
Is red, white and blue.
I cut my teeth on Kansas,
The heart of the brave and the free
And though I forsake 'er,
I love every acre
For she's like a mother to me-e-e.
She's like a mother to me.

When we needed a big patriotic rally number early on—for the Democrats to drive home their campaign slogan with, Esther tapped into her memory bank and came up with what we thought was a rouser to which I set the lyric "Ten Cent Loaves of Bread." For some inexplicable reason (I guess this sometimes happens) the final result was disappointing. It never really sounded inspirational. I revive it here only to give you a sample of what I did first with Esther, (presented to Kermit)—then did a second version of with Frisch (presented to nephew Hank.) Together the two contrasting lyrics make up one of those interesting bits of musical theatre trivia that I hope in the long run will make this book more entertaining for some musical theatre buffs and/or professionals other than me. First, the bomb.

What a day for the U.S.A.—
Ten cent loaves of bread!
Millions of hungry faces now agree
Soon they'll be well fed.
Oh, happy day; three cheers and hip-hooray
For one thin dime a head.
It's like a nineteen-twenty world of plenty
Nickel subways, quarter haircuts,
Ten cent loaves of bread.

What a year when we see appear
Ten cent loaves of bread.
When people frail and thin from dietin'
Now begin to spread.
Oh, happy year, rejoice and give a cheer
For one thin dime a head.
We're back in nineteen forty, flushed and sporty.
Nickel phone calls, quarter movies,
Ten cent loaves of bread.

Honest John Jonas, a friend of the people,
A kin to the little man is he . . .
Offers a bonus to all of the people.
Now, this is the man for you and me.
He's gonna see that we consumers get a break.
Each bite of bread'll taste as sweet as sugar cake.
I'll have my shiny new plane.
I'll have my trip to the moon.
Let's wreck the Adams campaign.
Let's bring in Jonas, and soon.

What a day for the U.S.A.,
Ten cent loaves of bread.
Millions of hungry faces now agree
Soon they'll be well fed.
Oh, happy day, three cheers and hip-hooray
For one thin dime a head.
It's like a nineteen-twenty world of plenty,
Nickel subways, quarter haircuts,
Ten-cent loaves of bread!

Now for Version II, called "Bring Back the Days," with music by Al Frisch—not that it was so much more polished lyrically, but at least it did have a bit more satirical bite, and after all "Kazoo" was a satire and needed the bite badly.

Bring back the days, the glorious days
Of the ten cent loaf of bread.

Too long has the country gone forward and onward.
It's time to go backward instead.
As prices go rocketing up, up and up—
Remember when coffee was five cents a cup!
Too many new trails are already ablaze.
Let's bring back the glorious days.

When the subway was only a nickel
And the neighborhood movie two bits
And you were in luck if you earned half a buck
Cause then you could mix with the ritz.
When your haircut was only a quarter
And your cigarettes fifteen a pack.
What I wouldn't give—
Why, it hurts where I live
To think of those days coming back.

Bring back the days, the glorious days
Of the ten cent loaf of bread.
Too long have the people been skinny and puny.
It's time we all started to spread.
Why, even with money to pay for champagne,
What I wouldn't give for an old two cents plain.
Enough of this progress, let's start a new craze
And bring back the glorious,
Gay and uproarious,
Bring back the glorious days.

Next, the first act closing in the original version of "Kazoo" with Esther, with everything falling apart for our hero Blade Reade: "Somebody's Got to Pick Up the Pieces"

BLADE

First Zelpha runs off with that bum (her hairdresser). Adams is behind 64 to 36. The Republican National Committee is set to fire me. Fanny Frazer (copy-chief of the enemy agency) can blow the whole set-up to hell anytime she strikes a match. Sour racket? You bet! Oh, well . . . (he sings)

Somebody's got to pick up the pieces
When your world comes tumbling down.
Somebody's got to hitch up the wagon
And go hustling into town
Hoot'n'hollering: "Hey there, wake up!
You have had your share of trouble.
Grab a shovel on the double
And clean up all that rubble!"
Somebody's got to pick up the pieces
After lightning hits your tree
And that somebody, yes, that somebody,
That somebody sure enough is me.

Somebody's got to pick up the pieces
When your moon-shot goes kerplunk.

Somebody's got to call you a taxi
When you pass out stone cold drunk,
Hoot'n'hollering: "Hey, there, get up!
It's your day to be recruited.
It's a cinch that you ain't suited
For lyin' there polluted."
Somebody's got to pick up the pieces
From the last catastrophe,
And that somebody, yes, that, somebody,
That somebody might as well—
That somebody what the hell—
That somebody sure enough is me!

In another brief excursion into "Kazoo II" and satirical patriotism, this number doesn't replace anything in particular from "Kazoo I," but it does provide another opportunity for cornfed candidate Adams to do his thing, this time with a small group of Boy Scouts. "Everything American"

HENRY
What do I stand for, boys? Why, that's simple. Zelpha, the flag, please,
    Ma'm.
Everything American
Is what I represent.
The prairie plains,
The subway trains,
The girl and boy scout tent.

Everything American
Like jazz and rock and roll,
Installment plans
And garbage cans
And Wheaties in a bowl.

Behold our splendors near and far—
A land so bountiful and free.
I'll fight to keep them as they are.
No change will come about with me.

Everything American
Like freedom at the poll,
And simple folk
Who thrive on Coke
And hot dogs on a roll,
Everything American
Warms my heart and stirs my soul.

After all, boys, my name isn't just Adams, you know. It's Henry Clay Adams,
and that stands for something extra.

Everything American
Like Sioux and Seminole.
From Harris Tweed
To signs that read

"Se habla Espanol."

The flag and every stripe and star
Belongs to every single man.
I'll fight to keep them as they are
Though manufactured in Japan.

Everything American
From Levy to O'Shea,
And plain chow mein
Which comes from grain
That's grown in I-o-way.
Everything American—
That's the good old U.S.A.

In another excursion into "Kazoo II" . . . we discover a number which again replaced nothing in particular in "Kazoo I," but which reinforces the validity in Joan's reason for thinking "Kazoo" would be a good project for me in the first place, my advertising background. I had fun with this one. The song: "Madison Avenue U"

The scene is the Enemy Camp: BS&J Advertising. Lance Banner, President of BS&J, has just discovered that his copy chief, Joe Quanto, defected to the Republican agency. He swears vengeance.

The role of Lance Banner is played by the same actor who plays the part of Blade Reade, only slightly disguised; purpose—to give the impression that all agency executives are cut out of the same bolt of cloth. (By the time *Kazoo* was written, I had already worked for a half-dozen small agencies, and was rather proud of this observation I had come up with concerning the similarity in all my bosses. That still holds true today.)

(One historical note: The mention of shirts of TV Blue—for those readers too tender in years to remember—refers to TV's requirement in its early days that men wear light blue shirts rather than white, in order to minimize glare.)

So that's the game that Reade is gonna play!
    Unprincipled and dirty all the way!
    Well, he will learn to rue the day
    He took me for a fool.
    The man forgets we're graduates
    Of the same hard-hitting school . . .

    Madison Avenue U.,
    Madison Avenue U.—
    Long may your graduates remember
    Your uniforms of charcoal gray
    And shirts of TV blue.

    Where any measley mailroom clerk
    Can score a forward pass
    And get an 'A' in dirty work
    By kicking someone in the . . .
    Ass—pirations are always skyhigh,
    And loyalty ever taboo
    At grand old Madison . . .
    All for gratis in

Madison Avenue U.

Now, supposin' that you've chosen to be honest
And sincerely work your fingers to the bone,
And your efforts are creative,
Never, never imitative,
Plagiarism is a practice you can't possibly condone.
And supposin' you're allergic to martinis
And at golfing you miss every putt by yards,
And you seldom pad expenses,
Cause you fear the consequences,
And you still don't drive a Jaguar
Or have twenty credit cards . . .

You're a misfit, you're a misfit,
And your letter can't be won.
You'll never get ahead.
You shoulda stood in bed.
You don't belong on campus, son.

Madison Avenue U.,
Madison Avenue U—
Long may we hear the alma mater
That's low in tars and big in bras
And rinses just like new.

Where every member first must pledge
For our fraternity:—
The Sigma and Omega Boys,
Or better known as S.O.B.
Experience money can't buy
At being a heel through and through
At grand old Madison,
All for gratis in
Madison Avenue U . . .
Madison Avenue U.

It's funny how much I thought I'd forgotten about "Kazoo" before I started writing this, and how much I've remembered since. And all of it fondly, too. My wife shared most of it with me, as she did just about all of my writing projects—and she always rooted from the sidelines with all her might. If it hadn't have been for her encouragement right along, this book would never have been written because there would have been precious little to write about. Indeed among the fondest memories of my writing career through the years was the experience of having her share so much of that career with me. I can't imagine having gone though it alone. So much of the joy (and disappointments and pain) would have seemed so pointless alone. With her gone now there is really no one else around who knows much of what working in this particular career was like for me. And even though my work is not as widely known as that of some of the masters in the field I've mentioned previously, I've just uncovered this one more reason for *Of Rhyme and Reason* to exist . . . because Joan can't help keep any of it alive anymore; because I'm the only one left who can.

One last nod to "Kazoo" before we leave it forever. Was the golden one ever really found and executed? Well, yes, it was, by John Schneider in his book, of course, and by Esther and me in our finale, "It's Free," capturing (or borrowing from) a little Gershwin flavor along the way, but in this instance, suitably so. Once again, it's too bad you can't hear the melody Esther created for this one. I think it's probably very close to what Geroge G. himself would have composed for the very same situation.

It's free, it's free,
It's free, it's free,
It's all for nothing, it's free!

The sun and sky and land and sea,
It's all for nothing, it's free.

Sing hallelujah!
On it's unwavering way
To yah's—
A new Utopian day.

It's free, it's free,
It's free, it's free,
It's all for nothing for you,

A day to play and save your pay
And give the devil his due.

Your future lies in
The new horizon.
It's free, it's free,
It's all for nothing, it's free!

A wagonload full of food,
One for every family,
A train so long it never disappears.
Why, they'll join in jubilation
Throughout this mighty nation
To praise the biggest giveaway in years!

It's free, it's free,
It's free, it's free,
It's all for nothing, it's free.

The sun and sky and land and sea,
It's all for nothing, it's free.

Sing hallelujah!
On its unwavering way
To yah's—
A new Utopian day.

It's free, it's free,
It's free, it's free,
It's all for nothing for you,

A day to play and save your pay
And give the devil his due.

Your fortune lies in
The new horizon.
It's free, it's free,
It's all for nothing,
IT'S FREE!

SEVEN

The B.M.I. Workshop: being admitted; meeting
and working with new collaborators Saul Honigman
and Karl Blumenkranz, and having a great
learning experience and a helluva time musicalizing scenes
from Streetcar, Sheba, and many more.

"One little pigeon sees me coming./That one little pigeon
spreads the word,/Telling two little pigeons, then a few little
pigeons,/And before you know it/The whole pigeon family has
heard."

B.M.I. STANDS FOR BROADCAST MUSIC, INC., a company which was developed as
an alternative to ASCAP. ASCAP in turn, is a society which at one time was the only
existing professional organization representing the writers and publishers of American music and lyrics and other professionals affiliated with the business.

As I heard it, B.M.I. was a less elitist, less exclusive group, which in the early
60's was trying to develop its own stable of Broadway show writers, since most of the
old-timers in the latter profession had automatically become members of ASCAP
before this second choice of B.M.I. existed. In order to expand its stable B.M.I.
formed this Workshop in which aspiring lesser known writers or newcomers could
develop their skills by performing weekly assignments which really got down to the
nitty-gritty of what writing for the musical theatre was all about. The B.M.I. Workshop was headed by no less prominent a man of the theatre than Lehman Engel, noted
conductor, composer, musical director and himself an author and thoroughly experienced scholar and student of what makes a musical tick (and click). What a happy
wedding—B.M.I. and Lehman, and what a lucky day for all of us who were accepted
into membership as participants!

I know I sometimes have a tendency to underestimate my accomplishments. But
evidently in the sphere of trying to build a writing career for myself my will did prove
indominatable because somehow or other, though I was generally not aggressive
enough, I made the necessary phone call to B.M.I. to learn what the requirements
were for applying for membership in the Workshop, and was then sufficiently moti-

vated to fulfill those requirements in no time flat. Though I don't recall specific help from Joan this time and on this process, more than likely if my memory could completely reconstruct the story, she would have at least had a staunch supporting role.

Lord knows, the requirements were simple enough for me to fulfill. I needed only to furnish the Workshop Administrative Director, Allan Becker, with a resumé of my background as a writer, and samples of my work as a lyricist. Thus, though it surprised me when it happened, I was readily accepted just on the strength of samples of lyrics from *Sylvester* and "The Golden Kazoo" and a few lyrics I wrote especially for the occasion of applying—never set to music, lyrics for proposed projects I selected at random. I'm hazy on the dates, and the evidence is incomplete, but as far as I can tell I was accepted some time in 1963 and remained active in the Workshop until some time in 1965. I would have stayed on as long as they'd have permitted me to, but finally had to withdraw after two years because my boss at the ad agency then paying my weekly salary, the Zlowe Company, was not happy about my continuing, on an indefinite basis, to be absent from the office several hours during one afternoon every week. I explained to him on more than one occasion that it was a terribly important obligation for me, and that that was the only time this group met, and I assured and reassured him that the work for which he was paying me was not suffering (and I made sure that it was not by returning to the office on Workshop afternoons and staying as late as necessary, and coming in as early as necessary the following morning, and never taking any other time off. But he made his unhappiness known by scowling a lot and being stingy with raises, and I finally had to cry "Uncle" and drop the Workshop from my schedule.

I wrote four lyrics expressly for B.M.I.—before being admitted—simply to show my "stuff." One, based on a situation in the play *Never Too Late*, seems to have disappeared with the years. The following three lyrics, however, are part of what did the trick in my being accepted:

"The Sarge in Charge" (as might be sung by Will Stockdale in *No Time for Sergeants*)

> When Uncle Sam called me
> To come to his aid
> I still was a lad in my teens.
> That's why it's so thrillin'
> So soon to be made
> The Sergeant in charge of latrines.
>
> The sinks, pipes, and plumbin'
> Are lined up so clean
> And stretched out so furr—wall to wall!
> My kinfolks'll never
> Believe that I've seen
> The plumb biggest outhouse of all.
>
> What an honor! What a glory!
> What a dream-hatchin', throat-catchin' story!
> Of all the joes they could have chose.
> The sarge in charge is me.
>
> The captain's inspection

Was just like they said.
He gave me a turrible fright.
That crazy old goat
Went and buried his head
Into everything here in his sight.

I've rubbed and I've scrubbed
And if I had my due,
I'd follow it up with a sign:
"This place if off limits,
And men, that means you!
It now is a national shrine."

What an honor! What a glory!
What a hand-wringin', wing-dingin' story!
The trail I led to get a-HEAD
Goes furr as you can see!
Who dreamed that this could be?
The task was large,
But it's no mirage.
The sarge in charge is ME!

In *Night of the Iguana*, Hannah Jelkes might sing this next song to Shannon about her relationship with Nonno. "We Make a Home for Each Other"

I'm not lonely, Mr. Shannon,
Not with Nonno at my side,
For we travel, Mr. Shannon,
Travel far and travel wide,
And we're never to be pitied
For in each new land we roam,
We have roots, dear Mr. Shannon,
And we always feel at home.

We make a home for each other
Wherever we may be,
Not a regular home as you think of a home,
No, not the kind you can see.

We make a home for each other
In just the way we feel.
Not a regular home as you think of a home.
No, not a home that is real.

Not of brick nor of stone,
Nor of steel nor of wood
Nor of chimneys and curtains and flowers,
But it's something we own
And it makes us feel good
Knowing this home is ours.

We make a home for each other,
Which needs no walls nor base—
Finding treasures in life

In the pleasures in life—
No hardship's too hard to face,
When the home in our hearts
Is such a comfortable place.

In *Toys in the Attic*, Julian addresses his sisters upon his successful return home:
"Big Successful Julian"

Big successful Julian,
The way you wanted me,
The man who was never good at anything
Made it big, you see.

Big successful Julian!
I like it fine this way.
A hundred and fifty thousand dollar bills!
Sisters, that ain't hay!

I'm through with hiding
To stiff the waiter.
Now, whaddya think, whaddya think of that?
Now when I go riding—an elevator,
I don't even take off my hat!

No, sir, folks!

Big successful Julian—
We knew it all along.
The failure who never did a damn thing right
Now can do no wrong . . .
Now can do no wrong!

You'll believe your eyes
When you wake up in the morning.
Then you'll know for sure
It hasn't been a dream.
When these checks are yours for signing
You'll go wining and go dining
And soon be ord'ring snails and French ice cream.

And you'll travel on the stoutest ships a-sailing
And be dazzling in the finest jewels and furs
And you'll soon pretend to love it
Hearing other women covet
"That over-genr'rous lover of hers." "And hers!"
Because of me,
Because of me
We'll wallow in luxury!
Big successful Julian—
We knew it all along.

The weakling who couldn't raise a half a buck
Came back big and strong.

It is surprising to me that the three preceding lyrics were as good as they are, since I hadn't yet worked at B.M.I. or started enjoying the benefits of the wonderful learning experience at the Workshop. Therefore it is equally surprising to me that the very first lyric I wrote for my first assignment at the Workshop ever was such a bust. Perhaps I was too nervous. Perhaps I misunderstood the assignment. But whatever the reason, I'll record the lyric here for the sake of thoroughness, inept as it was.

The assignment was one of the several we had for musicalizing a scene from *A Streetcar Named Desire*. As I recall it, the choice of the specific scene was not mine at the time, but the choice of the content was. Evidently I was not yet wise enough to extract any but the most trivial of concepts from this Williams vignette between Blanche and Mitch. So I wrote, with the collaboration of Saul Honigman's music, "A Pretty Silver Case." Saul may still have the typed lyric and scene in his files; I don't know; I didn't ask him. I do not have them on paper, but I did have a crudely-made audio tape recording from which I've transcribed them here—just the basic lyrics (sung) without lead-in dialog or narrative. The tape also has a spoken request by me to Saul that "before proceeding with any new work at hand, we record this one so that I would be able to play it for my wife over the weekend." [It was always important to me, when I was doing my collaborating at the home of my collaborator rather than at my own, to let Joan share in the work session by taking a recording of it home for her to hear.]

Anyhow, here is that first effort which was justifiably criticized by Lehman Engel as being trivial, and which was quickly dismissed by our fellow Workshop members and promptly never heard of or from again or since. Blanche sings.

> Such a pretty silver case she gave to you.
> How sweet of her to care
> And leave her words of love forever there.
>
> Such a sentimental thought she left with you
> From deep within her heart
> To hold you near though you were far apart.
>
> How lovely it must be
> To be so much in love,
> To see so much in love that you can give . . .
>
> Such a pretty silver case with words designed
> To keep the love you knew.
>
> I wonder if I still my find
> In gifts of love the very kind
> Of pretty silver case she gave to you.

That was it. Not only trivial, but pointless, meaningless, and a sad way to display one's talents to a new group for the first time. But I can't retract it, or erase it as one can a tape. So we faced our early embarrassment as bravely as possible and went on to new assignments.

I had met Saul upon entering B.M.I.; we were among the new members who had been admitted without partners, and were encouraged to try working with each other, with the understanding that we would be free to "change partners" in due time if we wished. Saul's music to the above lyric effort was certainly adequate; I can't blame *him* for it being uninspired if *my* lyric, which was written first, was devoid of inspirational content or form. I've never asked him if he knew then—going in—if it was that bad, and didn't tell me so because he didn't want to hurt my feelings. Perhaps that first flop should have foretold a gloomy future for us together in the Workshop. We may both have been too shy to be sufficiently communicative with each other. I don't know. We went on to improve only ever so slightly with our next several assignments from *Streetcar*, and then onto what for me was a more meaningful project.

By the time we started work on *Sheba*, I was evidently more tuned-in to how to make selections in content from the material at our disposal. In one of my first opportunities to come up with a good original idea in the Workshop I even dared in a song for *Sheba* to express my homosexuality without being suspected, I think. [I must now digress for a moment to explain that in the Workshop I was actually experiencing contact with a far greater number of homosexuals than I had ever run into in my life. It is generally well known that there exists an inordinately large number or percentage of gays in the performing arts and the theatre (although I didn't really know this for a fact until *Christy* in the mid-70's). And most of us in the entertainment industry now wear our gayness with pride and openness. (I hope my readers have noticed how I now identify myself officially with being gay by saying "most of *us*." That's important to me, for I expect to wear mine with pride for the rest of my life.) Well, in the early 60's most of us were not yet open about it. Certainly not I, who was still the respectable and traditional married man till almost 1986. But in the Workshop, where the atmosphere was more creative and less inhibited, I think many of the gay men present simply didn't care about concealing their gayness. I don't intend to imply that the Workshop was a breeding ground for one kind of sexuality or another. I do mean to imply, however, that there almost *seemed to be* an inner circle of gayness present, and that one almost had to be flaunting one's membership in it in order to win kudos, plaudits, and the unequivocal admiration of our leader, Mr. Engel. It may be that some of the overtly gay writers were actually more talented than some of the closet cases like me, or some of the straights like my collaborators, but in further exploration I offer the evidence with sour grapes not intended, that only once, in several years worth of working actively there, did my collaborator and I receive undiluted praise upon performance of any one particular weekly assignment. Only God knows now how my stature might have changed if anyone there other than God and I had known at the time about my real sexual preference!]

Back to *Sheba* and my one big chance to drool in the Workshop without being caught. One of my selections of content was written from a woman's point of view, and involved a complaint about the inequality that existed then between the total undraping of women for modeling purposes (they were permitted by society to do it freely) as opposed to the only partial undraping of men—this was long before the days of *Playgirl*, etc. The song, with music by Saul Honigman which has precisely the right feel of indignation, is called "Injustice"

    MARIE

You can change in there, Turk.

    LOLA

Change?

    MARIE

He's gotta take off his clothes. Those drawings are for my life class. Turk is the best male model we've had all year.

LOLA

You mean he's gonna pose naked?

MARIE

No. The women do, but the men are always more proper. Turk's gonna pose in his track suit.

LOLA (looking on longingly)

Injustice. That's what it is.

MARIE

What is?

LOLA (singing while moving in to inspect Turk while he models rigidly)

Injustice, injustice,
It must be a form of injustice
For women to bare all
While men have to wear all their clothes.
Are men so ungainly,
Or is it they plainly don't trust us
To glare at their flesh
Without getting too fresh while they pose?

Injustice, injustice.
Since Adam and Eve it's injustice!
With fig leaves and leather
The men always feather their nest.
If girls must undrape
To reveal just how shapely the bust is,
It's clearly a case of injustice
For men to be dressed.

MARIE

There ought to be a law.

LOLA

Take it off.

MARIE

There ought to be a law.

LOLA

Take it off.

MARIE

There ought to be a lalala lalala lalala lalala law.

LOLA

Take it off.

MARIE

To draw them in the raw.

LOLA

Take it off.

MARIE
To draw them in the raw.

LOLA
Take it off.

MARIE
To draw them in the rararah rararah rararah rararah raw!

LOLA
Take it off.

BOTH
A law bent on warming the heart
Of every true lover of art.

MARIE
Unfairly divided
And clearly one-sided malpractice.
They'd fume with frustration
Were this situation reversed.
If men couldn't witness
How physical fitness has stacked us
While we watched 'em nude
And we rudely reviewed first things first.

We've surely been tricked
With a fraud they've inflicted upon us.
It's time we demanded
A similar standard for all.
It's clearly well reasoned
For any well seasoned Adonis
To give us a hint of his
Spring, summer, winter and fall.

LOLA
There ought to be a law.

MARIE
Take it off.

LOLA
There ought to be a law.

MARIE
Take it off.

LOLA
There ought to be a lalala lalala lalala lalala law.

MARIE
Take it off.

LOLA
To draw them in the raw.

MARIE
Take it off.

LOLA
To draw them in the raw.

MARIE
Take it off.

LOLA
To draw them in the rararah rararah rararah rararah raw.

MARIE
Take it off.

BOTH
A law bent on proving to prudes
There's nothing indecent in nudes.

LOLA
In doodles in hallways
And statues it's always injustice,
For men keep concealing
While we are revealingly frank.
In any museum
Whenever we see 'em our lust is
Confined to the charms
Of the chest or the arms or the shank.

MARIE
In art publications
From all observations, injustice.
And even in France
The removal of pants is denied.

BOTH
I can't help the feeling
That man will keep dealing injustice,
For man is a dumb thing
Who thinks he has something to hide.

MARIE
There ought to be a law.

LOLA
Take it off.

MARIE
There ought to be a law.

LOLA
Take it off.

MARIE
There ought to be a lalala lalala lalala lalala law

LOLA
Take it off.

BOTH
Against . . . INJUSTICE!

TURK
Okay. If that's the way you feel about it. (Starts to remove his shirt and laugh
as the women shriek and scamper away.)

Obviously I had my own little laugh, explored that subject till I was blue in the
face, and got away with it, I think. However, because of overkill, or possibly because
it just made people uncomfortable, or possibly because it was far from being the
blockbuster I perceived it to be, my peers and Lehman Engel dismissed "Injustice"
without much ado as they had everything else we'd done up to that point, leaving me
to suspect I was indeed being judged "unjustly" at the Workshop, but with no choice
other than to persevere. Even so, I'm sure it was good for the soul for me to have
gotten my feelings for the subject matter expressed for the first time ever, albeit in
disguise.

Saul and I didn't work together in the Workshop for very long. As I remember it,
the group had reached either a summer or other holiday hiatus, and Saul decided not
to return afterward. A man by the name of George Linsemann and I briefly explored
working together, but did not follow through beyond my one meeting with him up at
his place.

Then I got a call from composer Karl Blumenkranz who needed a lyricist with
whom to collaborate and to whom I'd been referred by a teacher friend we mutually
knew. Karl had previously been in the Workshop himself and pulled out. Having me
to collaborate with, he now rejoined, and became my continuing partner from that
point on—through the run of our participation at B.M.I. and on many other projects in
later years.

In addition to assignments musicalizing scenes or sections of other plays, my
efforts with Karl in the Workshop included adapting scenes from several short stories,
and the fully-fleshed-out challenging final endeavor of a complete musical, in our
case *Johnny Belinda*.

Before *Belinda*, the next two lyrics recorded here were set to Karl's music for the
two other "practice" projects we spent the most time on in the Workshop—*Idiot's
Delight* and *Look Homeward Angel*. The former play in another version much later on
became the flop musical *Dance A Little Closer* by Alan Jay Lerner and Charles
Strouse; the latter play, the flop musical *Angel* by Gary Geld and Peter Udell. I doubt
if my contributions to either of the two projects would have affected the fates of the
other writers' works one way or another . . . but for the record, here they are.

In my *Idiot's Delight*, picking up on a suggestion by Lehman Engel, the locale
was changed to a South American country in the throes of a revolution. At Rise, Harry
and the Girls have just arrived at the hotel, suitably frazzled.

SHIRLEY
Look at the crowd, Harry. Do you think they're . . .

BEULAH (gasping)
Communists!

SHIRLEY

Oh, my God! A regular revolution! Harry, let's go home. This tour ain't safe.

BEULAH

I wonder what it would feel like being home now.

SHIRLEY

Let's face it, we don't have a real home anyway. (sings)
The bowers of flowers
That bloom in the Spring
Are somebody else's plantation.

BEULAH

The corn that's as high
As an elephant's eye . . .
A fanciful falsification.

SHIRLEY

Get her!

HARRY

The deer and the antelope frolic
On everyone's range but mine.

HARRY AND GIRLS

But modest or plain,
It's there I'd remain.
As long as it's *my* home it's fine.

GIRLS

Home . . . may be a cheap hotel
Without a welcome mat.

HARRY

Home . . . may be a rusty hook
But there I'll hang my hat.

GIRLS

Home . . . may be a lumpy mattress
On a squeaky spring.

HARRY

But I won't complain
For there I'll reign . . . a king.

GIRLS

Home . . . is where the shoes and girdles
Slip right off with ease.
Down . . . to bra and panties . . .

HARRY

B.V.D.'s.

GIRLS

As you please.

HARRY AND GIRLS
All . . . I pray is once more lemme
Find . . . the way to H-O-M-E.
Take . . . me back to H-O-M-E home.

(After a soft-shoe routine dance break.)

HARRY
Home . . . the place where I can hang
My etchings on display.

SHIRLEY
Then . . . to sleep I lie me down.

BEULAH
Or lay.

SHIRLEY
Either way.

HARRY AND GIRLS
Sneer . . . and jeer but don't condemn me;
All . . . I pray is once more lemme
Find . . . the way to H-O-M-E . . .
Show me the way to go H-O-M-E—home!

From *Look Homeward Angel*—Scene One at the railroad station—young Eugene Gant enters carrying a handful of circulars, and is greeted by the Station Master, Luke.

LUKE
Is that the new advertising circulars your Ma had printed up? Let me see one, will ya?

EUGENE
Have two or three. Ma says I gotta get rid of them before I show my face for dinner.

LUKE
You mean you ain't had dinner yet?

EUGENE
Ma feeds the boarders first. Boarders . . . hah! A house fulla frustrated old maids and floozies and has-beens.

LUKE
It sure is a right handsome piece of literature. My Lord, look what it says here. (sings)
Stay at the Dixieland,
Altamont's homiest boarding house.

EUGENE
What it means is . . .

Stay at the Dixieland,

Home of illicit romance.

LUKE

You don't say. That's interesting.

Friendly and cozy and
Modestly priced for a boarding house.

EUGENE

What it means is . . .

They'll take most anyone;
Just pay a month in advance.

LUKE

And the extras like the change of linen
Every three weeks—
Does the rent include them all?

EUGENE

Yup!

And fancy indoor plumbin' there
With hardly no leaks
If you don't mind walkin' down the hall.

LUKE

What a ball!

BOTH

Stay at the Dixieland,
Altamont's homiest boading house.

What we mean is . . .

Stay at the Dixieland,
Ho-ome awa-ay from home.

LUKE (chuckling)

Kinda makes me wanna move in myself.

EUGENE

Forget it, Luke. I wouldn't recommend it to my worst enemy.

LUKE (hearing train whistle)

I'll help you hand out the circulars when the train pulls in.

EUGENE

Good! The sooner I get rid of them the sooner I get to eat.
(Moves to where he can see the train approaching; looks at it longingly as
stage darkens. He sings.)

Far away train,
What a beautiful sight . . .
Far away train,
Where ya goin' tonight?

Wending your way
Through an ocean of trees,
Far away train,
Can't I come along, please?

Far away train,
What a beautiful sound,
Tootin' your blues—
With your wheels dancing round.
North, south, east, west—
Wherever you're heading, I swear,
Some day I'll go your way
On the road to anywhere.

Far away train,
What a beautiful dream . . .
Far away train,
What a beautiful dream!

(Several disembarking passengers emerge. Eugene has started making paper airplanes with the circulars and tossing them into the air. Luke follows the passengers; distributes the circulars.)

LUKE AND ENSEMBLE
Stay at the Dixieland,
Altamont's homiest boarding house

EUGENE
The floors creak . . . the beds squeak.

LUKE AND ENSEMBLE
Stay at the Dixieland,
Altamont's homiest home.

EUGENE
That's a misprint. It should read homeliest.

LUKE AND ENSEMBLE
Friendly and cozy and
Modestly priced for a boarding house.

EUGENE
The maid drinks; the food stinks.

LUKE AND ENSEMBLE
Settle at Dixieland,
Never again for to roam.

ENSEMBLE
And the extras like the change of linen
Every three weeks—
Does the rent include them all?

LUKE
Yup!

And fancy indoor plumbing there
With hardly no leaks

EUGENE
And roaches crawling on the wall.
And that ain't all . . .

LUKE AND ENSEMBLE
Stay at the Dixieland,
Altamont's homiest boarding house.
What we mean is . . .
Stay at the Dixieland.
Ho-ome awa-ay from home.

EUGENE (walking off, almost inaudibly)
Oh, yes.
(sending his last paper plane up)
Ho-ome awa-ay from home.

About a year before Karl and I left active participation in the Workshop each member or pair of collaborators was given the assignment of selecting a project of their own, developing the project as a complete musical, and following through to completion. Karl and I sought a subject for adaptation which would be both appealing to us, and yet not be one that fellow members would likely be selecting themselves. Our reasoning was that if we were going to be spending a year or two on the project, it might as well be one nobody else was doing. We'd then be free and clear in case we wanted to follow through later with aspirations for a commercial production, for the rights would be more available, we hoped, if not sought out and gobbled up by stiff competition. Not a bad idea.

I suggested *Johnny Belinda* to Karl and he liked my choice, and we then found ourselves on safer ground than we'd ever dreamed we'd be, because no one else in their right mind would choose a story for a musical in which the heroine was a deaf-mute who not only couldn't speak but couldn't sing. (Our rationale was simple enough. Everybody else in the cast would sing and Belinda would be a dancer.)

The advantage we had in developing the show while at B.M.I. was that we were able to try out various ideas on our leader, Lehman Engel, and our fellow members, and discard or perfect other ideas, themes, musical numbers, or whatever—as we went along. Thus our musical of *Johnny Belinda* took shape as our last project in the B.M.I Workshop, and took longer and accumulated more waste paper than any show I've ever worked on, and was more polished for its day and age than any work I'd done before. I'm not certain [no one ever is] that all the revisions that we made along the way were well-advised. We fashioned the show too much as a "typical" Broadway musical—with secondary male and female "comedy" leads—(at Lehman Engel's suggestion) when [by today's standards] typical "Broadway" comic characters didn't truly belong in that type of folk opera. But developing *Belinda* in that way, for all to see and hear and critique each step of the way, was nevertheless an enormously satisfying experience both educationally and emotionally, and I couldn't have asked for a better way to become the "pro" lyricist and playwright I'd aspired to being for so long a time.

As it turns out I made more money from this show than from any other writing project I've ever been involved in. But more on *Belinda* later. For now, in a fitting finale to this chapter on my stint in the Workshop, I must record for posterity that obscure lyric of the one and only number by Karl Blumenkranz and me ever to win unequivocal approval at B.M.I.: "One Little Pigeon," as sung by Dona Laura while on a park bench in a musical scene based on a short story called "A Sunny Morning."

Did I hear my friend, the pigeon? Is that you, Cisco? Ah, yes, there you are. How could I miss you? One little pigeon sees me coming.

> That one little pigeon spreads the word,
> Telling two little pigeons,
> Then a few little pigeons,
> And before you know it
> The whole pigeon family has heard.

> One little pigeon finds a bread crumb.
> That one little pigeon has his fill.
> Three or four little pigeons,
> Then more little pigeons
> Gather all around me,
> A bread crumb in every little bill.

> Why, hello, it's nice to see you.
> I'm glad that you could come.
> Won't you join with me
> In a cup of tea
> Or at least another crumb?

> One little pigeon is a rude one,
> And one little pigeon is polite,
> And that little pigeon
> Is a fat little pigeon
> For he never tires
> Of swallowing everything in sight.

And how are you today, Pablo? And you, Felicia?

> And there I see the shy one,
> Too timid to attack
> As he stares at me
> From a nearby tree
> Wond'ring how he'll get his snack.

I never forget you, do I? There you are.

> Then one little pigeon leaves the picnic
> And no little pigeons can remain.
> From the first little pigeon
> To the last little pigeon
> They go marching onward
> To find someone new to entertain.
> But tomorrow morning
> I know they will surely come again.

EIGHT

Miscellaneous projects concurrent with and immediately after the Workshop (including meeting and starting to collaborate with Al Frisch, trying to market "Belinda," and finding a fan in Joan Scott of I.C.M., which led to Clint Ballard and "Love in the Afternoon.")

"You had to be this wonderful, / I knew it all along. / You had to be this beautiful— / I couldn't be so wrong."

AL FRISCH WAS THE FIRST COMPOSER I WORKED WITH who actually earned his living composing. We met at a Catskill Mountains resort at a time when he had been thinking of expanding his career to include scores for the theatre, because his old world of pop songs had in recent years been changing from one of graceful and romantic music and lyrics to one dominated by loud rock accompaniments to tempestuous rhythms and largely unintelligible words. He justifiably felt that there was no longer an economically sound future in pursuing the kind of work he did best for the kind of market he had always done it, and he wasn't about to lower his standards and resort to trying to compose music for the new generation and crop of, to us, weird-looking rock stars flooding the pop music market.

At the time we met he hadn't yet been able to find another "pro" lyricist who wanted to join him on the adventure of working "on spec" (speculation) in order to present marketable ideas to theatrical producers; and he knew of no way to break into the theatre other than to write on spec and try to interest someone important in his work. He had no ready-made connections in the theatre, but he *was* very willing to invest his time. And so he asked me to join him on the adventure, and I accepted his invitation, flattered to have been asked to collaborate with the composer of such favorite old-time pop song hits as "This Is No Laughing Matter," "I Won't Cry Anymore," "Two Different Worlds," and "Roses in the Rain," all of which I had known from big-star pop recordings of them in years gone by. I did not really have the time to take on another composer collaborator, but I agreed anyway. (By now my urge to succeed in the field may have been every bit as strong as the unmentionable sexual passion, and I simply couldn't sublimate both.)

The first work Al Frisch and I did together was on the previously discussed project, "Golden Kazoo" (II), for which I called upon him to fill the bill as the "professional" composer John Schneider decided we needed in our attempted rescue of the project at the last minute. As stated earlier, both versions of "Kazoo" were finally aborted, and it was Al Frisch's affiliation with ASCAP that led him and me to our next joint project: A musical based on Moss Hart's autobiography, *Act One*.

ASCAP, it seems, was now keeping up with B.M.I., and starting a musical theatre workshop of its own (though a different format), and although I had already started working in B.M.I. a year before, I was permitted by ASCAP to join in collaboration with Al for his presentation to the more newly-developed ASCAP forum. We chose *Act One* for source material partly because we were amused at some of the similarities between the Kaufman and Hart collaboration and our own.

Our *Act One* work took place in 1964, when, though hardly still a juvenile at 39, I'd had only months of training behind me at the B.M.I. Workshop, and therefore only months of its seasoning and polishing effect on me, and did not yet feel I was quite professional enough a lyricist to be competing at ASCAP with the big boys. And perhaps I was right, for our material as performed for the ASCAP Workshop was met with only cool response and the event led us nowhere.

But Al was so sure we had created something special that he refused to let the project die, and in time some of his feeling of self-worth and quality of achievement must have rubbed off on me, for I eagerly joined him when he next pinned down friends and acquaintances he thought might be helpful, and we performed our half-dozen or so numbers for them, too—several times, to several groupings of them. Also to no avail. We then even made a half-hearted attempt to reach Mrs. Moss Hart (Kitty Carlisle) through a theatrical attorney we knew, to try to get *her* attention to our fledgling project. But in the end when we couldn't reach Kitty Carlisle Hart (I don't know why we didn't try harder) we finally abandoned the idea of further developing *Act One* and went on to something new.

The spectre of *Act One* actually hovers over me still, for I loved the source material so, and over the years I haven't lost the feeling that it would make a whopper of a show-biz stage musical. As a matter of fact in 1984 or early 1985 my wife met Mrs. Hart at some theatrical function, a benefit or tribute, and mentioned to her that we'd tried in vain to reach her some twenty years before, but then dropped the idea. According to Joan, Kitty was all ears about the project that evening, and sounded both receptive and encouraging. But at that time there were too many other problems for Joan and me to deal with, and we simply couldn't afford to spread ourselves too thin. Joan's health was failing, and our immediate commitment to *The Shop on Main Street* was consuming as much of our energy and time as we could spare. And so we never tried to capitalize on Joan's chance meeting with Kitty Carlisle Hart. But soon after it's published I shall send her a copy of this book, ask her to read this chapter, and perhaps we can renew our interest together, hers and mine, in musicalizing her husband's autobiography.

Here are a few of the lyrics I wrote to Al Frisch's music for it some twenty-five years ago. First, a teenage Moss and a possible production number opener: "Me and Aunt Kate"

> Me and Aunt Kate
> Have an eight thirty date
> In the world of make believe.
> Stylishly dressed
> In our Saturday best
> In the world of make believe.
>
> Comic or tragic
> Or sweet and sedate—
> Wonder what magic they'll weave.
> Won't it be great—
> Gee, for me and Aunt Kate
> In the world of make believe!

Row E on the aisle? What a break!

Thank you, thank you,
For having a play.
Thank you, thank you
Is all I can say.
There's a lump in my throat
And an onrushing tear
As the houselights grow dim
And the moment grows near . . .

Me and Aunt Kate
Have an eight thirty date
In the world of make believe.
Set for a treat
At the edge of our seat
In the world of make believe.

Don't let the villain
And heroine fight!
What's up his nasty old sleeve?
Please turn out right
At the ending tonight
In the world of make believe!

Tonight? Well . . .

Tonight I am Juliet's love.
But soft, she appears there above.
I long to embrace her,
I leap to ascend.
But who am I fooling?
Why must I pretend?
I know that I always
Lose out in the end
Whenever I'm Juliet's love.

Or . . .

Tonight I'm Marie Antoinette
By typical troubles beset;
My subjects are hungry
And begging for bread.
Of course I can offer them
Pastry instead.
Who cares either way
When it's off with my head
Whenever I'm M'rie Antoinette.

Me and Aunt Kate
Have an eight thirty date
In the world of make believe.
Stylishly dressed

In our Saturday best
In the world of make believe.

Comic or tragic
Or sweet and sedate,
Lost in the magic they weave,
Isn't it great
Gee—for me and Aunt Kate
In the world of make believe!

Soon after their meeting we find Moss and George S. Kaufman singing a duet about their new relationship as collaborators. They also find time for private asides to the audience—individually—to divulge what they really think. "That's Collaboration"

> BOTH
> Partners in co-laboration,
> Ten until six every day,
> Filled with such deep admiration,
> Each gives the other his way.
> Moved by the same inspiration,
>
> Close as the pod and the pea.
> The problems and dangers
> Of working with strangers
> Would never concern him or me.
> Partners in co-laboration . . .
> We have decided to be.
>
> KAUFMAN (aside)
> But . . . he smokes like a chimney throughout the day.
> So thick is the air from cigar bouquet
> That sometimes I can't even see my way,
> Yet never do I say a word.
>
> HART (aside)
> But . . . he works through the day with such driving heat,
> We don't even stop when it's time to eat.
> To him the word "lunch" must be obsolete,
> Yet never do I say I word.
>
> BOTH
> Yes, that's collaboration,
> Pure and extra dry
> When two true mentalities
> Skip the formalities
> And meet eye to eye.

Bigger than Barnum and Bailey,
Born to remain at his side,
Strings on the same ukelele,
Bonded like Jekyll and Hyde.
Grateful as Bell to Ameche,
Loyal as Tarzan to Boy—

We never could quarrel
Like Hardy and Laurel.
We're thicker than Trigger and Roy.
Partners in co-laboration
Doing a job we enjoy.

KAUFMAN (aside)
But . . . his speeches and thank yous are so sincere
That when one is coming I disappear
And head for the bathroom so I won't hear,
Yet never do I say a word.

HART (aside)
But . . . I'm not one to quibble or make demands—
Poor fellow can't help his abnormal glands.
I thank him and he runs to wash his hands,
Yet never do I say a word.

BOTH
Yes, that's collaboration
In the purest sense—
When two great abilities
Call off hostilities
And tear down the fence.

Moved by the same inspiration,
Close as the pod and the pea.
The problems and dangers
Of working with strangers
Would never concern him or me.
Partners in co-laboration
We have decided to be . . .
We . . . have decided to be.

In the song "You Had To Be," an older and wiser Moss Hart alone in a crowd on Broadway reflects on his feelings of wonderment upon seeing Broadway for first time many years before. This, incidentally, was so strong a melody and might so readily have been sold as a ballad "single" in days of yore, that when we abandoned *Act One*, Al did one of the things he knew how to do best—he arranged for a wonderful demo (demonstration record) of "You Had To Be" and tried to peddle it as a single to his music publishing contacts in Tin Pan Alley. No luck.

If Messrs. Sinatra or Bennett or anyone else who still makes beautiful music is looking in on this . . . by God, the song is still available for being recorded.

Long ago and starry-eyed
Took a one-way subway ride
Down to the street I'd dreamed about for years.
With that first big breathless view
It was all that I could do
Walking on and holding back the tears.

You had to be this wonderful;

I knew it all along.
You had to be this beautiful,
I couldn't be so wrong.
For everyone at any time
That you're made mention of
Just lights up at the thought of you
And speaks your name with love.

You had to be this comf'table
For me to feel at home.
You had to mean so much to me
That I could never roam.
And now I see you're everything
I pictured from afar.
You had to be,
And Broadway, you are.

To wind up my memories of *Act One* for these pages, here is "Big Tomorrow" as sung by Moss while in his hotel room overlooking the theatre at which his first opening night is taking place, on the threshold of that first success.

There's a big tomorrow,
A big tomorrow
That's heading straight my way.
Gonna lose my senses
And bust some fences
And throw the rule-book away.

Want no more
Subway roar.
Now it's taxis for sure.
Swank hotels
Like the swells
And a weekly manicure.

There's a new complexion
To my direction
That glows like that marquee.
There's a rising star
And a big tomorrow for me.

Can't you see that sight of sights,
Bulb by bulb my name in lights?
Blazing out with bright success
M and O and S and S . . .
H and A and R and T . . .
Hey, you guys, Moss Hart, that's me!

It's my big tomorrow,
My big tomorrow.
A whole wide world of fame.
There's no greener valley
Than Shubert Alley

When Broadway knows you by name.

I can hear
Thousands cheer,
See them standing on line.
That's my play
On Broadway.
Every word is mine, all mine.

There's a golden summit,
And up there from it
For all the world to see
There's a brand new star
That is shining only for me.
And that brand new star
Means a big tomorrow for me.

At about the same time as I was creating *Act One* material with Al Frisch, I was beginning to wind up *Belinda* with Karl Blumenkranz. Feeling we had a professional and marketable musical on our hands in *Belinda*, Karl and I started looking around for an agent, or a producer, or a "godfather" or champion. We again learned that agents don't want to be your agent until you've got a track record, and getting a track record without first having an agent is next to impossible. But we persevered. We got letters about *Belinda* off to several big-name producers of that era, including David Merrick and Hal Prince, and received courteous replies but no interest. We then did manage to attract the attention of several lesser-known though substantial enough theatre people such as Philip Rose and Edward Padula, and got to perform our *Belinda* score for them individually—each was respectful but not overwhelmed.

It should be noted that I had written *Belinda* as a big show, and the proposed size of the project may have helped to discourage them. But at least we left the door open with them, and actually got to see both Messrs. Rose and Padula on several other projects later on. I concluded we were at this point evidently now coming across with some stronger degree of professionalism.

We were also able to make a presentation on *Belinda* to Joan Scott of I.C.M. (International Creative Management) which led to nothing in particular on *Belinda*, but did establish Ms. Scott's being enough impressed with my own potential to introduce me to another of her promising clients, a composer named Clint Ballard, for the possibility of setting up Ballard and me as a new team on a whole new project. I'll discuss the results of that attempt a little later on.

Back to *Belinda*: We were getting nowhere with it—till we started exploring the question of the rights to the original property of *Johnny Belinda*—the play and/or the film. Then we learned that Sheldon Abend of American Play Company controlled the rights to the play, handling them for original author Elmer Harris. And so we next went to see Mr. Abend about our completed work. After appropriately chastising us for not having inquired about the rights *before* starting the adaptation, he permitted us to perform our score for him, and then found that he liked it so much that he was prepared to put in a good word for us, and we actually got the exclusive rights for a fixed period of time on a "spec" basis, with no fee involved (we couldn't have afforded that).

In a sense he started acting as our agent on the project—by contacting his own resources on our behalf while we were contacting ours. But the only marketing ideas I can recall from that point on were a letter to and reply from Lee Remick in our attempt to enlist her interest, and an actual live presentation of the material to Shirley MacLaine in Shelly's apartment on East End Avenue. Neither contact resulted in anything overwhelming, though I've always thought that at this point we were really starting to talk big-time.

But I must return chronologically to the "almost wedding" of Spiro and Ballard through Joan Scott of I.C.M. Just what I needed at that time—another collaborator and another new project, right? But how do you say "No" when a big agent is expressing interest in you, and engineering the "use" and screening of a hot property evidently with potential for its outright optioning.

The project Joan Scott had in mind for Clint and me was *Love in the Afternoon*, a musical to be based on the film which starred Gary Cooper, Audrey Hepburn and Maurice Chevalier. It was a charming movie (although surprisingly dated now) of which Ms. Scott had arranged a private screening for us (this was in days long before the advent of the VCR). She even provided conference room space with a piano where Clint and I could meet to work. Funny, I don't remember how or why or how soon we abandoned the project and parted, but I do recall that Clint and I were simply not on the same wavelength, and couldn't get used to each other's style and product, and so another worthy attempt was soon aborted, and with it my contacts with Joan Scott and Clint Ballard. Clint had a musical produced off-Broadway several years later (*Johnny Appleseed*), and I saw him briefly at the theatre when I looked in on the show, but we have not been in touch since, and at this date I don't know what's become of him. Last I heard about Joan Scott, she had relocated to I.C.M.'s California office. And that was that, except that we still have those few lyrics based on *Love in the Afternoon* to include here, lyrics which I think prove that once more I'd let a really hot one slip through my fingers.

I have copies of only the following four lyrics from *Love in the Afternoon*. Briefly, the narrative concerns an innocent young French music student, Arianne (Audrey Hepburn), her private detective father (Maurice Chevalier) and her romance with the worldly wise American businessman Flannagan (Gary Cooper). First she confronts Papa about the lurid aspect of his work; then she yields to Flannagan's charms while trying to pass herself off as a woman of the world; then Papa pleads with Flannagan to throw the "little fish" back; then Flannagan finally admits to his defenses being down. This is lovely romantic fluff. Too bad the idea was scuttled. "That Was Love"

PAPA

Arianne, have you been into my files? You've been told to stay away.

ARIANNE

But some of those cases are so romantic.

PAPA

What cases? That filth?

ARIANNE

Not filth, Papa. Romance. I've read some over and over again. My favorite was in File D. The Duchess. (sings)

The Duchess who adultered
With a handsome Alpine guide . . .
That was love.

PAPA
That was lust.

ARIANNE
That was love.

PAPA
The Duke, a man insulted,
Had me trail them far and wide.

ARIANNE
That was love.

PAPA
That was lust.

ARIANNE
That was love.
She gave up wealth and title
For her frosty paradise.

PAPA
I followed day and night till
They had sinned not once but twice.

ARIANNE
They proved their love was vital
As they died entombed in ice.
That was love.

PAPA
Nonsense, Arianne. There was an avalanche. And what do you think started
it?
It was lust.

ARIANNE
It was love.

Who could ask for more than to die locked in her lover's arms forever?

PAPA
They'll thaw out this summer, and that will be the end.

ARIANNE
Well, how about this one, under M—for "Monk"? (sings)

That young Alsatian widow
And her Benedictine Monk . . .

That was love.

PAPA
That was lust.

ARIANNE
That was love.

PAPA
A monk with his libido
Has no business getting drunk.

ARIANNE
C'est l'amour.

PAPA
That was lust.

ARIANNE
That was love.

Forsaking sworn obedience,
He let their arms entwine.

PAPA
She wanted the ingredients
For Benedictine wine—
A case of sheer expedience
In getting to the vine.

ARIANNE
It was love.

PAPA
Face up to it. It was good business bottling it commercially. You see it in every wine store you pass.

ARIANNE
Love.

PAPA
Lust!

ARIANNE
It was love!

Papa, you're a cynic. You enjoy your work. You'd enjoy it even if you weren't paid for it. You enjoyed exposing Madame LaRoche.

Next came "Don't Be Scared, Mr. Flannagan"

FLANNAGAN
It's just hard to believe—a girl your age—all those men.

ARIANNE
Would you prefer to think you're the only one? Or that I've taken pills or carried on like the girl in Venice?

FLANNAGAN

If I thought that I'd scat like a scared jack-rabbit.

ARIANNE (singing)
Don't be scared, Mr. Flannagan.
I'm not that kind of bore—not at all.
Don't be scared, Mr. Flannagan.
My chase is hardly more . . . than a crawl.

I play the game alertly,
This game called love and run,
Maneuvering expertly
To keep it just plain fun.

Worry not, Mr. Flannagan,
I couldn't fall in love . . . if I tried.
There's no plot, Mr. Flannagan,
To seal your doom with groom—kissing bride.

Take my word, Mr. Flannagan—
I know the rule, and you'll be spared.
Come kiss me, Mr. Flannagan,
Come kiss me, and don't be scared.

FLANNAGAN
You put that nicely.
We think the same.

ARIANNE
It always works out neatly all around.

FLANNAGAN
That's it precisely.
No guilt, no shame.

BOTH
Two grown-ups each with two feet on the ground.

ARIANNE
That is, of course, till we become horizontally inclined?

FLANNAGAN
Well, anyway, you don't have to worry about me.

They can't scare Mr. Flannagan
With plans most girls have planned—not a bit.
They can't scare Mr. Flannagan.
One whimper or demand and I quit.

No reason to embellish
The reason why we're here.
Just jump right in with relish,
Sincerely insincere.

ARIANNE

Have no fear, Mr. Flannagan.
We're models of good cheer, you and I.
Disappear, Mr. Flannagan,
And see how brief a tear I would cry.

So, my dear Mr. Flannagan,
You'll see I'm really well prepared . . .

FLANNAGAN

Yes, I see.

ARIANNE

Come kiss me, Mr. Flannagan.
Come kiss me, and don't be scared.

FLANNAGAN

Mr. Flannagan wants to kiss you,
And kiss you, and kiss you,
And kiss you, and he's . . . not . . . scared.
Next, "Such a Little Fish"

PAPA

Your records show that whenever a girl gets serious you run. She's very serious, so you'd better start running.

FLANNAGAN

But it's a little different this time.

PAPA

How different? Instead of the usual two weeks it will last four or six. (sings)

Throw her back, M'sieu,
She's such a little fish,
Such a little fish, this girl.

Swimming where the water
Is dangerously deep.
Sure, I know you caught her,
But she's too young to keep.

Throw her back, M'sieu,
What does she know of life,
Such a little fish as she?

Wet behind the ears she is.
Green enough for tears she is.
Give her time to frolic and be free.
There are many others in the sea.

FLANNAGAN

Look, I hired you to give me information, not advice. How much do I owe you?

PAPA

There will be no charge.

FLANNAGAN
Why not?

PAPA
Because she's my daughter. (sings)
    Think again, M'sieu.
    What does she know of life,
    Such a little fish as she?

    Wet behind the ears she is.
    Green enough for tears she is.
    Catch yourself a catch and leave her be.
    There are many others,
    Bigger, better others . . . in the sea.
    And last, "Of All the Women in the World"

FLANNAGAN
Who does she think she is—
Anyway?
Anyway—
Anyway!
What does she think she's got—
Anyway—
That would make me
The least bit interested in her?

Of all the women in the world,
Of all the women in the world—
What makes her think it's she
That I prefer?

Her figure isn't great.
I think she tints her hair.
Her hips are much too straight.
Her teeth—just fair.
Her eyes too far apart,
Her chest a mite too flat.
In short, a winsome wisp of a girl—
No less or more than that.

Yet I can't shake the longing
To be near her,
To protect her,
To revere her
And to be with her each moment of the day.

And I can't shake the feeling
That this strangely unappealing
Little creature is the rarest
And the loveliest and fairest
Of all the women I have ever known,
Of all the women I am yet to know—
Of all the women,
All the women in . . . the . . . world.

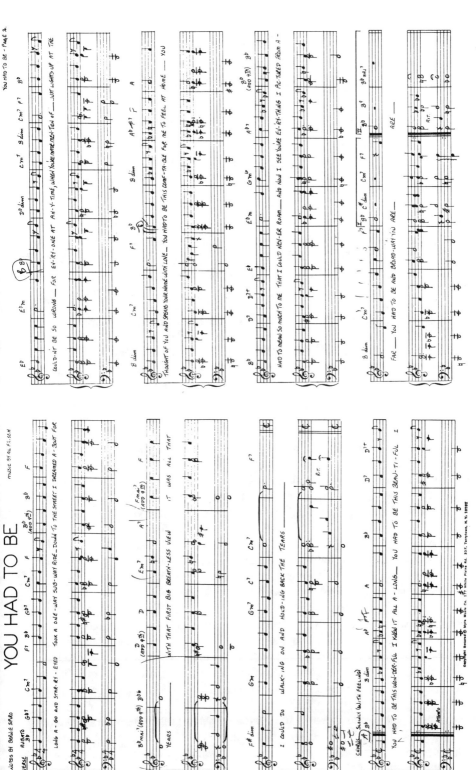

"You Had To Be," Moss Hart's love song to Broadway
from *Act One*—music by Al Frisch

NINE

"Johnny Belinda"—the production

"Let's start with the sign for 'sign'. / Let your fingers circle in the
air. / Move them up and down—and around and round, / And
that's how you sign for 'sign'."

OUR EFFORTS TO TRY TO GET *BELINDA* PRODUCED had pretty much reached an
impasse in 1967 when from out of nowhere Sheldon Abend, the literary agent who
handled the original property, received a letter of inquiry about the rights from Robert Dubberley of the Charlottetown Music Festival, Prince Edward Island, Canada.
Charlottetown was a popular summer resort where a new "Centre for the Arts" had
opened a few years before, for which a musical version of *Anne of Green Gables* had
been written and produced, and where it played to great popular acclaim. In effect
Charlottetown was telling the world: "Now it's Canada's turn." The grant-giving arm
of the Canadian government, called the Canada Council, was behind this cultural
move with necessary financing, and the Centre was justifiably receiving much favor-
able publicity, particularly since *Anne* was native to that region, and Canadian talent
and facilities were being tapped and employed, and that's really what the expense
and hoopla were all about.

We here in the United States don't often have the need to pat ourselves on the back,
so it may be hard for us to realize that other less formidable national entities more often
do have that need. For them a musical based on *Johnny Belinda* was a likely candidate
for a follow-up success to *Anne* at the Charlottetown Festival because *Belinda*, too,
was native to that region. But the Festival people wanted badly to do their own thing
with the property, their own musical adaptation, not Karl's and mine (which they
learned about from Sheldon Abend), and so although Karl and I in Shelly had a sup-
porter behind us and behind our adaptation, Shelly simply could not turn down, in all
good conscience, on behalf of himself and the heirs to the estate of original author
Elmer Harris, a concrete offer for a production by the Charlottetown Music Festival of
their own musical version of *Johnny Belinda* in the summer of 1968.

What Shelly *did* do to help protect Karl and me was to get them and us all
together, to try to work out some feasible arrangement between the Charlottetown
group and lawyers and himself and Spiro and Blumenkranz, (they kiddingly called us
Rosenkrantz and Guildenstern) so that we'd all be protected, and so that the work
Karl and I had done would not go totally down the drain. What finally happened was
that Karl and I did get slighted creatively. But we had little choice, because we did not
have a definite offer ourselves from someone in the U.S. to produce our own version.
In lieu of a possible court case (and we would have been babes in the wood if it had
come to that and would probably have fared no better in the long run), Karl and I
finally agreed to give artistic control and credits to the Charlottetown group in exchange for a percentage of the gross proceeds which they agreed to allow us as
originators of the idea of doing *Johnny Belinda* as a musical, and as providers of the

source material for *some* of what was used in their final production. Our hands were tied; we did not have ongoing rights to the original, particularly if our work was going to sit around without bringing in any income. We had to agree.

As I've stated earlier on, *Belinda*, the title of which was changed back to *Johnny Belinda* by the Festival team, did prove to be more lucrative for Karl and me than any other work for the theatre that either of us has ever been involved in, but while most of what took place onstage there was similar to how we had envisioned and created the musical, it must be remembered that ours too was an adaptation. Once a merger of writers and material like this takes place, it is difficult to figure out what ideas and material belongs to whom. But in the final analysis, while it was exciting for me to see *Johnny Belinda*, the production, in its final form, it was also terribly disappointing to know that it was far from really being mine, all mine (and Karl's).

Before negotiating, the business and creative heads of the Festival flew us up to Toronto so that Karl and I could make a presentation of our work to them. They were courteous and attentive, but I surmise pre-sold against us from the beginning, inasmuch as they more than likely had to come up with a complete Canadian creative team of their own so as not to clash idealistically with the financing program behind them. So, for whatever it's worth, they first unmercifully criticized our version (probably to get us in a defensive position), before eventually agreeing that much in it was just right for them. Their chief complaint was that our work was too "Broadway," not true enough to the simple folk style and quality of the original source material. We had known that ourselves, but had deliberately created our show in the "Broadway" style at the direction of Lehman Engel in the Workshop, whose one fear for our version at the time was that it wasn't "Broadway" enough.

In this instance we were up against "foreign" people out of the very background Karl and I as New Yorkers had taken the trouble to try to write accurately about, only to find them insisting we were way off target. They knew their country and the manners and ways of their people better than we ever could. And we could not be presumptuous enough to disagree. At any rate, with Shelly's inability to stave off their intervention because they were able to wave the cold hard cash in front of the Harris heirs et al, we finally decided it was a no-win situation for us and we acquiesced. Had we held on firmly to what was ours, had we resisted and insisted, we could conceivably have come out with more credit for our own work, or possibly blocked their production and seen our own production come to light *some* day; but we also could have gotten nowhere ourselves, and, in our preventing them from getting anywhere, we could have all wound up a lot poorer from having spent much more money for legal representation or whatever, without ever seeing a production, and without any of us ever receiving any income from the show at all. Anyhow, typical of me, I backed off from confrontation; I accepted the easy way out.

The final printed program cover for the musical *Johnny Belinda* as produced in Charlottetown in 1968 and 1969, and in Toronto, Montreal, Ottawa and Quebec—and later as a TV special on CBC—gives authorship credit to Mavor Moore and John Fenwick, with the following concession in small type below: "*MUSICAL ADAPTATION SUGGESTED BY KARL BLUMENKRANZ AND BERNARD SPIRO*," and an asterisk inside the program attributes authorship of certain lyrics to Karl Blumenkranz and Bernard Spiro. Particularly with this one, my avocational career continues to sound like a long history of "settling for."

Johnny Belinda, the musical, was actually a big hit in Canada, and it was the

Festival's intention to tour it in the U.S. and U.K. as well, with particular aim toward Broadway and London's West End eventually. I tried to intercede in their behalf (anything benefitting them would have financially benefitted me in the long run) and use some of my own connections during the ensuing years, to help with the transfer to either New York or London. My intentions were honorable, but nothing ever materialized in this respect either. As re-written by the Festival creative team, *Johnny Belinda* was still an extremely expensive production. While they could support it there because the Festival was subsidized, I'm afraid that here (I don't know about London) it could well have become one of those colossal flops that loses its giant opening investment in one fell swoop and never has a chance to recoup.

In my opinion, *Johnny Belinda*, the musical, as produced in Canada, lost much of its intimacy and therefore many of its most touching moments—not because it was too big, but because it was "too arty." It needed more of the Rodgers and Hammerstein style flavor Karl and I had sought to bring to it. Somehow that got lost in the transition. They aimed for much more dance (although ours, too, was a dancing show) and they settled for much less warmth of melody and earthy humor than what I had in mind. In the end, (again my opinion) they may have brought professionalism to it, but in the process they lost its heart. One thing is certain—the property does indeed work as a musical—it works quite well. But in their production *Johnny Belinda* became too mechanical and predictable, and suffered from the lack of its original sense of discovery and inspiration. Most of the Canadian reviews were ecstatic.

Joan and I flew up to Prince Edward Island to see *Johnny Belinda* during its first summer there, and we stayed long enough to see *Belinda* twice, and the other two shows with which it played in repertory once each. The others were *Sunshine Town* and *Anne of Green Gables*. The theatre was physically magnificent, and the Centre most impressive, and the Island itself more cold and gloomy than one would normally expect for a summer resort. It was too cold to swim! We managed to get out of town a bit to take in the sights, including the actual "Belinda's" home. Karl couldn't make the trip that year, but finally did get to see the TV adaptation of the show some years later when Robert Dubberley of the Festival team agreed to send us a couple of copies of the videotape as the one memento we held out for at a point at which there seemed to be no hope that the show would ever be performed in the U.S. The videotape confirms my contention that *Belinda* had lost its warmth and intimacy and heart in this adaptation. It did come closest to capturing the right quality in the one scene the Charlottetown creative group "lifted" with only minimal alterations from my own text. Knowing that I actually "created" this scene myself (with Karl's music, of course) and that it works so well when performed, has provided at least some of the compensation I've needed over the years to help ease the disappointment in our having had to part with our "baby" in its formative stages.

Therefore, for my token sampling of work from *Belinda* in this book, I start with "The Sign Song"—because, more than anything else, that's what *Johnny Belinda* is all about. Charlottetown, incidentally, inexplicably changed the music for this number, but it is Karl Blumenkranz' original melody, in its simple yet eloquent ability to complement my lyrics and the dramatic theme, that remains memorable for me to this day. After "The Sign Song" scene, without breaking the continuity in this reprinting, Belinda's father follows, in an extension into the next scene, with the strong soliloquy "When A Man's Alone," which was not used in the Charlottetown version, but which Karl and Shelly and I have always thought surely should have been.

(From Act I Scene 3 of *my* original version of *Belinda.*)

Outside the farmhouse where Belinda lives with her father, Black McDonald. Dr. Jack comes along carrying his rod and creel, prepared to go fishing in Black Pond. He calls out for McDonald but there is no answer. Then he sees Belinda for the first time and tries speaking to her, having heard about her in town and knowing she can't hear or speak, but not realizing she also can't communicate or lip read at all. Finally he speaks aloud to himself.

DR. JACK

You strange, tragic creature. I wonder if I could teach you. I wonder if you could learn any signs like the deaf children in the ward I used to work in. Belinda! (No response.)
Belinda! (He reaches out to take her hand. She cringes.) Don't be afraid. Come here. Come. (He beckons her toward him. She approaches.)
Belinda, where are the—fish*? The fish*? (She doesn't understand the sign for fish. He indicates his creel and pretends to cast a fly, and repeats the sign for fish. She now understands and points in the direction of the pond.)
Good. You know what I mean. Belinda . . . this is the sign* the deaf* use for fish*. (She tries the sign for fish and is fairly successful.)
That's just fine. Would you like to learn some other signs? Of course you would. Well, then—follow me. (He sings, and she follows his signs as he makes them, not always understanding, but mimicking him as well as she can.)

(NOTE: Asterisked words denote accompanying physical sign-language sign.)

Let's start with the sign* for sign*.
Let your fingers circle in the air.
Wave them up and down
And around and round,
And that is the sign for sign.

And how would you sign* for deaf*?
First you place your finger on your ear.
Then your hands must lock
To suggest a block
And that's how you sign for deaf.

For me* . . . point your finger inside.
For you* . . . point your finger outside.
For Baby* . . . how would a cradle be?
And a Mother* holds her baby here, you see.

Now, what is the sign* for speak*?
Let your fingers circle near your mouth
Till you almost feel
That the words are real.

Perfect!

You're talking a mean blue streak.
It's hard to believe
You've just begun to speak.

(She motions to him, but he can't make out what she means. Then she signs for sign.)

Oh, you want more, do you? Hungry for knowledge already? Well, let's see what I can remember. (Pause—while scratching his head.) All right. Ready now?

Now what is the sign* for sad*?
Stretch your fingers out before your eyes.
Bring them down to show
That you're feeling low,
And that is the sign for sad.

And how would you sign* for glad*?
Let your palm brush up against your heart.
Do it once or twice.
It's like "making nice."
And that's how you sign for glad.

A man* . . . tips his hat and he's tall.
A boy* . . . tips his hat and he's small.
A woman* . . . fastens her bonnet string,
And a girl*, you see, does the very same thing.

Now, what is the sign* for heart*?
With your fingers on the very spot
Draw a nice round sphere
With a point down here.

That's fine!

You're getting a good head start
And proving to me
You're really very smart.

(Belinda signs "sign" vigorously, then makes a huge circle with her hands and arms.)

Yes, Belinda? You mean you want to put all the words together? (She points to him and signs for speak.) You want me to say the words, too? All right. Go ahead.

(Belinda dances and performs the signs as he translates.)
— — — — — — — —girl
— — — — — — — —you, Belinda
— — — — — — — —deaf?
— — — — — — — — —oh, sad
— — — — — — — — —man
——signs
——girl
——glad

That's almost a story, isn't it? Your story. And you must be trying to thank me. Well, I* thank you* for learning* so well. That makes me* a good teacher.* (Belinda signs "sign" again.) More signs? All right. But just a few more. I've still got to go fishing.

> Now, here is the sign* for pray*
> And your prayers* are said before you eat*.
> And they're also said
> When you go to bed*—

Wonderful!

> You're coming a long, long way
> Toward saying the things
> You've always longed to say.

(McDonald returns and he tells Dr. Jack he thinks Belinda is a hopeless case. He has been able to teach her little other than to keep an account book at the grist mill. But Dr. Jack, insisting she is intelligent, asks for McDonald's permission to work with her further on the sign language. When Doctor Jack finally leaves to go fishing, Belinda joins him to show him the way to the pond. McDonald, left by himself, soliloquizes:)

McDONALD

Imagine him filling her head with fancy notions she can hear or speak like an ordinary girl. She ain't no ordinary girl. She's a dummy. Still, her mother wanted her to have a chance, didn't she? But dammit, there's work to be done and I need her to do it! And I can't afford to pay a hand.

Her mother . . . Cathy . . . my Cathy. You understand, don't ya, Cathy? I know I promised ya I'd look after the child, and treat her good. Maybe it would have been easier if I married again. And it looks like I might have the chance to pretty soon, if the Widow Maggie has anything to say about it. But all these years, Cathy, it's you I missed, you I thought about every night. (Sings: "When a Man's Alone")

> When a man's alone
> It ain't no good,
> It ain't no good at all.
> No comfort when he's tired
> When night begins to fall.
> No chance to feel desired
> Or ten feet tall
> When a man's alone.
>
> Although I'm on in years
> It happens now and then
> When springtime reappears
> I am young again.
> And suddenly I feel a spark
> And chills run down my spine
> And it's moments like these I remember
> And dream of the nights you were mine.

When a man's alone
It ain't no good.
He walks a lonely mile.
With no one to look after
And share his cares a while
Or laugh to hear his laughter
Or need his smile—
When a man's alone.

It's true, Cathy, I miss you all right. We weren't together very long, you and me. And maybe I didn't tell ya then or even know it myself. But I know it now, and I can say it and mean it with all my heart. I love ya, Cathy, and I done my best for Belinda.

I gave her a home
And three square meals a day,
And clothes to wear
And kept the boys away.
What more could any man do
That I ain't done?
What more could any man do!

I learned her to work in the grist mill
And handle a sack full of grain,
And scoop up the grain in the hopper,
And I never once heard her complain!
No, I never once heard her complain!
What more could any man do
That I ain't done?

My money, it never came easy,
So how could I send her to school?
Besides, they'd be all of them laughin'
And calling her dummy and fool!
What more could any man do
That I ain't done?

Besides, I can't forgive her,
No, not in all my life,
For she was the one
Who took away . . . my wife.

When a man's alone
It ain't no good,
It ain't no good, I swear,
For while he's growing older
He sees her everywhere.
His arms reach out to hold her
But she's not there . . .
When a man's alone.

(He walks off slowly as the lights fade and the scene ends.)

Part of the first chorus of "The Sign Song," music by Karl Blumenkranz

I think we can thank the B.M.I. Workshop for the improvement if the above scene and both musical segments have a touch more polish, professionalism and class than any of my other work to this point. Earlier I acknowledged that it was at about this time in my career that my work started reflecting more maturity, and I think we have finally reached that stage.

For instance, thank goodness I realized in advance that there was no way I'd be able to achieve creating something comparable to "The Sign Song" without having instruction in the sign language myself. I had to accept the responsibility of viewing each new work project at the professional level it warranted, rather than "just for the fun of it." And so I spent a few sessions at a class at the Manhattan School for the Deaf, just enough to learn whatever signs I'd need to write the lyric for what resulted in "The Sign Song." And when "When A Man's Alone" needed my digging into McDonald's character and background perhaps a bit more extensively than Elmer Harris did, I was up to that task, too; but it was more like a voyage of discovery than a task, because I was truly collaborating with Harris, the original author, in creating and extending motivation for the character he created.

In a sense avocation was finally becoming as serious as vocation, and from this point on I seldom let go of it for long. By the early 60's my wife had started working (as a teacher). My own career in advertising, while still important, by then no longer needed to be the end-all. And with Joan still encouraging me all the way through my journey as lyricist and playwright, I was letting myself become carried away by the creative urge, and spending more and more time addressing it, though the 40 to 50 hour week in advertising never left me enough time to feel truly fulfilled.

Thus far I've limited myself to including just a selection of lyrics, not all of them, from each show I've been involved in. Having previously recorded the two "key" numbers from *Belinda* to start with, we now return to committing some of the fourteen others to print. My ensemble-type opening number was called "Bum Luck"; and its negative approach was possibly an outgrowth of an element of lyric-writing learned in the Workshop having to do with expressing ideas in opposites. (Odd that the opener for the Canadian counterpart had a title precisely opposite mine: "A Fine Catch.")

(Outside Dr. Jack's office in town.)

FLOYD (A fisherman)
Are you the new doctor in town?

DOCTOR JACK
Yes.

FLOYD (holding up his empty net)
What can you do for a lousy catch, Doc? (Bystanders laugh)

HECTOR (A farmer)
What can you do for a sparse crop, Doc? (He pulls two skinny ears of corn out of a sack. More laughter)

A PATIENT
My arm feels like it's gonna fall off, Doc. (The doctor takes him inside. The fisherman sings, followed by the farmer, and then others, as villagers gather around and join in.)

FLOYD

There's a world full of fish in the ocean
So slipp'ry and wet
That they're all of them still in the ocean
And none in my net.

HECTOR

There's a field full of seeds that I planted
To feed us this fall.
But aside from some weeds where I planted
There's nothing at all.

ENSEMBLE

Bum luck this time round.
Lobsters is stubborn, and so is the ground.

HECTOR

And my wife jes' turned up
At the town Lost & Found.

FLOYD

Tough break, fella!

ENSEMBLE

Bum luck, bum luck today.
But maybe tomorrow
I'll be back in form
And find me a clover
To help tide me over the storm.
I'll shine up a horseshoe
And make sure t'pray,
And maybe tomorrow
I'll have me a luckier day.

(Stella, the doctor's assistant, comes out of the office with the patient whose
arm is now in a sling.)

FLOYD

Hey, Stella! Hear Locky popped the question.

STELLA

I ain't said yes—yet!

There's a diamond I saw at the jeweler's
That's meant just for me.
But the ring Locky won in a crapgame's
As much as I'll see.

PATIENT

There's a goldmine that I've been a diggin'
Since back in the Spring.
But the only result of my diggin's
My arm's in a sling.

ENSEMBLE
Bum luck—this time through.
The goldmine is worthless.
The diamond is, too.

HECTOR
And my girlfriend is almost
A week overdue!

FLOYD
That's it, brother. You've had it!

ENSEMBLE
Bum luck, bum luck today.

But maybe tomorrow
My star'll be bright,
For I'll put a rabbit's foot
Under my pillow tonight.
I'll shine up a horseshoe
And make sure t'pray
And maybe tomorrow
I'll have me a luckier day.

REVEREND (entering)
Did I hear someone say "pray"? Glory be to God, it always helps.

HECTOR
How's business at the church, Reverend?

REVEREND
Not good enough, I'm afraid. (sings)

There's a town full of souls to be saving
Who've all misbehaved.
But the town full of souls I'd be saving
Don't want to be saved.

FLOYD AND HECTOR
There's a house full of gals in the city
We hate to refuse.
But the house full of gals in the city
Won't take I.O.U.'s.

STELLA
Cash on the line—or git!

ENSEMBLE
Bum luck, this time sure.
Some's too expensive,
The other's too pure.

HECTOR (sniffing)
And I think I just stepped in

A heap of manure!

FLOYD
Now, there's the clincher!

ENSEMBLE
Bum luck, bum luck today.

PATIENT
Wait a minute! Did he say what I thought he did? Why, that's the best *good* luck sign I ever heard.

HECTOR
Good luck? I wonder what it feels like.

FLOYD
I don't know. But it sure smells pretty all of a sudden.

ENSEMBLE
It's coming tomorrow—
A future that's bright.
No need for a rabbit's foot
Under my pillow tonight.
To hell with the horseshoe!
Why bother to pray?
It's coming tomorrow,
It's coming tomorrow,
It's coming tomorrow—
My happy-go-luckiest day!

Though some of the above lyric may seem a trifle obvious, dramatically it serves the purpose so well—(of expediently introducing the town, its people, some of its leading occupations, its piety, its superstitions and its local color—all in one number)—that twenty-five years later I doubt if I'd want to change a word.

Next to be remembered here is "Belinda," the closest thing we had to a romantic ballad, sung by Dr. Jack to Belinda as he observes her practicing writing alphabet letters in the sand—after she has accompanied him on another occasion to Black Pond for his weekly fishing excursion.

Innocent and starry-eyed
Though you still may be,
Seems to me you're growing every day.
Why, even now you're dreaming dreams
Of dashing, shining knights.
Well, don't you worry,
One will find his way.
Never mind the things
You cannot say . . .

Belinda,
He will hear you, Belinda,
He will hear all the joy of a child,
Reaching high, running wild,
Feeling free.

Belinda,
He will hear you, Belinda,
And he'll know from the moment you smiled
How bewitched and beguiled
One can be.

He'll answer the cry
Of a child who is lost in the night,
And show you where sunlight
Waits to be found.

Belinda,
He will hear you, Belinda,
For your heart is awake
Though your lips cannot make
A sound.

One of my favorite "naughty" "laundry list" numbers ever of those I've written, and I wrote a few for *Belinda* [I always do have an immense amount of fun with them even though it sometimes surprises me that other people don't always appreciate them as much as I do], is called "Little Black Book" . . . a favorite because it literally runs the gamut from A to Z—and that was no easy problem to solve. The villain of the piece, Locky, (the fellow who later winds up raping Belinda) is, in this number, sitting and drinking beer at the tavern with his buddies.

FLOYD
Say, Locky, what are you going to do with that diary of yours now that you're getting hitched?

MCGUFFEY
You mean Locky the he-man keeps a diary? Like a girl?

LOCKY
Just a little book I make notes in now and then. Here, take a look.

MCGUFFEY
How do you like that? Alphabetized—and filled up—A to Z.

LOCKY
I believe in learning by experience, fellas. It was the only way I could get to master the alphabet.

FLOYD
Which one was Ada, Locky? I don't remember no Ada.

LOCKY
Ada? It was all accounta her I got started. (sings)

Ada was an aging beauty,
Somewhat highly strung.
When she got to feeling moody
She craved someone young.
I could hardly do my duty

Being just turned ten.
But once we hit the sack
In time I got the knack
And joined the ranks of men.

FLOYD AND MCGUFFEY

In his little black book of playmates
Check off letter "A"—
Then Beth and Claire and Dora
And Eleanor and Flora.
Our boy is on his way.

MCGUFFEY

I see you got Gladys and Hildy too, eh? But who's this Iris?

LOCKY

Iris was an ice cold snooty,
Straight laced as could be,
Smart enough to keep her booty
Under lock and key.
Nach'rally I did my duty
Competing for the prize.
The crushing blow was dealt
And I made Iris melt
By dotting both her I's.

FLOYD AND MCGUFFEY

In his little black book of playmates,
Dot the letter "I."
Then Jenny, Kate and Lizzie
Who also kept him busy.
Oh, what a way to die!

LOCKY

And then—ah, Meg! New Year's Eve 1899. I remember it well, because
1900 sure began with a bang!

Meg was mad for making merry
Starting New Year's Day,
Lasting clear from January
Half way into May.
Conceding it was necessary
To free me from her nest,
I heard the doctor say
As I was hauled away
"This boy needs six months rest."

FLOYD AND MCGUFFEY

From his little black book of playmates.
Now add M-N-O.
Then Penny, Queenie, Rosy—
Who also were so cozy.
That leaves just eight to go.

MCGUFFEY

Next it was Sue and Tessie, I see. Right?

FLOYD

And how about them three sisters, Ursula, Vera and Wilma? Remember?

LOCKY

Yeah. Then Yetta.

FLOYD AND MCGUFFEY (in unison)

Yetta???

LOCKY

Okay. Okay. (sings)

> Yetta was a wild young bruiser
> Built like solid brick.
> Any guy who dared refuse 'er—
> He'd get his, but quick.
> Every time I tried to lose 'er
> She tied me to a tree.
> I guess you can assume
> Just who was had by whom—
> But that's how I reached "Z."

FLOYD

What happened to "X"?

LOCKY

That one's all up here, fellas. (He taps his head.) It ain't written down . . .

FLOYD AND MCGUFFEY

In his little black book of playmates . . .
Now it's all but gone.
From Ada to Zenobia
He's managed to disrobe ya,
But it's time to pass it on.

(They scramble for it.)

LOCKY

Okay! To the highest bidder. But with the understanding that any time I want it back for the night . . . it's mine, all mine.

ALL THREE

It's time . . . to . . . pass . . . it . . . on.

Almost everything I wrote for *Belinda* holds up well enough for me after many years. But, knowing it won't be all that easy for my readers to pore through endless lyrics (particularly without knowing or hearing the music) after this next entry I'll forsake the balance of my work on *Belinda* to wind up with an even half-dozen and move on to a new show. We close with the self-explanatory "I Want a Boy."

DR. JACK

You've been alone so much, Belinda. But you're not going to be alone anymore. You're going to have a baby. (She looks at him in awe, and slowly makes the sign for "mother.")

Yes, Belinda.

(She shows amazement and fear. She stands up and looks at and touches her body. And she signs, and alternately he translates—in song. The musical phrases accompany her signs.)

(Music, sign)

    How can it be?

(Music, sign)

    What will it feel like—

(Music, sign)

    Having a child

(Music, sign)

    Growing in me?

(Music, sign)

    How did it happen?

    Where is it from?

(Music, sign)

    How will I know

(Music, sign)

    When to be ready?

(Music, sign)

    When will there be

(Music, sign)

    Something to see?

(Music, sign)

    Why am I trembling,

    Trembling with joy?

(Music, sign)

    What will it be?

    I want a boy.

    Why not a girl?

(She signs: "No, a boy." She begins swaying, raising her arms as if holding a baby in them.)

Hey! You're supposed to be resting.

(She shakes her head "No" and swirls freely about the stage as he watches in amazement. Finally she signs again, and he translates aloud.)

You want to name him J-O-H-N-N-Y? All right, you can name him Johnny.

(She signs again, and he translates in song again.)

(Music, sign)

    How will I know

(Music, sign)

    If he should need me?

(Music, sign)

    How will I hear

(Music, sign)

If he should cry?
(Music, sign)
    Somehow I'll know,
    Somehow I'll hear him
(Music, sign)
    Just like I know
    I want a boy.

Like so many other worthy Spiro-Blumenkranz gems, "I Want a Boy" wasn't used in the Charlottetown production. Pity!

TEN

Juggling the first of two composers, Karl Blumenkranz (with Al Frisch) from the mid-60's to the mid-70's . . . and "Never on Sunday," "The Twenty-Seventh Wife," "Catfish Bend," and a little "Purlie" & "Iguana."

"Diff'rent . . . we're each himself/With diff'rent things to say and do and give/To make this world the same for you and me— / A better place for diff'rent folks to live."

THE TITLE OF THIS CHAPTER suggests that for ten to twelve more years I was working simultaneously with two composers, but that's only partly true. There were dry spells with each, so there wasn't always an overlap. But there was usually enough of an overlap to keep things humming. And in 1970, at about the middle of this period, Joan and I moved from Brooklyn to Manhattan, and the move changed some of my collaborating habits, too. More work with Al for the next five years and less with Karl. (I was always influenced by geographical convenience.) But before that, from the mid-60's on, Karl and I were riding on the crest of our high after having completed two years in the B.M.I. Workshop (and *Belinda*) together. So we were intent on keeping that high in gear.

One of us had read in one of the trade papers that Kermit Bloomgarden had plans to do a stage musical of the enormously successful film *Never on Sunday*, but no writers had yet been chosen to do the score and adaptation. Since the subject matter appealed to both Karl and me, and since I had already broken the ice with Kermit on the earlier project, "Kazoo," what could have been more natural than for me to take a stab at writing some material for *Never on Sunday* on spec in hopes of having an opportunity to present it and be considered for the final job? The only problem was—how do we (Karl and I) absorb enough of the film from one viewing to write half-a-dozen songs accurately enough to impress a prospective producer?

Well, Karl and I spent not one but two sessions at a local cinema where the film coincidentally was playing in re-release, and we took copious notes in the dark. But this process worked only minimally, and we soon found a better way, which was engineered by—who else—my wife! Joan had a friend whose husband did some work for a movie company, and who was able to gain access for us for a weekend to a copy of the typed film scenario of *Never on Sunday*. Bingo! That was all we needed.

We recognized this opportunity as being an extraordinarily good one, because, we imagined, not too many would-be contenders for authorship of the musical would have access to the same source. Karl and I therefore worked very hard for a couple of months (in our spare time only, since we still had to earn our respective livings—Karl's as a teacher), attempting to out-do ourselves. And we came up with a reasonably professional presentation, the words bound in a folder entitled "FIRST FIVE SCENES AND SIX SONGS OF SUGGESTED MATERIAL FOR A MUSICAL STAGE VERSION OF NEVER ON SUNDAY written and composed expressly for presentation to Kermit Bloomgarden."

And we did indeed get to make that presentation live to Kermit and several of his associates. With Karl's wife doing a lovely job of performing the women's songs, and Karl as usual being at least adequate vocally, and with the material generally sounding authentic and smart, one would think someone in the Bloomgarden office would show some animation and appreciation. Forget it. As I mentioned earlier, this kind of presentation is one of the most difficult things in the world to do.

Karl and I read somewhere a short time later that the Greek composer of the acclaimed and popular title song from the film *Never on Sunday* had finally been signed to do the score for the musical play, Joe Darion the lyrics, and Jules Dassin the book, and so Karl and I were out before we were ever in. In the end, none of the acknowledged contracted writers of record impressed us terribly when we caught up with an early performance of the Broadway production of *Illya Darling*, the show's new title.

The book was the book was the book; there was nothing much to restructure, refine, or recreate in it one way or another, although a little more humor surely would have helped. But if ever there was a question as to whether performers in musicals should be cast in lead roles only if they have at least minimally pleasant singing voices, *Illya Darling* supplied the answer every time one of the leads delivered a song. Ms. Mercouri and Mr. Bean may be wonderful actors, but with them carrying much of the burden of the score, had I been in composer Manos Hadjidakis' shoes, I think I would have cut my throat (or theirs) long before opening night.

From *my* version of *Never on Sunday*, the musical

SCENE ONE: A seemingly deserted shipyard in Pyraeus, Greece. Time: The Present. On stage are Tonio, a handsome new shipyard worker, and four other workers, a man referred to as The Captain, and the beautiful whore, Illya.

TONIO (to Captain)
You think I have a chance?

CAPTAIN
Why not? But you'll have to wait your turn.

ILLYA
I'm busy till eleven.

TONIO
Eleven then.
(He blows a kiss as she leaves, then turns to the Captain.)

Yippee! What a way to start life my first day away from home!

(He begins the musical number, "Eleven O'Clock")

I've got a date with Illya.

4 WORKERS IN UNISON
I've got a date with Illya

4 INDIVIDUALLY
At seven . . .
Eight . . .
Nine . . .
Ten . . .

TONIO
Eleven o'clock, eleven o'clock . . . with Illya.
Won't it be great with Illya?

4 IN UNISON
Won't it be great with Illya

4 INDIVIDUALLY
At seven . . .
Eight . . .
Nine . . .
Ten . . .

TONIO
Eleven o'clock, eleven o'clock . . . with Illya!

Mine in an hour,
A lifetime of bliss.
Mine to devour
With every kiss . . .

4 INDIVIDUALLY
Kiss . . .
Kiss . . .
Kiss . . .
Kiss . . .

TONIO
Say . . . won't it be fun with Illya,

4 IN UNISON
Won't it be fun with Illya,

4 INDIVIDUALLY
At seven . . .
Eight . . .
Nine . . .
Ten . . .

TONIO
Eleven o'clock, eleven o'clock . . . with Illya?
Fun to be one with Illya—

4 IN UNISON
Fun to be one with Illya—

4 INDIVIDUALLY
Alone.
Alone.
Alone.
Alone.

TONIO
Alone . . . with Illya.

4 IN UNISON
Please ring the bell when you get there
Or you may be in for a shock.
When my hour is up I may want her again

4 INDIVIDUALLY
Be it seven . . .
Or eight . . .
Or nine . . .
Or ten . . .

TONIO
Or eleven . . .

ALL
Oh, heaven! . . . o'clock.

Next, the American tourist, Homer Thrace, meets Illya and her Captain friend at the Bouzoukie Cafe. "Where Aristotle Walked"

ILLYA
What you doing in Greece if you not rich tourist or writer?

HOMER
I'm an amateur philosopher, looking for something in Greece.

CAPTAIN
Maybe you'll find it just from walking around this port. The old philosophers often walked here, you know.

HOMER
Wow! How thrilling! (sings)

Just think! Just think!
Aristotle stood upon this spot!

ILLYA
Big deal. This man—
Aristotle—what made him so hot?

HOMER
Just think! Just think!
Socrates might well have spoken here!

ILLYA
Waiter! Waiter!
Better bring another round of beer.

CAPTAIN
Illya wouldn't have gotten on well with Aristotle. His opinion of women was
rather low.

HOMER
Socrates and Aristotle—
May their virgin wisdom reign again!

ILLYA
Socrates and Aristotle—
Virgins? Hey, they don't sound much like men.

Aristotle, Socrates,
I like better men who's not so pure.

HOMER
Aristotle, Socrates—
Long may their philosophies endure! . . .

I want to walk
Where Aristotle walked
In days of Ancient Greece;
Talk to your youth
Where Socrates once talked
Of wisdom, truth and peace;
Dig through your ruins,
Roam your sands,
Holding your culture
In these hands.

Yes, I want to walk
Where Aristotle walked
In days when men were wise;
Learn first hand
And try to understand
Why man has closed his eyes.
The world is sick with trouble,
But we can make it strong—
Asking where, why, when, how

It started going wrong.

CAPTAIN

That's a tall order, my friend.

HOMER

I know, but a man must try.

ILLYA

I think he tries too much.

CAPTAIN

What she means is . . . look around all you want, but don't meddle.

ILLYA and CAPTAIN (in a counter melody)
Leave us alone, Homer Thrace.
This is a most happy place.
Leave us as happy
As when you found us.
Don't try to bring gifts of peace.
We have enough peace in Greece.
See the famous sights around us,
Then go home.

HOMER

I have no intention of meddling, honestly.

(At this point Homer reprises his "I Want to Walk" theme while the Ensemble joins the Captain and Illya in counterpoint with "Leave Us Alone, Homer Thrace.")

This number, I'm afraid, was simplistic and yet pretentious, both—not really as adroit as I'd hoped. One of our mistakes, therefore? Perhaps. But not such a grim one as to have warranted the icy reception we got in the Bloomgarden office, or their lack of courtesy in not even notifying us by mail or phone that someone else had been signed when finally that happened. Ah, well, that's show biz.

In a later scene, Illya and a presumably only temporarily impotent sailor share a sweet and touching few moments. "Many Things Are Love"

SAILOR

But what's the use if I can't . . .

ILLYA

If you can't what? Make love? Do you like music? (Starts phonograph going.) This is Greek love song music. Men like this music. You like? (sings)

Many things are love,
Many things are love,
Tenderness and gentleness
And friendliness are love.

Sympathy is love.
Harmony is love.
Listening to birds in Spring
Or Illya sing is love.

Smiling if you're smiling
From the heart is love.
Or helping someone else's smile
To start is love.

And memory is love,
Yes, memory is love,
And this is true
For me and you
Though all we do is kiss.
I'll remember,
You'll remember
Lovely love like this.

In another scene a bit later on Homer and Tonio have just bid goodbye to Illya, and each of them describes how she has impressed him, each for different reasons. Homer is sold on her intellect, Tonio her physical charms. Watching as she slinks away, they sing "There Goes a Woman"

TONIO
Che belleza!

HOMER
Extraordinary!

TONIO
There goes a woman.

HOMER
There goes a woman.

TONIO
There goes the perfect mate to mate with.

HOMER
To debate with.

TONIO
There goes a woman.

HOMER
There goes a woman.

TONIO
There goes the very best for whoring.

HOMER
Or exploring.

TONIO
With lips that set me burning,

HOMER
A mind that's ripe for learning.

TONIO
She's worth her price and more.

HOMER
Worth looking into.

TONIO
And ah, what fun to pry there!

HOMER
What depths of soul must lie there!

BOTH
Such depths t'would be a sin to
Not have been to.

HOMER
There goes a woman.

TONIO
There goes a woman.

HOMER
There goes a challenge for a teacher

TONIO
There goes a warm and luscious creature
To her toes . . .

BOTH
And there . . . she . . . goes.

HOMER
How surprising is her classic taste,
Yet unrefined a mind.

TONIO
Have you ever seen such slim, trim waist
And classical behind?

HOMER
Is it really that she's all corrupt,
Or is it more complex?

TONIO
And how perfectly each bosom's cupped
Like a pinnacle of sex!

HOMER
Taste . . .

TONIO
Waist . . .

HOMER
Mind . . .

TONIO
Behind . . .

HOMER
Complex . . .

TONIO
Sex . . .

BOTH
Oh-h-h!

HOMER
There goes a woman.

TONIO
There goes a woman.

HOMER
There goes a subject for a thesis.

TONIO
There a piece is.

HOMER
A riddle so infernal,

TONIO
A vision so nocturnal,

BOTH
She's given me a mission
To be true to.

HOMER
The stuff to reach new heights with

TONIO
The stuff to spend my nights with.

BOTH
The stuff t'would never do to
Not get through to.

TONIO
There goes a woman.

HOMER
There goes a woman.

TONIO
There goes a reason for existing.

HOMER
And I must grant you—
Sometimes trysting, I suppose.

TONIO
Well, what are you doing here, Tonio—

HOMER
Well, what are you doing here, Homer—

BOTH
When there . . . she . . . there . . . she . . .
There she goes?

Sitting at one of the tables at a sidewalk cafe, we next find three of Illya's "hooker" friends, Olga, Sandra and Despo, complaining to one of his henchmen, Garbage, about being swindled by their pimp, No-Face. "An Honest Drachma"

GARBAGE
No-Face has a message for you.

DESPO
And I give you a message for him. Tell him to drop dead.

GARBAGE
He wishes to inform you that due to increased maintenance costs your rent is being raised twenty drachmas. (He exits)

OLGA and SANDRA
Twenty drachmas!

DESPO
Will it never end?

(The THREE WOMEN sing)
Where does he get his nerve?
Where does he get off raising the rental?
Monthly the rent grows more monumental.
Where does he get his nerve?

We've given years of
Working our rears off
Verily to the bone.
What have we got to
Show for it—not two
Drachmas to call our own.

An honest drachma,
An honest drachma—
It's all but extinct and erased.
The landlord's commission
On acts of coition
Or similar work we've embraced
Has drained us and hurt us
And yet may convert us
And render us practically chaste.

For an honest drachma,
An honest drachma—

– 141 –

God forbid, he will render us chaste.

OLGA
Who is he anyhow?

DESPO
King of the harem.

SANDRA
Cock of the walk. (They look askance.) Oh, excuse me.

ALL THREE (singing)
Why should I slave for him?
Why should he reap the fruits of my barter?
What do I look like, some kind of martyr?
Why should I slave for him?

We're getting poorer,
He's getting richer,
But—is he satisfied?
Soon you may see us
Roaming Pyraeus
Sunlighting on the side.

An honest drachma,
An honest drachma,
Alas, it must be obsolete,
Cause where's the enjoyment
In hustling employment
Like regular tarts of the street—
And still we're complaining
When through entertaining
The whole Yugoslavian fleet!

For an honest drachma,
An honest drachma
God forbid, we'll back on our feet.

And so we bid a fond farewell to Illya and her cohorts, and proceed onto more innocent smut (one of the hardest things to write) with Karl and *The Twenty-Seventh Wife*.

I commented earlier that a writer of adaptations like me should never get involved with material he isn't crazy about, or at the very least material he doesn't think will work as a musical. On my next project with Karl, I fell into the trap again.

For whatever Karl's reasons, he had become particularly fond of a ponderous book by Irving Wallace called *The Twenty-Seventh Wife*, and wanted me to read it and then try my hand at libretto and lyrics. I'm an especially slow reader, and let alone do an adaptation of it, I couldn't even get through reading the book. That should have been clue enough for all of us to not get involved. But I couldn't say no. Karl had had enough chutzpah to write to Mr. Wallace, and to our amazement, Mr. W. agreed to give us six months, I think, to show what we could do . . . after an initial presentation of several representative lyrics I wrote for the occasion, once again evidently professional enough to whet the appetite of the impressive literary figure to whom they were being submitted.

If I had desperately needed the practice at that point the project probably would have served adequately as another exercise—but that was no longer the case. More than likely I was even probably simultaneously deeply entrenched in some other project with Al Frisch, so I could have gotten along quite well without the extra time commitment to *The Twenty-Seventh Wife*. Thus again, because I was not comfortable with the material, and as I had done with John Schneider, I had to disappoint about half-way through the prep stages of our "option" time and apologize for not being able to deliver an adequate outline for the book. I felt extremely remiss about that. Lyrics were not a problem, but the ponderous biographical source material simply could not work as a musical.

Nevertheless, in order to not totally disappoint, I did furnish an outline, on which I'd based the lyrics, which followed the chapter-by-chapter outline of the book itself. And Karl and I completed a half-dozen songs. And wrote letters to a couple of "name" librettists of the time, Abe Burrows and Howard Teichmann, trying to enlist their interest in the project, so that we could make a full-fledged presentation to Mr. Wallace. But we couldn't come up with the right libretto concept or the right librettist in time, and our option ran out, and eventually so did our contact with Mr. Wallace, though we did submit our completed material to him.

In itself, as far as it went, our work was more than just passable, but it did fall victim to a trap that the entire project would have fallen into, too, if we'd gone ahead with it. Once you've established that polygamy is the subject, and that funny things can happen in polygamous relationships, where else can you go? If there was another route or point of view, it escaped me then and still does. Certainly in my treatment of *The Twenty-Seventh Wife*, as far as it went, I couldn't get much past the one-joke, one-note level. See for yourself.

Our suggested rip-snortin' and rather ambitious opening was invented to be performed by a young husband returning from a hard day's work, being confronted by a few of his young buddies outside a hotel barroom and then by a group of his wives in their parlor on the opposite side of the stage. "Headin' Out West"

> BILL

What do you say, Tom? How about a beer for your pals before you hit the road?

> JOE

Where's he going?

> TOM

I'm packing in this town and starting a new life. Heard it on good authority there's still one place left that's heaven on earth. (sings)

> Headin' out west to Salt Lake City.
> Building a nest for thirty-three . . .
> Dora, Flora, Mary and Bess,
> Ellie Mae and Tillie and Tess—
> That seven wives and twenty-five kids and me.

> FRANK

Seven wives? Twenty-five kids?

TOM

Sure.
Haven't you heard in Salt Lake City,
Heard of the man called Brigham Young?
He took himself some twenty-odd wives
I hear they have the time of their lives.
Well, that's the folks I'm aiming to live among.

I can picture me now, coming home from work, all my wives waiting with open arms to greet me, eager to please, ready to serve. Well, six of the seven anyhow. Where's Ellie Mae?

6 OF THE 7 WIVES INDIVIDUALLY

Darling, may I fetch you your paper?
Darling, are you ready to eat?
Darling, may I bring you your slippers?
Time to rest your weary old feet.
Darling, would you like to be read to?
How about a brandy or beer?
Darling, may I get your tobacco?

ALL 6 IN UNISON

How else may I comfort you, dear?

TOM

And what did you girls do to keep yourselves busy today?
And where's Ellie Mae?

WIVES 1 to 4 INDIVIDUALLY

I milked the cow and fed the pigs
Just like you said I should.

I chopped us down a great big tree;
We're low on firewood.

I tended the stable and watered the geese.

I pitched ten bushels of hay.

WIVES 5 and 6 IN UNISON

We weren't much able. Activities cease
When you're in the family way.

ALL 6 IN UNISON

And now we're very weary . . . oh so very weary . . . so . . .
Darling, if for pleasures you're caring,
And you're ready for passion to rise,
May we be so bold and so daring
As to now suggest a surprise.
Ellie Mae's upstairs and she's raring
To bestow a pleasure or two,
After all day's resting preparing
For her great big moment with you.

TOM

Yahoo!

> Headin' out west to Salt Lake City,
> That's where I long to settle down.
> With all them gals to tickle my lust
> I swear I'll keep 'em busy or bust.
> I'm headin' out west . . .

ED

Hey wait for me!

TOM

Headin' out west . . .

BILL

What time we leavin'?

ALL

Headin' out west for Salt Lake City town.

In "I'm Not Crying" as sung by Ann Eliza, soon-to-be twenty-seventh wife to Brigham Young, while alone on stage, she reaches the decision to accept his proposal. (Students of lyric-writing will catch a glimpse of Lehman Engel's previously alluded to theory of "opposites" at work in this one.)

> Hail to the powerful leader
> Who wants me!
> Once he has spoken,
> Then so must it be.
> Surely if I were to try
> To oppose him,
> God would be angry
> And punishing me.

> Hail to the powerful leader
> Who wants me!
> I should be flattered
> And run to his side.
> Why, then, have I so despaired
> Since he asked me?
> Why have I wakened at nighttime
> And cried?

> He offers me wealth and position
> And even a promise of fame.
> And all he expects is submission . . .
> In return for his name.

Well, Ann Eliza, it's time to face it. No more tears now. At least not while he's looking. (Drying her eyes.) Crying? Who, me?

> I'm not crying.
> It's tears of joy you see.
> No one's dying

And no one's harming me.
Other marrieds manage
Very well, I've heard.
What if I don't love him?
Love is just a word.

I'm not crying.
Life's amusing and gay.
See? I'm trying
To think of sunnies to say.
Everything will turn out fine—
No fears, no tears, no pain;
And I'm not crying—
Not a bit.
Is it starting to rain?

Next is "I Wonder,"—sung by a group of people waiting to see Brigham outside his office, and then sung by Brigham inside.

Which one did he sleep with last night?
Which one gave the beast his delight?
I wonder by what standard
He chooses and decides
When someone has philandered
With twenty-some-odd brides.

(Eeny-meeny-miney-mo—
No no no no no yes no.)

Which one, pray, last answered his whim?
Did she do her duty by him?
Which doll was his to wind up
And wriggle her behind up
From all of them who lined up on his queue?
Which one did he sleep with last night, I wonder.
And I wonder, too. Don't you?

BRIGHAM

They wonder, they wonder
What lucky girl was under my spell.
They wonder, they wonder,
They wonder too wisely and well.

When strangers come to meet me
In sermon, prayer and song
I preach that God is everywhere in sight.
But each new friend to greet me
Is wond'ring all along
If that was God in bed with me last night.

Well, as a matter of fact, yes, brothers, it was. We slept on one universal bed, the bosom of our mother earth. And we all slept together.

Oh, how I pray to impart

The virtue that's deep in my heart—
But still I keep hearing
More whispers and jeering
The moment my sermon has start-ed.

Which one, pray, last answered his whim?
Did she do her duty by him?
Which doll was his to wind up
And wriggle her behind up
From all of them who lined up on his queue?
Which one did he sleep with last night, they wonder.
And I wonder, too.
Don't you . . . and you . . . and you?
And you . . . and you.

"Someone He Loves," is sung by a group of Brigham's wives at Lion House when they learn the news of his marriage to Ann Eliza. Some lines are sung by individuals; some by the group.

Come on, now, girls, where's our generosity?
Aren't we forgetting
She's someone he loves?
Set her table setting.
She's someone he loves.
So we'll work a little harder,
Eat a little less,
Share what little ardor
We get from his caress . . . God bless.

Bravely let us meet her,
This someone he loves.
Gently let us treat her.
No pushing, no shoves . . . D'Y'HEAR!
For if we bid her welcome,
And play no dirty tricks
We can make this heaven
For twenty-seven
As it was for twenty-six.

It can't be true, it can't.
You know how rumors spread.
Must he collect a wife for every
Hair upon his head?
It can't be true, it can't.
The man has lost his mind.
Must he collect a wife for every
Freckle on his be . . .

Be . . . have yourselves, ladies! Temper!

Aren't we ignoring
She's someone he loves?
Can't we share his snoring

With someone he loves?
So we'll double up on duties,
Bake some extra bread,
Knit two extra booties
And make more room in bed.

But how?

Fondly let's receive her,
This someone he loves.
Liz, put down that cleaver!
She's someone he loves.
And if we bid her welcome,
Accepting of our fate
We can make this heaven
For twenty-seven
As we wait for Number Twenty-Eight.

And for the last entry on this project, "Plural Pleasures" is yet another sum-it-all-up endeavor for Brigham and several of his followers.

Where are the plural pleasures
Polygamy should bring?
As yet it's only brought me
A rude awakening.

Where are the plural pleasures?
The myriad of joys?
Is anything increasing
But living costs and noise?

Monogamists are envious.
To them our life's sublime.
But even when polyga-men
Are in their prime as I'm,
The best of us can handle
Just one woman at a time,
And so I ask again . . .

Where are the plural pleasures
In almost sixty shoes?

(Just think of it!)

Or wond'ring in the morning
Which toothbrush I should use?
If these are plural pleasures
When all is said and done
I'd be happy being lonely
With a one and only only
Only single sing-u-lar one.

* * * *

Where are the plural pleasures
When off to bed I creep

– 148 –

If half are nursing baby
And half are fast asleep?

Where are the plural pleasures
Presumably I've got
If they have either headaches—
Or monthly you-know-what!

Monogamy, polygamy,
Which-ig-amy you're taught-
It seems to me they equally
Are disappointment fraught.

And so I ask again . . .

Where are the plural pleasures,
Or is it all a hoax?
Has Fate decreed to fashion
The cru-el-est of jokes?
There can't be plural pleasures
When one is struck with awe
At the sight of all his frightful, hateful,
Dour and spiteful, grim, ungrateful
Plural mothers-in-law!

Now that I've been spending time with these old projects again, I rather like the latter one more than I'd remembered, and the preceding *Never on Sunday* less. But, as was true back in the late 60's with *The Twenty-Seventh Wife* project, my kingdom for a qualified book-writer! Although now more than ever I would venture to say that the sheer enormity of the cast of characters for a musical of *The Twenty-Seventh Wife* would in itself prohibit this project from ever being economically feasible.

The last of the major efforts by Karl and me during this roughly ten-year period was an odd one, but one that is still dear to our hearts. We'd read that producer Ed Padula had optioned Ben Lucien Burman's *Catfish Bend* stories for musicalization, and having had contact with Mr. Padula previously on *Belinda* and finding him to be warm and receptive, we figured we had a good chance of at least getting to present to him whatever spec work we cared to invest time on . . . hopefully to then be considered seriously enough when the time came for the producer to get the production off the ground. So, we did seven on spec for *Catfish Bend*, and Ed Padula was indeed accessible, and also invited the wonderful Mr. Burman to listen in on the presentation.

Both of them seemed impressed enough with our work, if not exactly overwhelmed. But the project itself lost its steam along the way and Messrs. Padula and Burman re-thought their original plans and went off in another direction (animation). Later those plans faded, too, and so we never really got a chance to climb on board because the project itself never got off the ground.

For those of my readers who are unfamiliar with *Catfish Bend*, I am retaining Doc Raccoon's following long-winded lead-in to the first musical number, "Diff'rent," thereby hopefully providing all the background necessary for understanding the story while the lyrics are used to advance the fable and flesh out the characters.

DOC RACCOON
Good evening, friends and neighbors of the people world. I emphasize "peo-

ple" because I trust there are no fur, feather or scale-bearing animals among you. The management would frown.

What you are about to see and hear is a story peopled by members of the animal world. But don't despair, or steel yourselves for some absurd little fairy tale. There are similarities, you see, between human and animal traits and characteristics.

For instance, did you know that animals can talk? I, for one, speak most effortlessly and literately, and I am a raccoon. Doc Raccoon. Mayor of our Mississippi community of Catfish Bend, where there is a simple key to the peaceful, harmonious life we lead. We accept each others' differences.

(He begins to sing and is joined by other members of the cast, Rabbit, Snake, Frog and Fox as he proceeds.)

> Diff'rent
> In how we talk,
> In where we're from,
> And in the dreams we dream.
> Diff'rent—
> It outwardly would seem.

> Diff'rent
> In who we are,
> In what we're like,
> In how we spell our name.
> Diff'rent,
> Yet very much the same.

> All we want is being loved and needed,
> All we want's to feel secure and free.

> Diff'rent.
> We're each himself
> With diff'rent things
> To say and do and give,
> To make this world the same for you and me—
> A better place for diff'rent folks to live.

> DOC RACCOON

And now may I introduce Judge Black, our gentle vegetarian blacksnake, who is personally trying to live down the terrible reputation of all snakedom.

> JUDGE BLACK
> Once I hissed when I talked
> And I squirmed when I walked,
> And I'm scary black to see.
> But my friends now all agree . . .
> Black . . . is beautiful . . .
> And I'd never harm a flea.

> CHORUS
> Not a flea, not a flea, not a flea, not a flea.

DOC RACCOON
And J.C. Hunter, our proud Red Fox! (Bugle accompaniment)

J.C.
I was fast, I was sly,
I would cheat, I would lie,
And I loved my rabbit stew,
But I've started now to mew
Like a pussycat
And my hunting days are through.

CHORUS
Thru and thru, and thru, and thru.

DOC RACCOON
And here's our giggly rabbit
Who dreams of carrot salads
And has a silly habit
Of rhyming silly ballads.

Recite something for us—

(Rabbit giggles and runs off.)

And our bullfrog (Croak),
Our old bullfrog (Croak)
Who rehearses night and noon
To keep the Indian Bayou
Bullfrog Glee Club in tune.

GLEE CLUB
Tune . . . tune . . . tune . . . tune.

DOC RACCOON
Then there's me, Doc Raccoon.

CHORUS
Then there's he, Doc Raccoon.

Diff'rent
In how we dress,
In what we think,
And in our hopes and fears.
Diff'rent,
But less than it appears.

Diff'rent
In what we eat,
In how we sleep,
And how we wear our hair.
Diff'rent
With sameness that is rare.

Sign a pact to live in peace together.
Live in peace and perfect harmony . . .

Diff'rent.
We're each himself
With diff'rent things
To say and do and give
To make this world the same for you and me—
A better place for diff'rent folks to live.

Next came a wonderfully lazy, bluesy piece of music by Karl to my simple bluesy ballad lyric "Drifting Home."

Drifting home
Down the winding river.
Catfish Bend
Is journey's end for me.

Home again.
Walking by the river.
Hey, old friend,
You're so good to see.

Summer days:
Sitting still and fishing,
Watching clouds
Drifting in the sky.
Wintry days:
Keeping warm and wishing
Winter time
Soon would hurry by.

Here she comes,
Steamboat down the river,
Wonder who
The next old friend will be
Drifting home,
Drifting home,
Drifting home
To Catfish Bend like me.

Next is a perky celebration of the general philosophy of the animal community: "Ararat"

I have days when I'm so ornery
Just a corner re-mains
Of the sentimental lamb I am, but then—
Just before all sense has ceased in me
And the beast in me reigns,
I become my gentle old sweet self again.

Whenever I get angry
I say ararat.
Ararat.
That's my routine.
And 'stead o' staying angry,
Saying ararat,

In nothing flat,
I feel serene.

And when I feel like cussin' up
A storm or two,
What to do?
Well, ain'tcha guessed?
Instead of fume and fussin',
I say ararat,
And off the bat
It's off my chest.

It has the sort of silly sound
That makes a frown turn upside down
And changes disagree into agree.
It has that kind of catchy beat
You keep repeating with your feet
Until you're feeling fine and fancy free.

So if you're getting angry,
Try it—ararat,
And just like that
You're sure to see
Your grief and gripes'll quickly end
When you become a faithful friend
Of ararat—like me . . .

Your grouch and grumps are on the run
When you become a champ-i-on
Of Ararat—like me.

Next, "Garbage Party" is sung individually and in ensemble by the leading
animal citizens of "Catfish Bend" as they awaken and emerge from their respective
sleeping places in the woods.

Mornin' . . . mornin' . . .
Feels like I just went to sleep.
Mornin' . . . mornin' . . .
Mornin's like this you can keep.

But wasn't . . . that a high old time last night?
When we do it, we really do it right.

So help me . . .

That was the greatest garbage party we've had in years,
Simply the greatest garbage party we've had in years.

Thanks to the church pie supper made to support the priest
He got his contributions, we really got the feast.

Scraps of every flavor, every taste and spice,
Ours to savor . . . a gourmet's paradise. Sheer heaven.

Singing and dancing, stuffing up to our very ears,

That was the greatest garbage party we've had in years.

*****

Oh, what a garbage ball we had for ourselves last night.
Oh, what delicious garbage, ate every bite in sight.

Fav'rites of frogs and foxes, rabbits, raccoons and snakes.
Ate till my sides were busting. Lord, how my tummy aches!

Scraps of every flavor, every spice and taste,
Ours to savor . . . a multitude of waste—and refuse.

Singing and dancing, stuffing up to our very ears,
That was the greatest garbage party we've had in years.

> Pots and pans and garbage cans
> All bountifully brimmin!
> When have I . . . when have I . . .
> So richly wined and dined?
> Chocolate chips and carrot tips.
> An over-ripe persimmon.
> Piles on high, miles on high
> Of watermelon rind.
>
> Crumbs of crackers,
> Pits of fruit,
> Bits of nutshells—
> Wow, what a lot of loot! A goldmine.
> Mounds and mounds of coffee grounds,
> Hooray! Hurrah! Three cheers!
> All in all, what a ball!
> The best we've had in years.

And one of the most uninhibited musical jamborees I've ever had a hand in. Karl's music was joyous, and when the "Garbage Party" theme returned to play and sing in counterpoint to the "Pots and Pans" theme, I think even ancient Ben Lucien Burman was clapping his hands and tapping his foot. Hot dog! Every once in a while this line of work can sure reward the writer with something to be happy about!

Next we find the outlaw villainess coyote, Mata, (also known as The Killer), an expert hypnotist, having her way with our genial swamp animal friends: "Repeat After Me" (to Karl's satirical tango).

> I've made the most delicious diagnosis.
> You're much too smart,
> Too well-informed and wise.
> Hereafter you'll think only in hypnosis.
> It's time to start.
> Come look into my eyes.
> Mata means "The Killer", you will find.
> From now on, it's Mata over mind.

MATA	ANIMALS (Repeating)
Repeat after me (music repeat)	
You're beautiful, Mata	Beautiful, Mata.

I'm under your power	Under your power.
I can't get away	Can't get away.

Repeat after me (music repeat)	
I'm dutiful, Mata	Dutiful, Mata.
I'm your to devour	Yours to devour.
Come take me. Olé	Take me. Olé.
I'll go where you want me to go	Want me to go.
I'll do what you want me to do	Want me to do.
I'll say what you want me to say	Want me to say
Or I'll be still	Shhh! Shhh!

Repeat after me (music repeat)	
I'm at your discretion	At your discretion.
A paltry possession	Paltry possession
To cuddle or kill	Cuddle or kill.
I love you, Mata	Love you, Mata.
And I always will	I always will.
I love you, Mata	Love you, Mata.
And I always will	I always will.

To bid a fond adieu to the *Catfish Bend* project—our rousing finale, "Count Me In"

JUDGE

Don't despair, Doc. We'll think of some way to drive out the outlaws. (sings)

When you are met with unbeatable odds,
That's when to count me in.
When it is you against the gods,
I'll tend and guide you
And fight to the end beside you.

When you're beset with unplayable cards,
Certain that you can't win,
Don't wait till all destruction descends—
Give me a call; remember we're friends.
Start counting, and count me in.

DOC

But how can we drive them out when there's just two of us?

J.C.

What do you mean just two? From where I stand . . . (sings)

When you must break that unbreakable foe
That's when to count me in.
When you must brave the undertow
In stormy weather
We'll sink or we'll swim together.

When you can't shake that unwavering woe,
Certain that you can't win,
What good's a boat with only one oar?
Let's stay afloat and give 'em what for.

Start counting, and count me in.

　　DOC

All right. That makes three. But three can't fight against a whole army of them.

　　(CHORUS enters, chanting)
One-two-three-four,
Where there's three there has to be more.
Five-six-seven-eight,
Coyotes retreat before it's too late!
Nine-ten-fifteen-twenty—
If it's hell they want, we'll give 'em plenty.

　　CHORUS (singing)
When you are faced with disaster and doom,
That's when to count me in.
When you can hear the cannon's boom
Take heart in knowing
You won't be alone in going.

When skies are laced with foreboding and gloom,
Warning that you can't win—
Give me a ring and watch 'em turn blue.
That's what this thing called friendship can do.
Start counting, and count me in!

Finally with Karl, over this ten year span was a brief involvement with getting something going, through Philip Rose (whom Karl and I had had previous contact with on *Belinda*) on *Purlie Victorious* (prior to the produced musical *Purlie*, which Mr. Rose launched with other writers a short time later).

These two experimental numbers were not intended to infringe in any way upon the fine final version as written by Ossie Davis, Gary Geld, Peter Udell and Mr. Rose. These were written on spec only. First: "A Few of Us Left"

　　OL CAPN

Just the other day I was talking to the Senator about you, Gitlow, and he was telling me how hard it was—impossible, he said, to find the old-fashioned, hard-earned Uncle Tom type Negra nowadays. I oughta invite him over here. We'd show him a thing or two, wouldn't we, Git?

　　GITLOW

You the boss, boss. (With crew, he sings)

By the grace of God
There's a few of us left,
Still a few of us to scrape and shuffle,
Shut my mouth,
Faithful to the spirit
Of the grand old South.

By the grace of God
There's a few of us left

To tote that barge and lift that bale on high,
So coddle us and be forgiving
We may be the last ones living.
Count your blessings, boss, the well is dry.

There's a few of us left, you see,
One or two of us left, or three,
Just a few of us left
Who still remember days gone by.

OL CAPN
Would you say that blacks and whites
Should school together?

GITLOW
Never, never.

OL CAPN
Does it please you to be at my beck and call?

GITLOW
Day and night.

OL CAPN
Do you dig this integration bit
In public transportation, Git,

GITLOW
I'd sooner travel nowhere, boss, at all.

OL CAPN
Would you change a single thing about the Southland?

GITLOW
Never, ever.

OL CAPN
Would you say that you're contented with your lot?

GITLOW
Pure delight.

OL CAPN
Would you rule out segregation
In a public comfort station?

GITLOW
Boss, I'd sooner bust than dare to share your pot.

OL CAPN
That's the spirit!

By the grace of God
There's a few of you left,
Still a few of you
To scratch and grovel,

Glory be!
Cotton chompin' champions
Of Cotchipee.

ALL

By the grace of God
There's a few of us left,
Who mean to leave the scene with head hung low.
So keep on hummin', banjos strummin',
I'm a-comin', I'm a-comin',
We shall overcome has got to go.

There's a few of us left, praise be,
One or two of us left, or three
Just a few of us left
Who still remember . . . old . . . Black . . . Joe.

For me the above lyric works well in reversely stating my own views about racial prejudice, or any other kind of prejudice—the old B.M.I. Workshop/Lehman Engel "opposites" approach again, with me hopefully making it ironically clear how deeply I feel about the subject and the cause. I know some of us are working on it and it takes time, but I'm impatient lately, thinking it's about time there were "*none* of us left,"—at all—for all time!

And now to close this time frame and creative period with Karl, a simple ballad for Lutiebelle from *Purlie Victorious*, again self-explanatory, called "All the Good Things in My Life," which I consider to be one of my most heartfelt lyrics ever. I think now that I may have experienced more sadness than I realized at the time in letting this one get away.

LUTIEBELLE (to Missy)

Oh, I just knowed, just knowed there was something . . . something just reeks about that man . . . (sings)

He brings to mind
All the good things in my life.
He brings to mind
Whenever I have smiled.
The kind of welcome
That doesn't happen often,
The kind of welcome
From a wide-eyed child.

And now I find
All the good things in my life—
They come to mind,
Returning from the past;
And I see them again,
And I feel them again,
And I know now they'll never grow dim . . .

All the good things in my life
And now there's him—too—
All the good things in my life

And now there's him.

The picnics, the fish fries,
And plucking huckleberries,
And shucking corn when cotton picking's done;
The gospel singings,
Roasting groundpeas,
Sunday barbecuing—
Oh, Missy, being colored can be fun!

    MISSY
When nobody's lookin'.

    LUTIEBELLE
And now I find
All the good things in my life—
They come to mind,
Returning from the past.
And I see them again,
And I feel them again,
And I know that they'll never grow dim . . .
All the good things in my life,
And now there's him—too—
All the good things in my life,
And now there's him.

ELEVEN

Juggling the second of two composers, Al Frisch
(with Karl Blumenkranz) from the mid-60's to the mid-70's
. . . and "Moulin Rouge" (later to be "Bordello"), "Dick Daring,"
"The Rothschilds," and "Christy" ("The Playboy of the Western
World")

From the ridiculous of "Seventy thousand murderous Berbers /
Scaling the mountains, sweeping the
desert . . ." / to the sublime of "Amschel, Nathan,
Kalmann, Solomon, James— / Where have you
heard five such dependable names?"

OUR NEXT MAJOR EFFORT (for Al and me as a team) was Moulin Rouge. We selected
this particular work once again after my wife's or my or Al's having read in a trade

paper that Jose Ferrer (after having been involved in the successful film) had optioned the novel about Toulouse Lautrec, *Moulin Rouge*, by Pierre La Mure, evidently intending to produce and/or direct a musical version of it on Broadway. While Al and I proceeded with some songs on spec as usual, we also simultaneously tried to reach Mr. Ferrer. To no avail. I recall some contact (through Joan again, I think) with a lawyer who represented Ferrer—but we could arouse no interest in our work through the lawyer, and gave up too soon. To my knowledge, Ferrer never even knew of our attempt, or of the existence of the spec work we had done on the property.

While still unsure as to whether we were going to reach Ferrer or not, I did try to do an outline for a libretto based on the novel. But with this project, too, as with a few others already discussed, I could not find the right concept or format or key for the episodic biography being whittled down to a skeletal-sized libretto for a musical. I therefore settled for the best that I could come up with—a dozen or so situations in the novel that I thought would lend themselves to musicalization. Al and I then wound up with nine or ten complete songs (six to be printed herein in lyric form)—from all over the biographical source, without any particular point of view or story line. Evidently Ferrer gave up on the idea, too, for there was never any further "press" about his project except for the announcement several months later that he was then newly associated with a "name" Hollywood composer on it. (Where have we heard that before?) We later assumed that eventually Ferrer's option was dropped.

It paid, indeed, however, to continue this working relationship of mine with Al Frisch, because he, more than any other of my collaborators (possibly because he had no other source of income), was intent on becoming and was going to have to *depend* on becoming a successful composer for the theatre. He never actually quite achieved that goal, but he came closer than any of the other composers I knew or had worked with.

Several years after our first attempt at *Moulin Rouge*, Al got into a conversation on a return flight from California with a music business executive named Carl Denker. They discussed their backgrounds with each other, which resulted in Carl's taking an interest in Al's work, which further resulted in Carl's winding up visiting Al's home some time soon afterward, and listening to Al's repertoire at the piano. That repertoire included Al's work with me on *Moulin Rouge*, and that's how Carl first became attracted to the idea of a musical based on the life of Toulouse-Lautrec. Carl soon returned to one of his home bases, London, intent on finding an experienced librettist to whom the subject matter would equally appeal. He found such a writer in Julian More, the librettist/lyricist of the English version of *Irma La Douce*, and the British stage successes *Expresso Bongo* and *Grab Me A Gondola*.

One of the first problems they faced, however, in proceeding with the project with Al, was what to do about Bernie Spiro. With Julian's being a lyricist, too, you see, he'd have to crowd me out. Nothing had been contractual between Al and me, but Al felt that removing me from the project altogether would have been unfair, inasmuch as it was because of me that he was involved in the first place in a musical about Toulouse-Lautrec, whatever its eventual name. Therefore, through Al's persistence in defending my position (for which I shall be eternally grateful), Carl and Julian offered me an arrangement whereby I'd be co-lyricist on the project, if that was okay with me. I'm a firm believer in "half a loaf is better than none." I agreed, not really giving the chances for a successful *Moulin Rouge* much of a second thought at the time. After all, hadn't I myself tried to do an outline for a libretto on it and come up empty handed? "Whoever you are, Julian," I thought to myself, "good luck to you." And I left Julian and Carl and Al to their own devices and kept a low profile, busying myself with other work.

Thus it was with considerable surprise that soon afterward I was asked to evaluate a concept and first rough draft by Julian (with co-concept by Carl Denker) and soon thereafter meeting with visiting Briton Julian for the first time, actually having a couple of introductory work sessions as collaborating lyricists. To be perfectly honest, I didn't think much of Carl's and Julian's concept, or the first draft, or Julian's lyrics. But they were both charmers, and collaborating with them was becoming fun.

What Julian and Carl had done in order to proceed with their version, incidentally, was to go to France and absorb first-hand as much accurate biographical material about Lautrec as they could, invent their own story line, and then therefore be totally independent of Pierre La Mure's *Moulin Rouge* and Jose Ferrer. Their solution worked well, for they were now indeed rid of La Mure's biographical novel as source material. There was little even remotely resembling the situations in the earlier *Moulin Rouge*. However, their elimination of it also meant that there was less likelihood that there'd be any use for the earlier songs that Al and I had written when we undertook the project on spec with an eye toward interesting Ferrer. Well, what the hell! If half a loaf is better than none, I suppose so is a quarter loaf. So that's the attitude with which I went to work on my share of the newly re-created Lautrec musical, now named *Bordello*.

Collaborating on *Bordello* leads us well into the 70's (though the *Moulin Rouge* project originally started in '65). I devote a separate chapter to that part of the history of the *Bordello* that was produced when we chronologically reach the point of backers' auditions, the hiatus while waiting for money, the pre-production stage and the actual production itself. For now, for me, the most memorable aspect of what we were doing consisted of the relationships that were forming between the four of us . . . Denker, More, Frisch and myself—people from very different backgrounds working together with great mutual admiration and enthusiasm. This period was unquestionably one of the highlights of my professional career, with Joan sharing in many of the goings on, if only by her very presence, since much of the actual collaboration work was done in our apartment.

However, all of *Bordello* so far has been a digression, inasmuch as chronologically in the lyrical scheme of things we have yet to include herein lyrics written from my original attempt at musicalizing *Moulin Rouge* which we'd hoped to present to Jose Ferrer, long before Denker and More got involved.

First, "Ma'moiselle Montmartre," a kind of obligatory general colorful production number set to an existing melody of Al's which was very French in flavor and melodically too lovely to exclude, even though it wasn't really a "book" song. The music was so lovely, in fact, that it wound up being the only one of Al's tunes that was used first by me in my version, then by Julian with a different lyric in a different "book" situation in his final version of *Bordello*.

> Never give your heart away
> Until you've been to Paris.
> Save your love for Ma'moiselle Montmartre.
>
> Warm and wild, alive and gay,
> You'll thrill to all of Paris

In the arms of Ma'moiselle Montmartre.

Colors—splashing brightly
From the sidewalks paved with art.
Lovers—meeting nightly
Over matters of the heart.

If I ever go away,
I'll leave my heart in Paris
'Neath the spell of Ma'moiselle Montmartre.

* * * *

Bistros—fairly spilling
With their laughter, wine and song.
Women—all too willing:
"Eh, M'sieu, you come along?"

If I ever go away,
I'll still be true to Paris
'Neath the spell of Ma'moiselle Montmartre.

Of course I myself had not yet been to Paris at the time I wrote this, so obviously the research material was gathered from memories of every pseudo-French/Hollywood-made movie I'd ever seen.

Next, as a young and still discouraged aspiring artist, the aristocratic Henri de Toulouse-Lautrec receives some earthy advice from his less refined friend Rachou in "For the Sake of Art"

RACHOU
Nonsense, Henri! You can draw!

HENRI
Thank you, Rachou. If only you knew how much such compliments mean to me.

RACHOU
Shut up and don't thank me so much. You're too gentlemanly. That's the only real trouble with you. (sings)

You've got to swear a lot,
Swear a lot,
And spit and throw a fit
And tear your hair a lot.
And mutter "Sacre bleu!"
"Nom de Dieu!"
Such is the course we take
For the sake of art.

You've got to drink a lot,
Drink a lot,
And take mam-sel-le bel-le
To the brink a lot.
You've got to dissipate.

Why fight Fate?
Such is the bed we make
For the sake of art.

I must condone you
Your timid past
But I'll disown you
If you don't learn to be a bas-tard.

Sneer a lot, jeer a lot,
Deface your reputation
Being queer a lot.
You've got to learn ab-saird
Words like "merde."
Such is how hearts must break
For the sake of art.

HENRI

Anything but that. It's not in my makeup.

RACHOU

Then we'll put it there. I'm here to help you, no? Now—suppose you and I
we're having an argument.

I say the greatest painter
Who ever lived . . . is Rubens.
What would you say?

HENRI
I say the greatest painter
Who ever lived . . . is Rubens.
Far and away.

RACHOU
No no no no no, Henri,
You must learn to disagree,
For the truth is only reached through pro and con.

HENRI

Oh?

Should I spit you in the eye
And with deep emotion cry:
"Hmph! I wipe my derriere with your Rubens"?

RACHOU

Yes, that's it exactly.

HENRI

You mean it?

RACHOU

Sure! See! You're learning already.
(They now sing and exclaim simultaneously.)

RACHOU	HENRI
You've got to swear a lot	I never ever uttered Sacre Bleu.
Swear a lot	I really must remember Nom de Dieu
You've got to spit	Ptuey! Ptuey!
Throw a fit	Shriek! Shriek!
Well, that's showing	
some improvement!	Can I graduate next week?
You've got to drink a lot	They sit me and permit me Grenadine
Drink a lot	But so much Grenadine may turn me
You've got to leer	
And sneer and jeer	
Appearing queer a lot	(Accompanying gestures.)
You've got to . . . say that "waird"	Merde! Merde! Merde!
Wonderful! Just the right intonation!	
Such is the course we take	Such is the bed we make . . .

BOTH
Such is how hearts must break
For the sake of art.

At art school Henri de Toulouse-Lautrec met a number of young students who, not as well off as he, had to struggle to make ends meet while they were studying. One day in a bistro Henri and his friends discuss the economic pros and cons of becoming an artist in the musical number "Anyhow."

GRENIER
Henri is the gentleman we all could have been if we hadn't become artists.

ANTEQUIN
In my case gentleman farmer. My brother inherited the farm. He's been up to his neck in money ever since.

GAUZI
My dentist uncle was going to let me study under him. I gave up a chance to be a professional. (All THREE sigh)

ANTEQUIN
I could be tending pigs and hay.

GAUZI
I could be fighting tooth decay.

GRENIER
I could be eating evry day.

HENRI
Comrades, what foolish things you say!
I'm surprised at you.

GAUZI
Sorry, Henri.

ANTEQUIN
You're right, of course.

ALL
First, last and foremost—we're artists.

Well, we never liked to eat, anyhow.
We can't paint a stroke when overfed.
We much prefer the street, anyhow,
To room and board and bed.

We're seldom on our feet, anyhow,
So why mend a shoe that has a hole?
And anyhow, heart to heart,
Strictly for the sake of art,
Suffering enlightens . . . the soul.

GRENIER
So we remain poor but dedicated, right?

HENRI
Right, Rene.

GRENIER
But I'm so hungry.

GAUZI
Think of the prestige that comes with a steady job.

ANTEQUIN
The feeling of security.

GRENIER
I could be learning to invest.

ANTEQUIN
Saving and building up a nest.

GAUZI
Shaving and fashionably dressed.

HENRI
Comrades, you leave me unimpressed.
I'm ashamed of you.

GAUZI
Sorry, Henri.

GRENIER
You're right again.

ALL
First, last and foremost, we're artists.

Well, we never liked to shave, anyhow.
By now we're accustomed to the itch.

We'd squander what we save anyhow,
And still be poor when rich.

The ending is the grave anyhow,
So why save a sou or leave a will?
And anyhow, word is out—
When you learn to do without,
Deprivation heightens . . . your skill.

GRENIER

So we remain true to the spirit of art, eh?

HENRI

Right!

ANTEQUIN

Poor but noble, eh?

HENRI

Right.

GAUZI

But I like women, and for them you need money.

GRENIER

Why? Two can live as cheaply as one. I'm proof. My wife and I both starve.

GAUZI and ANTEQUIN

Who's talking about wives?

Think of the pleasures we'd pursue
Having a mistress we can woo
But who can woo without a sou?

HENRI

Comrades, I sympathize with you,
But it just won't do.

GAUZI

Sorry, Henri.

ANTEQUIN

I lost my head.

ALL

First, last and foremost, we're artists.

Well, we'd rather sleep alone anyhow,
So why add a mistress to our woes?
The mistresses we've known anyhow
Expect expensive clothes.

We must be made of stone anyhow . . .
We look at a nude and think of art.
And anyhow, sound advice,
What's a little sacrifice?

Suffering enlightens . . . the soul;
Deprivation heightens . . . your skill;
And sex is very bad for . . . the heart.
But now . . . and then . . .
To prove . . . we're men . . .
Let's dream of auld lang syne again
And any-anyhow.

"Inspiration" is sung by the girls in the brothel when Lautrec visits for the first time after he had several abortive attempts at conventional romance. They adopt him as a mascot, and make a big fuss over him as they recall other artists they have known.

VERONIQUE
I once posed for an artist-painter.

SUZANNE
Didn't you feel shy?

GIANNINA
An artist looks at you like a doctor, not an ordinary man.

BERTHE
You don't mind showing off your derriere to the doctor every Monday, do you? Well, an artist, it's the same thing. We are their inspirations.

VERONIQUE (singing)
When I spent my night with a painter
He proved to be harmless but quaint.
As I got undressed
I'd never have guessed
The canvas was not what he'd paint.
He whistled the national anthem
While I hummed a chorus or two
And let him paint hearts
On my intimate parts
Which he rendered in red, white and blue.

ALL
Inspiration, inspiration,
Many's the wonder of inspiration
When even a tart inspires the start
Of somebody's masterpiece.

GIANNINA
A student who dabbles in sculpture
Induced me last winter to pose.
I sat on his chair
With bare derriere
And slowly but surely I froze.
He mumbled: "To hell with the sculpture!
This model herself is a jew'l!"
He lacquered my hair,
Smoothed me out here and there

And I won him first prize at the school.

ALL

Inspiration, inspiration,
Many's the wonder of inspiration
When women of shame win fame and acclaim
As somebody's masterpiece.

DANIELLE

I once met a near-sighted dauber
And posed in exchange for a meal.
He asked—would I mind,
His being near-blind—
What he couldn't see, could he feel?
My heart was so stricken with pity
That how could a girl disapprove?
The feeling and touch
Helped his painting so much
That my bust is now hung in the Louvre.

ALL

Inspiration, inspiration,
Many's the wonder of inspiration
When even us broads start winning awards
As somebody's masterpiece;
When creatures of lust lend beauty or bust
To somebody's masterpiece;
When hung on the wall or giving our all
We're somebody's masterpiece.

During the period in which we put *Moulin Rouge* aside, Al and I drove on to several other new projects using the same formula: Watching the trade papers for announcements of proposed new musicals, and trying to beat somebody else to the punch with spec work. Thus it was that we stumbled upon an unlikely but thoroughly delightful project, *Only You, Dick Daring*.

I had met with producer Arthur Cantor once before (re *Belinda* with Karl) and he seemed like a friendly and approachable enough person to stay in contact with. Therefore, when I read that he had optioned for musicalizing for the theatre a book by Merle Miller by the name of *Only You, Dick Daring*, I called him first to try to set up a deadline by which Al and I could make a presentation of a few spec songs for him. That's how we then proceeded on that one, with me even dropping off samples of a few lyric ideas at Mr. Miller's hotel for him, too, to approve first, before further involvement.

Evidently my lyrics were good: Merle liked them, and Arthur seemed to genuinely enjoy and respond to both the lyrics and Al's wonderfully inventive music and rhythms when we finally made our presentation to him a month or so later. This time our only problem was that Arthur himself had to altogether abandon the idea of doing *Dick Daring* as a musical play because of legal problems. I'm not sure of the details, but I believe CBS said "No," and since they and some key people there figured prominently in the story, Mr. Cantor evidently respectfully withdrew, leaving Al and me with the following potential winners. For those unfamiliar with the book Merle Miller co-authored with Evan Rhodes, it deals with Miller's experiences in writing the pilot for a new TV series proposed as a starring vehicle for the then hot TV star Jackie Cooper.

First, in order to give you a feeling for the kind of off-the-wall humor the source material is chock-full of, the title song: "Only You, Dick Daring," with Al's accompanying music being suitably comic. This is sung by a network exec to fledgling pilot-writer Merle.

> "I've had experience with pilots . . . You've got to capture them (the audience) in the first thirty seconds, and they've got to stay captured. In the first thirty seconds, the pilot should go like this . . . "

> Seventy thousand murderous Berbers
> Scaling the mountains, sweeping the desert,
> Heading for Cairo, streaming from Timbuktu,
> Threatening nearer, sworn to enslave us;
> Only our hero, Jackie, can save us . . .
> Only you, Dick Daring, only you.

> Enter the villain, friend of the Berbers,
> Watching our Jackie run for assistance,
> Cleverly evil, snickering right on cue,
> Guarding the entrance dressed as a sentry,
> Giving the Berbers peaceable entry . . .
> Hurry, do, Dick Daring, Daring do!

> Unthinkable atrocities
> Must certainly await us
> Unless you rescue us but soon, dear friend.
> We may survive the sponsor's
> Sixty seconds of hiatus—
> But after that we're doomed;
> We've reached the end.

Or have we?

> There in the distance, on the horizon,
> Leading the British, waving them onward,
> Sounding a trumpet, well, can you all guess who?
> Temples now graying, looking maturer,
> Saving the day with quiet bravura,
> Only you, Dick Daring—
> Fine, upstanding, clean, un-swearing
> You, Dick Daring, only you.

Now you see how it's done? Real easy, isn't it?

> You introduce the characters
> And give them all direction.
> You've gotta keep them moving, moving fast.
> No contemplating navels
> And no deadly introspection.
> No time to let the folks at home get gassed.

Once more, now. Look!

> There in the distance, on the horizon,
> Leading the British, waving them onward,
> Sounding a trumpet, well, can you all guess who?
> Saving his people, brushing his tears back,
> Routing the Berbers, pinning their ears back,
> Only you, Dick Daring,
> Stalwart, humble, feeling, caring
> You, Dick Daring, only you!

Next is "Isn't Nature Wonderful?", a deliciously goofy assessment by Merle Miller of his new place in the country, again with a marvel of an original, inventive and melodious musical composition by Al Frisch.

> I have me a place
> Up in Brewster, New York,
> Where I hide in quiet retreat,
> Where life is so restfully sweet,
> Just me and the sky and the wheat.
> I think it's a wheatfield,
> Or is it a cornfield
> Or maybe it's weeds. Well, who knows?
> At least it looks healthy and clean
> And it's green and it grows.
>
> The branch that I cut
> From my wild apple tree
> Is ready to burst into bloom
> And render my whole living room
> With wild-apple-tree type perfume.
> I think it's wild apple,
> Or else is it maple,
> Or maybe wild cherry. Well, gee,
> At least it has buds that are pink,
> And I think it's a tree.
>
> Now isn't nature wonderful?
> Isn't nature grand?
> From city humdrummin'
> I fast am becomin'
> The best greenest thumb in the land.
>
> How well I enjoy
> Life In Brewster, New York,
> When I see the first sign of Spring,
> A robin at last on the wing,
> And singing as robins will sing.
> I think it's a robin
> Or is it a sparrow
> Or vulture? No, that's too absurd.
> At least it is building a nest

So I've guessed—it's a bird!

Yes, isn't Nature wonderful . . .
A field, a bird, a tree!
Wonderful and absolutely grand to see . . .
Wonderful and absolutely grand . . .
Especially for city folk—like me!

The pilot Merle writes is for a projected series called "County Agent." But his series has nothing to do with what the studio has in mind. In an off-the-wall scene, here is what I had the studio executives singing after reading Merle's first fully developed outline. It's called "Operation County Agent," and once again Al's music was suitably comic, though in this case I feel my lyrics were unquestionably too arch. Lines are sung in succession by various individuals of the executive committee.

Here we are united,
And sworn to a common goal.
Calm and unexcited
And models of self-control.
Polishing a pilot
Is done in one-two-three.
Shape it, mold it, style it—
It's easy as A-B-C.

You fool! Don't you know you can't use those call letters around here? Make that . . .

Polishing a pilot
Is simpler than you'd guess.
Shape it, mold it, style it . . .
It's easy as CBS.

Well, I'm certain the third act curtain
Comes much too late to help the pace.

At the worst we could switch the first
And third and never lose our place.

We could sneak in a Puerto Rican
To help advance the cause of race.

No, let's bring in some monster thing in—
You know, a threat from outer space.

Sounds right, doesn't it?

The story is perfect, the characters great.
In no time at all we can make this first rate.

Operation County Agent . . .
Bring the scalpel, get the axe.
Stitch his head on Ruthie's body.
Then let's call him Auntie Max.
Cut some words out. Put a song in.
Sew it tightly bit by bit.
Operation County Agent . . .

This could be a hit.

Well, it really is very nearly
Approaching perfect as it stands.

With a hero to end all heros
In all the western desert sands

With our Jackie in wrinkled khaki
And sunburned face and dirty hands.

Yeah, but maybe his little baby
Ought not to die from swollen glands.

Sounds bad, doesn't it?

The outline's improving, the plotline is clear.
Before we're all finished we'll air this this year.

Operation County Agent,
Fetch the razor and the tape.
Slip his pants on, trim his hair off,
Don't let on he's going ape.
Take the kids out, bring a dog in,
Let the crops get very sick.
Operation County Agent . . .
This could really click.

And just think! A part for Barbara Stanwyck, too!

Thrilling, isn't it?

If Stanwyck'll do it, by this time next fall
Her name will be bigger than . . . Lauren Bacall.

Operation County Agent—
Rush the scissors and the glue.
Flood the farmland, burn the orchard,
Whoop it up with mountain dew.
Then let Barbara rescue Jackie.
There's a switch to start a trend.
Operation County Agent . . .
This could be it, this could be it . . .
This could be the end.

So the sun now sets on Dick Daring—and rises on *The Rothschilds*. We'd read in *Variety* that Hillard Elkins had optioned *The Rothschilds*, by Frederic Morton, with intent to produce a musical version of it on Broadway, and that no composer and lyricist had yet been signed.

I'd been in contact with someone from Elkins' office previously, though we had never done a presentation for them, but they seemed reachable, and so Al and I did our thing all over again—again only four songs—this time based on the Morton book, and we actually got a date to present them. I don't know how poor Al was able to play that day; his fingers were practically numb. Talk about chilly receptions—Mr. Elkins took the cake! I don't remember the date, but I deduce that it must have been summer time, for the air conditioning was on; it was an especially good machine, set to its coldest setting. I expect Mr. Elkins liked it that way, otherwise he would have lowered it. I happen to like it cold, and so did Al, but this was ridiculous. What a way to try to warm up to a performance or even to a conversation, with your teeth chattering!

At any rate, we never did learn whether or not we really bombed out. (Another highly demonstrative and appreciative judge and audience, you see.) All I know is that we read soon afterward that Jerry Bock and Sheldon Harnick had been signed as composer and lyricist, so we figured no one in their right mind would settle for Frisch and Spiro if they had the team that wrote *Fiddler* and *Fiorello* waiting in the wings, and we let it go at that. Indeed Bock and Harnick's score, when the show finally got off the ground, proved to be wonderful. But Frisch and I had made a not-too-bad college try ourselves with the following few on spec.

First, with Mayer Rothschild beginning to achieve his initial success as a merchant and dealer in coins, a great honor is bestowed on him one day by Prince William. A wooden sign is nailed to his door proclaiming him Court Factor. The people of the ghetto gather around to watch in amazement, and read the inscription on the sign.

CROWD VOICES
... I never thought I'd live to see the day ... Imagine! One minute a ghetto Jew, next a Court Factor ... .What a beautiful sign! Is the lettering real gold? .... .We have to treat Mayer with respect now. He has a title ...

(THE CROWD sings "By Appointment")

By appointment to his Serenity,
Court Factor to the Prince!
Mayer Rothschild was a no one
But he's someone ever since.

By appointment to his Serenity,
Rewarded by the Crown,
Mayer Rothschild has position
And renown.

Position enough to marry
And raise a family.
Just a small wooden shield
May some day yield him
A whole new family tree.

By appointment to his Serenity,
If he keeps making mints—
He may yet become as wealthy
As the Prince.

(Mayer's new wife, Gutele, is seen, carrying a baby.)

See? There he goes already. Just married to Gutele, and the first Rothschild heir, just like that! ... Tell us, Mayer, how did you do it so fast ...

MAYER
Do what? Become a success? Or have a baby?
It started in a modest way

While working at the bank.
While tidying my till one day
I spied a rare old franc.
From that day on I took my pay
In coins both rare and old . . .
And soon my coin collection
Was a treasure to behold.

    CROWD
And soon his coin collection
Was worth twice its weight in gold.
And there he is . . .

    MAYER
And here I am . . .

    CROWD
A smart, successful business man
With brand new sign upon his door
Proclaiming, as we said before . . .

By appointment to his Serenity,
We're happy to report
Mayer Rothschild of the ghetto
Now is welcome at the Court.

By appointment to his Serenity,
A rising star ascends.

    MAYER
But there'll always be a discount
For my friends.

    GUTELE and MAYER
We'll move to a house that's bigger,
With gardens in the rear
So there's plenty of space
For the brand new face
We introduce each year.

    ALL
By appointment to his Serenity
Court Factor to the Prince
Mayer Rothschild was a no one,
But he's someone, really someone,
Yes, he's someone, really someone
Ever since.

In a flashback, when Mayer returned as a young man of twenty to the Frankfurt ghetto in which he had been brought up, and where his family still lived, he walked through Jew Street, or "Judengasse" as it was called, remembering its poverty and squalor, and vowing to rise above it.

Judengasse,

Judengasse . . .
I've come home,
Home to the street of Jews
Where I was born;
Home to hear the ghetto's voices
Throbbing in the air,
Sobbing in despair,
Forlorn.

Judengasse,
Judengasse,
I've come home
Ready to join my people as a man;
And if there is a ray of light
Anywhere in this dismal night,
If anyone can find it, Mayer can.
Remember, Judengasse—
Mayer can.

When Mayer's five sons are of an age where they have started to venture forth into the business world and help their father expand his holdings and make names for themselves, they proudly review their modest success to date in "The Song of the Five Sons"—with as wonderful a piece of comic music composition by Al Frisch as has ever been written for the theatre. Too bad I can't share it with you here.

Amschel, Nathan, Kalmann, Solomon, James . . .
Where have you heard five such dependable names?
At your command, your beck and call,
With no request too great or small
For Amschel, Nathan, Kalmann, Solomon, James.

So we trade a few trinkets,
We give a few bargains,
We pull a few swindles,
We buy and sell.
And by and large we're selling
Fairly well.

(They now split the parts and sing simultaneously.)

Amschel, Nathan,	
Kalmann, Solomon, James	So we trade a few trinkets.
Where have you heard	
Five such dependable names?	We give a few bargains.
We're at your service,	
Beck and call	We pull a few swindles,
With no request	
Too great or small	We buy and sell
For Amschel, Nathan,	
Kalmann, Solomon, James	And by and large we're selling
Fairly well.	

Poor Prince William soon may flee his estate.
Bonaparte is close to crashing his gate.
But Willie's gold the French can't seize
For he'll entrust it when he flees
To Amschel, Kalmann, Solomon, James-e-le, Nate.

So we'll fool with some ledgers,
We'll forge a few papers,
We'll cross a few borders
But when we're done
Prince William will be richer
Five to one.

Poor Prince William
Soon must leave his estate   So we'll fool with some ledgers.
Bonaparte is close
To crashing his gate   We'll forge a few papers.
But Willie's gold
The French can't seize   We'll cross a few borders,
For he'll entrust it
When he flees   But when we're done
To Amschel, Kalmann,
Solomon, Jamesele, Nate   Prince William will be richer
     Five to one.

If your interests lie in things financial,
You are someone we would like to know.
What you start with needn't be substantial
In our hands—just trust us—it will grow.

Making fortunes isn't one of our aims.
We are not as rich as everyone claims.
It hardly seems that we're at fault
If gold just streams into the vault
Of Amschel, Nathan, Kalmann, Solomon, James.

So we run a few errands,
We juggle some figures,
We lend a few gulden,
And knock on wood.
We must admit: How's business?
Pretty good.

Making fortunes
Isn't one of our aims   So we run a few errands.
We are not as rich
As everyone claims   We juggle some figures.
It hardly seems
That we're at fault   We lend a few gulden.
If gold just streams
Into the vault   And knock on wood—
Of Amschel, Nathan,
Kalmann, Solomon, James   We must admit—how's business?

	Pretty good.
Of Amschel, Nathan, Kalmann, Solomon, James	We must admit—how's business? Pretty good.
Of Amschel, Nathan, Kalmann, Solomon, James	We must admit—how's business? Pretty good.

After Mayer dies, his five sons carry on the traditions and business he started. Before they leave for their various outposts elsewhere in Europe, they have a reunion with their mother, Gutele, at her home in Judengasse. She sings "My Family" and takes turns dancing with them.

My family, my family,
My seeds, my roots, my heart.
What else in life
Is important to know?
Pleasure for me
Is in watching you grow.

I see you before me
Like eager young trees,
Reach for the sky,
Bend with the breeze.
I see you before me
And smile through my tears,
Treasuring the joys,
Measuring the years.

I have no other needs in life,
No other sights to see . . .
For all I know and all I am
Are you, my family.

AMSCHEL (taking her around to dance)
You still dance like an angel, Mama.

GUTELE
And you still lie with a straight face.

NATHAN (cutting in)
You can't have her all to yourself.

AMSCHEL
Of all the chutzpah!

GUTELE
Just like your father, both of you.

JAMES (cutting in)
My turn.

GUTELE
Just like him . . . all five!

JAMES

Do you still miss him so much, Mama?

GUTELE

Of course. But when I have you, I also still have him.

> I see you before me,
> And there he is, too,
> Partly in you,
> Partly in you.
> I see you before me,
> And there is his chin,
> Suddenly his eyes,
> Suddenly his grin.
>
> I have no other needs in life,
> No other sights to see,
> For all I know and all I am
> Are you—my family.

Somewhere in the late 60's Al and I also embarked together on the major project I'd always dreamed of doing: A musical based on Synge's *The Playboy of the Western World*. This was to be more than a presentation for someone. It was to consist of an actual libretto that I wanted to write along with the score, more or less as a follow up to the major playwriting work I'd done on *Belinda*. It was therefore expected that *Christy*, which was its title, would take a lot longer to complete than any of the spec presentations I'd been working on with Al in the immediately preceding years. One problem I had with Al, however, was beginning to surface at this point. After the first draft of a scene or even a song number was completed, it was difficult to get him to accept alternate ideas and to discard work already completed if I later thought the work could be improved upon. And by this time "alternate" and "discard" had become two of my middle names. It's hard enough to be objective when you're writing, and hard to know for sure while you're doing it that it is just right or not quite right, or not right at all, or whatever in between. But give it a month or two, or sometimes as little time as a day or two, collecting dust in a folder or on the shelf, and often you can't wait to tear the work apart upon next glance and start all over again. Thus, the first draft of *Christy* had many elements in it that were not as right as they should have been, and at any point thereafter they could and should have been revised, but Al was usually stubbornly opposed to any change.

Nevertheless, I think I was doing my best work as a librettist on this project, editing, cutting, embellishing, inventing, shifting, opening up a bit from the one set of the original, and yet staying true to the spirit and language of Synge without destroying the poetry and dark humor of the original.

During the several years we worked on *Christy*, Al and I (with Joan along) went to see a new production of *Playboy*, directed by Siobhan McKenna, at Long Wharf Theatre in New Haven, just to make comparisons. We met with Ms. McKenna for a moment and told her about our project, but she seemed otherwise distracted and we pursued the "opportunity" no further. Al and I also saw the film that had been made of the play, starring Siobhan McKenna at a time in her life when she was really too old to be performing the role of Pegeen Mike. Again we were making comparisons, and studying the play close up, though after the fact. The film was a gorgeous adaptation (bless the good old *Thalia* movie revival house on Manhattan's upper West Side which has since been torn down), and yet it, too, only confirmed our opinion that we had done a commendable job.

Coincidentally, there was even more exposure around that time to *Playboy* in which to drench ourselves, including an ambitious Queens College production, and a none-too-successful professional revival at Lincoln Center's *Vivian Beaumont Theatre*.

I truly believe *Playboy* is a play that can't ever be mangled too badly—some of its intrinsic quality and worth will always come shining through. And feeling that, I, too, had retained all possible respect for *Playboy*—my hopes for *Christy* remained high through all the years we nursed it through submission, rejection, final revision, and, at long last, the production in 1975.

As soon as the first draft was completed, we started showing it around. In a period of perhaps two years it was submitted first to the two biggest names in the producing world, Hal Prince and David Merrick, and then to the few lesser luminaries I'd previously made contact with on other projects (including Philip Rose, Arthur Cantor, Ed Padula, Edgar Lansbury, and Hillard Elkins). Then on to a few new names, such as Albert Selden and David Black and Lawrence Kasha, and then to a few miscellaneous theatre people who did not necessarily fit into the category of producer but who were willing to listen to our presentation and help guide us, if not become outright involved themselves—people like Sylvia Herscher, Burgess Meredith, Alan Jay Lerner, and esteemed agent Flora Roberts.

Our visit to Burgess Meredith at his Rockland County home was even more memorable because Elsa Lanchester was his house guest at the time (sorting through some material for her work on her biography of Charles, she said), and she was devastatingly charming. Burgess himself was the wonderful listener I suspected he'd be, because he had starred in the first production I'd ever seen of *The Playboy of the Western World*—on Broadway—in the 40's, and I guess we were bringing back memories of his youth to him with our presentation.

I think in many instances people who like theatre are fascinated by the mechanics and process of conversion from straight play to musical, and appreciative of the opportunity of being exposed to the early stages of such a project. My guess is that Burgess Meredith was, too. And Alan Jay Lerner was thoughtful and gently warm in his reception of us and our presentation to him in a private room he'd arranged for at the *21 Club*. He even suggested his participation in a production of *Christy* (as writing collaborator and possibly director), if we could come up with half the money for it. (Thanks so much for the generous offer, Mr. L.) Flora Roberts gave us credit for a thoroughly professional "if ersatz Irish" attempt.

Basically what we got from almost everybody was that *Christy* was "good," but it wasn't "great." (How often I've heard that with other projects, too!) But the market for *Christy* would be very limited, they all said.

"How dare they," I thought. "This is *my Playboy* as well as Synge's they're talking about, and if I love the original so, and it is considered by all to be one of the great classics of modern literature, and if I have treated it with such tender, loving care and expertise and theatrical know-how, why shouldn't it be equally appreciated by all the theatre-going public!" We do have our moments of grandiosity in our lifetimes, don't we?

Yes, I wrote a pretty damned good adaptation! What I didn't do is know enough or learn enough about the regional or off-Broadway theatre markets or scene at that time. It was "Broadway or bust." We might not have had to have *Christy* collecting dust for so long if we'd been knowledgeable enough or willing enough to try to get it into the right hands at the time. Fact is, I now see in retrospect, there was no way that *Christy* was of Broadway caliber. We simply didn't know it or wouldn't accept it then. So Al and I finally left *Christy* to rest when action on *Bordello*, became hot enough to warrant all our attention. And we didn't pick up *Christy* again till after the *Bordello* production in 1974.

TWELVE

The "Bordello" production—1974.

"Let the human race / Lead its merry pace.
Let the clock be still / Until I see her face.
I have all the time in the world."

AS I'VE STATED EARLIER, once you get bitten by the show-biz bug, you stay bitten for life. Last time around it applied to just being produced. This time around it refers to a full scale production, such as one would usually associate with Broadway. In this instance it happened not to be Broadway, but, depending upon which side of the ocean you're looking at it from, it was either second best to or even better than Broadway: London's West End. All the hullaballoo and hype and publicity and hum of activity that goes with it, and the royal treatment—in my limited capacity as "co-"lyricist for this "small" but full scale musical—I experienced this one time. I'd love to experience it again—and wouldn't mind if next time it's Broadway instead of Shaftesbury Avenue. But with the economy of the Broadway scene being as difficult as it is to deal with at this point in time, and with my now having undertaken writing books instead of a new musical for the theatre, I still may be a very long way away from experiencing Moss Hart's "golden summit" while "up there from it" or his "no greener valley than Shubert Alley." I must fully accept the likelihood that I may never get there at all. Yet if I never do, at least I'll have had that London opening to remember, and though I wasn't one of the major creative contributors, I *was* one of the minor ones, and so I'll always have the pleasure of those memories to fall back on, along with an album of some wonderful photos of the experience taken by my daughter Teri and her husband Ken, and the warmth I feel every time I think back to the great two and a half weeks Joan and I spent in London—from final dress rehearsal through previews and just past opening night. A word of advice for those of my readers still with stars in their eyes and 3 dreams in their hearts: keep striving; it's worth it. If it happened to a lesser known talent like Bernie Spiro, it can truly happen to anybody else. It surely involves perseverance and struggle, continuing the pursuit and not giving up, and starting all over again when necessary, and spreading yourself thin when you have to, and perhaps sacrificing other interests or pursuits along the way. And usually a little bit of luck, such as meeting the right person at the right time just once. But in the end it's nice to know that it really can happen, and with *Bordello* it did to me.

When we left *Bordello* in the preceding chapter, it had just become transformed from "Moulin Rouge," and had been taken over by Carl Denker and Julian More. One of the great pleasures provided by Julian's and Carl's concept for *Bordello* lay in their selection of moments out of Lautrec's past which could be dramatized and musicalized while the drama was being heightened by a projection of that very painting or illustration of Lautrec's drawn upon from his own experience which related to the scene being played out on stage. In the end the concept was fine, and the execution of it theatrically exciting as far as it went. But the show itself simply proved to be too fragmentary, and the fragments were being held together by what was criticized as being too frail and unbelievable a story line, that of the whores of the bordello where Lautrec lived for a brief time putting on a show about his life for the benefit of the new chambermaid the madam has hired, in order to acquaint her with the history of their most famous client.

During the course of the creative period of this show, Julian More more than once spent several weeks at a time in the U.S. working with Al Frisch and me, although some of our collaboration continued till the very end to be by mail. And Carl Denker set up offices in New York trying to raise money for a U.S. production. And we held backers' auditions in my apartment in Manhattan, and at Al's home in Rockland County, and when necessary also in rented studio presentation rooms. But money wasn't coming easy. Feeling only peripherally involved, I stayed as far away from the business end as I could. But I did get drawn minimally into some of the backers' auditions activity, and even rehearsed for and performed in several of them. I have a couple of rehearsal tapes to remind me of what great fun they were.

I really didn't have much faith in the project, but hopefully always tried to appear as enthusiastic and encouraging and cooperative as possible. Julian's American agent was the prestigious Audrey Wood, and I even recall my modest apartment on the Upper West Side (as yet then not as fashionably gentrified as it is today) literally bursting with people one evening, listening to our infant of a show and discussing its future with Audrey and company. But, as always, money was hard to raise, and eventually Julian More packed it in and went home to England, and Carl Denker moved on to other pursuits, and creatively I simply continued my other work with Al Frisch and Karl Blumenkranz on an alternating basis, and gave up all hope of our ever getting anywhere further with *Bordello*.

Then unexpectedly a remarkably smooth and bright and bouncy and sexy sounding "demo" appeared from across the Atlantic, (courtesy of Julian More's and Carl Denker's perseverance, and presumably some of the front money Carl had been able to raise while still in the U.S.), and soon afterward in late '73 there were rumblings from England that a producer named Tony Chardet had agreed to present *Bordello* in London, and that one of Denker's money sources from the U.S. was about to invest heavily in the show, and that an actual production schedule was being prepared. I was asked about my availability to be involved in the pre-production planning for the show in the U.K., but I simply had to turn down any thought of spending more than a token amount of time in England at that point. It would have meant giving up my ad agency job, and although Joan was working, we still depended too heavily on my income for me to quit. It would have been great fun attending auditions and casting sessions and confabs with director and designers and the like, but since I was only co-lyricist, not only was it unnecessary for me to be there, but I might also have been looked upon as being excess baggage.

The solution as we worked it out was fine. Julian and I used the mails freely through which to collaborate on any long range lyric needs, and when there was something lyrical that required immediate attention Julian took care of it in England and had carte blanche from me to do so. If I had been there I might have disputed a few of Julian's final choices that I didn't agree with creatively, but the luxury of my being able to do that was one I could ill afford.

In due course I received a cablegram from Al (who did have to go to England before me) asking me to become an ASCAP member immediately. B.M.I. would have sufficed, and Al knew I was already a member of B.M.I., but I didn't want to make any waves at that late stage, so I acquiesced and changed my affiliation for the duration of the show. (Soon after *Bordello* I changed back.) And I received another cablegram asking me if I would accept Spokesmen, Ltd., as my agent in the U.K., since Spokesmen already represented Julian and Al, and it would make matters simpler if they repped me too. I accepted, gladly. Then I was asked to furnish a bio to be printed in the show's programme (which I was pleased to do, but which I wound up feeling guilty about for having to embellish, inasmuch as I thought my actual credits at the time were still too modest to admit to without embellishment).

Soon thereafter I received a detailed letter giving me the company's projected schedule for dress rehearsals and previews and opening—with a request that I let them know when I was coming so that they could furnish me with my first class plane ticket. I inquired of them whether I might convert the one first class into two coach seats in order to include Joan, and in no time flat perfectly satisfactory transportation was arranged for both of us.

Joan was able to call upon her "sick days bank" for a two-weeks-plus leave from school. I chose to pay out of my own pocket for a retired pro advertising production manager to handle my work at the agency, because just taking off two-weeks-plus at a very busy agency at the height of their busiest season for any reason other than illness would have been unthinkable, perhaps even grounds for my being canned. I wanted to enjoy this London adventure and not have to worry about what was happening back at the office.

The particular ad agency I was with at the time was one where the management thought nothing of interrupting vacations. They had once in fact had the audacity to phone me at a resort on Shelter Island while I was on a long Labor Day weekend vacation, had me paged, and when they were advised that I was out on a sailboat on the bay, arranged for a lifeguard to motorboat out to reach me and haul me in. Talk about indispensability!—and I use that word with ridiculing sarcasm only—who knows to what lengths they would have gone to reach me while in London over some idiotic or mindless detail I had tucked away in my memory, if I hadn't taken adequate steps to insure my job's being covered by a pro?

Al Frisch was needed in London long before I was—for music re-writes, selection of conductor and musical director, orchestrations and arrangements, selection of voices of cast members, and supervision of incidental music. When the time finally arrived for Joan's and my joining the company, all was practically set at the *Queens*

THE QUEEN'S THEATRE

Proprietors:
A.T.P. (London) Ltd.

Chairman:
Sir LEW GRADE

Deputy Chairman:
LOUIS BENJAMIN

Managing Director:
TOBY ROWLAND

Manager: WYBERT R. ALLEN

Box Office: 01-734 1166

Carl Denker
Anthony Chardet Productions Ltd
(in association with David Parkes)
present

BORDELLO
a new musical

Based on an original idea by
Julian More & Carl Denker

MUSIC BY
AL FRISCH

BOOK BY
JULIAN MORE

LYRICS BY
JULIAN MORE &
BERNARD SPIRO

WITH

CRISTINA AVERY
LYNDA BELLINGHAM
JUDY CANNON
NORMA DUNBAR
ANGELA EASTERLING

PADDY GLYNN
BRENDA KEMPNER
STELLA MORAY
ANGELA RYDER
JACQUI TOYE as
LEE WHITING

ALSO
HENRY WOOLF as Toulouse-Lautrec

DIRECTED BY
JOHN COX

CHOREOGRAPHY BY
MALCOLM GODDARD

MUSICAL DIRECTION BY
ALEXANDER FARIS

SETS DESIGNED BY
ROGER BUTLIN

LIGHTING BY
JOE DAVIS

COSTUMES DESIGNED BY
ELIZABETH DALTON

ORCHESTRATION BY
PETE MOORE

First performance at the Queen's Theatre, Thursday 18th April 1974

The *Bordello* programme

Theatre for the show to go on. At first I felt pretty much like just a spectator, though a warmly-welcomed one, I'll grant. Flowers were waiting in our hotel room—from Al and Julian—when we arrived. And big and hearty handshakes were offered from all around—from producer Tony Chardet, director John Cox, choreographer Malcolm Goddard, musical director Sandy Faris, company manager Hubert Willis, and the dozen cast members to whom I was introduced at an impromptu meeting shortly before the dress rehearsal of Act Two early the first afternoon I was present.

Joan and I had been to London for the first time ever just a year earlier—a particularly warm and soul-satisfying trip, inasmuch as we got to spend a good deal of our week with British family of mine I'd not previously met, and I got involved with seeking out my "roots." Because this trip to London for the second year in a row was entirely unexpected, I was indeed glad to have at least seen part of London itself the year before, for on this second occasion I could afford no time for sight-seeing; it was a working vacation. Right after the first dress rehearsal there were continuing confabs and re-write sessions which didn't end till the show was "frozen" several performances before opening night. During the almost two weeks of previews we all pitched in to try to save the show—but it was too flawed and we were too late. The show opened to mostly poor reviews, though we were able to extract several flattering quotes for promotion purposes. Producer Tony Chardet bravely let *Bordello* hang on for a few weeks, but finally had to post its closing notice.

Joan and I had traveled with our daughter Teri and her husband. They stayed for only one week—and we had long family meetings with tea and sandwiches in the lobby of our wonderful old dinosaur of a hotel (the Tavistock) during the first week of previews—every night after every performance—in which I brought the family up to date on what had been transpiring at rehearsals in the theatre that day, and in which they brought me up to date on their reactions to that evening's performance, and to any of the improvements or lack thereof they were seeing and hearing. They attended *Bordello* every night, the kids did. Poor kids, having had to miss out on the rest of the London theatre scene! But it was their choice; they were having too much fun being in on the inside track of a previewing show—Dad's, yet! They couldn't stay on for the opening, though, but that was just as well, because we couldn't have swung an invite for them to the wonderful opening night party, and they would have felt very much left out, after having been so intimate a part of the show as spectators and insiders through me prior to opening, for seven days in a row.

After Joan and I returned to the States, feeling badly that our younger daughter Jeri had been the only one in our immediate family to not have seen *Bordello* first hand, we sent her off to jolly old England, too, where she spent a bit of time under the wing of one of my first cousins, and got to see *Bordello* three or four times herself before it closed. Our 'generosity' in sending her on her own was motivated partly by appreciation for her assistance in our trying to pull off a last minute promotion job for the show immediately upon our return to the U.S. (while the show was still struggling to catch on in London).

Promotion job? Well, before leaving London, assuming that *Bordello* couldn't last too long after its poor reviews, I asked if I might meet with Producer Tony Chardet's ad agency or press reps prior to my returning to the States. My plan was to take back some publicity photos with me, and to quickly write an article about the show, and to submit the article with the photos to publications which might be interested in publishing the story of an English show struggling to overcome unbeatable odds, publications which might be read by travelers en route to London. We knew it wasn't very likely we could overcome difficult deadlines and appear in print before *Bordello* closed, but as long as it was even remotely possible, extreme longshot though it was, I felt we should at least try. For the record, I got a few courteous rejections, but the article was never published.

Anticipating the worst, but with foolhardy intensity, Joan and I continued to reach for ideas for promoting the show here in New York, any way possible, in order to try to help stimulate box office sales over there. Just when we'd almost given up, one last idea evolved, and with my advertising production know-how to help me, I had some flyers designed and printed at top speed and a few giant blowups prepared and mounted and converted into sandwich signs. Armed with several thousand flyers, four of us—Joan, daughter Jeri, her friend Eugene, and I, at end of the work day, on two successive days, drove out to Kennedy Airport, donned sandwich signs, and "hawked" *Bordello* to all the soon-to-be-departing London-bound passengers we came in contact with at the terminals of British Airways, Pan Am, Air India, and TWA. We nearly got tossed out on our ears a couple of times, but we proceeded, undaunted, to defy the sheer insanity of this labor of love, till we had gotten rid of all the flyers we came with. We were taking a risk with the printed matter, of course, because about-to-depart passengers are so busy with bags, baggage checks, tickets, coats, passports, and the like, that our efforts could possibly have worked at cross-purposes and inspired little more than antagonism and contempt for *Bordello* and toward anyone handing out an additional piece of paper to everyone standing on line. The fact that the flyer also had a deliberate double entendre invitation in it: "When in London, drop in on BORDELLO* and come out smiling!"—etc.—may also have served only to outrage a few of the more conservative travelers rather than pique their curiosity—but we risked offending and handed out the thousands of invites we came with—and only the Lord knows (we don't, of course) if the effort was ever responsible for selling even a single ticket at the box office once these passengers got to London. Anyhow, we tried.

What else is there to say about *Bordello*, the production, and its aftermath? A couple of years after the show closed, a "pirate" recording surfaced, being sold in New York record shops, which passed itself off as an "original cast recording," but which actually was an illegal duplicate of the demo of part of the score, which had been recorded in England and used for raising money. Some enterprising "pirate" or other had gotten hold of a copy of it and tried to capitalize on it without authorization to do so. We never did find out who. But Celia Frisch got off a strong letter to the name and address on the album cover, and to my knowledge all copies of the record were then withdrawn from retail outlets and the record was never heard from again.

Shortly after I returned to the U.S., Al and Julian spent a day at Pye Records in London supervising the recording of a 45 rpm "single" on two of the songs—both instrumental. Record sales were practically nil. My income from the show, based via standard Dramatists Guild contract on 1% of the box office gross for the forty-some-odd performances, was practically negligible. But for me the experience had been dazzling. I made a short-term good friend of Dick Odgers, of Spokesmen, my new agent in London. Al Frisch and his wife Celia seemed crushed by the failure of the show and returned to New York sounding impoverished and depressed, and angry about the mismanagement (in their opinion) of the show and its misfire. I've kept in touch with and seen Julian More a half-dozen times since, and Carl Denker more than several times since, and consider them friends to this day. And who knows but that some day one of us may yet be responsible for getting another, hopefully improved, version of *Bordello* going again. I've always thought that I'd like to try to have the show done in the U.S., but only after the conceptual kind of rewrite takes place that I think is not one of my own strengths as a creative writer. As a matter of fact, with Julian's permission, I already did make one try at it (soon after the production) without achieving any vast improvement in the book. I may still try again some day—with perhaps the fresh viewpoint of a new collaborator, as long as Julian doesn't mind. But I'm torn. If we really buried *Bordello* in 1974 in London, then more than likely, I should be willing to let sleeping dogs lie. I guess time will tell.

Though Julian and I were billed as co-lyricists, in the end we actually collaborated on only five of the numbers that were used. Most of the others were his alone; a few mine alone. In selecting those to appear here, I am using none of the lyrics written by him alone. His lyrics were fine, but this is after all a book intended to be about and including mine, not his. Therefore, of the six *Bordello* lyrics that follow, three are mine, and three were written jointly by Julian and me. And once they've become part of this manuscript, it will be time for me to put *Bordello* to rest, if not forever, then for at least the remainder of this book and the foreseeable future.

When Toulouse-Lautrec visits the House of Dreams for the first time, the occasion inspires a production number called "The Business Tango." performed by Madame Blanche and the girls (with some of the girls costumed in the fantasy roles their clients pay to have them assume). Lis Dalton, our costume designer, had a ball using her imagination.

HENRI

Do I pay now?

BLANCHE

As you wish, M'sieur. Elsa looks after these trifling matters. You can open an account with us if you like.

HENRI

I'm only a painter, Madame.

BLANCHE

In that case, cash! (sings)

When a client comes to play,
He's the sculptor, you're the clay.
He's the vulture, you're the prey.
That's business, good business.

If you thrill to his physique
And you tell him he's unique
He may come back twice a week.
That's business, good business.

GIRLS
Feed him his illusions
Of masculine rank.

BLANCHE
He'll feed my bank
Franc after franc.

GIRLS
Tell him he's the picture
Of prowess and skill.

ELSA
Bend to his will.

BLANCHE
He's yours for the kill.

As you lead him to his doom,
Once you're cozy in that room . . .
Don't let on who's having whom.
That's business, good business.

(Dance sequence as the archetypal client is passed from girl to girl getting more and more exhausted. ALL sing tag-line at end of dance sequence.)

That's business, good business!

ALL
Always treat him with respect.
Never let him once detect
You've a hint of intellect.
That's business, good business.

BLANCHE
If he's different in his taste,
Upside down or triple-spaced,
Or that new one, face-to-face . . .
That's business . . .

ALL
Good business.

You are but a plaything
He's paying to use.
Down with taboos.
What can you lose?

BLANCHE
He must never utter
A single request
Left unaddressed.
The man is your guest.

ALL
If he begs you to reprise,
Though you always aim to please,

BLANCHE
Longer hours, higher fees.

ALL
That's business. Good business.

Next, Henri has just sketched his favorite girl, Mireille, after sharing some intimate moments with her. This is one of the lovely scenes enhanced by the use of the projection device previously mentioned. In this case the projection is Lautrec's famous: "Woman Pulling on Her Stockings." The song: "Simple Pleasures," to Al's deliciously romantic melody—(the "hit" number).

MIREILLE
Can I see it?

HENRI
If you like. (She comes and sits by him, glancing at the sketch, laughing and cuddling affectionately. He tries to kiss her.)

MIREILLE
Sorry, we're not supposed to kiss. You might give me a cold.

HENRI
What a complicated life you lead.

MIREILLE
Not at all. It's really very easy. (she sings)

Why do people want so much?
The world is going mad.
It's such a waste to cry about
The things they've never had.
The grass may be a brighter green
In someone else's park
But who cares what the color is?
It's brightest after dark.

Give me the pleasures of life,
The simple pleasures of life,
A little music and wine
And I'll be satisfied.
Why should I reach for a star?
My life is richer by far
With simple pleasures
When you are by my side.
(Opening and pouring wine during next lyrics.)
People in this crazy world
Can lose a lot of time
In trying to reach the summit
Of a hill they'll never climb.
Why push ahead the hours too fast
Pursuing wealth and fame?
It's only hell we're heading for—

We'll get there just the same.

Give me the pleasures of life,
The simple pleasures of life,
A little music and wine
And I'll be satisfied.
Why should I reach for a star?
My life is richer by far
With simple pleasures
When you are by my side.

(She walks to the bed with the two glasses. He gives her a quick playful kiss which she can't prevent because of the glasses in her hands.)

That's cheating!

    HENRI
    Give me the pleasures of life,
    The simple pleasures of life
    A little music and wine
    And I'll be satisfied.

(She hands him a glass; they link arms and drink.)

    BOTH
    Why should I reach for a star?
    My life is richer by far
    With simple pleasures
    When you are by my side.

In a later scene, Henri arrives at his favorite Fantasy Restaurant to wait for his true love, Misia, to arrive. "All the Time in the World"

    WAITER
Good evening, M'sieur Lautrec.

    HENRI
Good evening, Bernard. Good, you've got the roses. Her favorite kind. And my favorite kind of champagne.

    WAITER
Will you order now?

    HENRI
No. I'll wait for my guest, Bernard. No hurry.
(The waiter bows and leaves. Lights come down to a spot on Henri, who sings like a young Chevalier, dapper, tilting his topper over his eyes.)

Let the human race
Lead its merry pace.
Let the clock be still
Until I see her face.
I have all the time in the world.

Let the waiter wait.

Let the band stay late.
Let the candles flicker
And evaporate.
I have all the time in the world.

The mellower the wine,
The sweeter flavor.
Imagine what sweet memories
I'll have to savor.

Leave me here to be
Deep in reverie
For the contemplation
Of her love of me . . .
I have all the time,
All, yes, all the time,
All the time in the world.

* * * *

Let the night grow old,
Let the wind grow cold.
I'll feel young and warm
When she is mine to hold.
I have all the time in the world.

Tonight's the night the world
Goes on around me,
For once she steps inside the door,
Yes, once she's found me . . .

Let the plague occur,
Revolution stir,
In the sweet fulfillment
Of tonight with her
I have all the time,
All, yes, all the time,
All the time in the world.

Early in this chapter I referred to the concept and technique in *Bordello* of Julian's selection of moments from Lautrec's past which were dramatized and musicalized in the show, with the drama heightened by a projection of his very painting illustrating our very scene. One of the better examples of this process was in the scene written for *Bordello* based upon Lautrec's painting "Le Passager Du 54." (The scene's author is Julian More. The lyric is mine.)

(Cabaret artist Yvette Guilbert and Henri are engaged in conversation near the end of the play.)

YVETTE

You spend too much time in that . . . place, Henri. Suffocating in voluptuousness. Come up for air.

HENRI

I know. But I'm about to embark on an orgy of celibacy.

YVETTE

England again?

HENRI

No. Going to sea. Coasting round to Bordeaux by steamship. I shall attach my soul to the stars—instead of one star like you. Fresh air in my lungs, two kilometers around the deck every day, and a complete abstinence from women.

YVETTE

I'll bet on that, or better yet, make up a song about it.

HENRI

Oh, no, you won't. There'll be nothing to write about.

(A Fantasy Ship's Cabin opens up, revealing "Le Passager Du 54" getting dressed. Projection: "Le Passager Du 54." Yvette watches the Girl in Cabin 54 put on her boater and come out on deck.

Lighting changes to bright sunshine. The Girl in Cabin 54 sits in a deck chair in the same position in which she sits in Lautrec's picture. Yvette assumes her cabaret style, acid and sharp.)

YVETTE

Mesdames et Messieurs, a little number entitled "The Girl in Cabin 54." What a beauty. Her hair gold as a cornfield. Figure slim as a rake. Brow noble as a princess. In fact for the wife of a mere Senegal consular official, she was no slag.

(Henri puffs out his chest, sniffing the sea air. He sets off on a turn around the deck, but freezes as he spots The Girl in Cabin 54. At certain times during the ensuing song Henri moves closer to the girl, like an animal stalking its prey, hiding, watching. Yvette sings.)

> As pretty as a picture
> As she leaned against the rail,
> He watched her from the moment
> That their ship began to sail.
> He wanted so to meet her,
> For he had so much to say.
> He hoped somehow she'd notice
> But she never glanced his way.
>
> She filled his heart with longing
> As they sailed across the sea
> With visions of a romance
> Somehow could never be.
> And when they reached the harbor,
> As he watched her step ashore,
> He knew he never could forget her—
> The Girl in Cabin 54.

The simple lyric and scene are then reinforced by a choreographed sequence in which Henri tries unsuccessfully to establish contact, a sequence which includes a howling gale, during which Henri finally confronts The Girl in Cabin 54 only while being thrown against her by the storm. It ends with a livid green light hitting her face as she runs unromantically from the stage holding her hand to her mouth, leaving Henri poised, words frozen on his lips.

The juxtaposition of the real and imagined and the present and the past, and the bittersweet, romantic and comic, all worked so well in this small and peripheral scene, that one had the feeling after watching it that this is what real theatre is all about. The final result was due to a collaborative effort that I, as lyricist only, was proud to be a simple part of.

THIRTEEN

The "Christy" production—1975.
And with it, at long last, the agent.

"All my words are still unsaid. / Who was I to say them to, Knowing they should stay unsaid / Until the likes of you."

FROM A BOOK in which it may sound like almost every project I write about was dearest to my heart, if I had to choose my own very special favorite, it would be *Christy*. I'm still so very dazzled by the language of the original *Playboy of the Western World* and ever fascinated by the darkness of its humor and the clever plot machinations and lusty characters, and so pleased with my own work as a playwright on the adaptation, and so full of rounded fond memories of the project of musicalizing it and seeing the production come to pass, that there it is, all-in-all my favorite child! I've said it and I'm glad!

The what, when, why and how of *Christy* as produced could in itself come close to being enough to fill a book. But I'll try to condense the story, although I shall have to report some of it to you in a rather *Rashomon*-like fashion, as various events occurred in my eyes and in my recall, as they occurred in the eyes of the composer, the late Al Frisch, and in the recall of his widow Celia.

Bordello was over with in May, 1974, and in the final analysis it had behaved more like a fizzled firecracker than a bonanza. Imagine the letdown, particularly for Al and Celia Frisch. Joan and I and all the London people involved had old jobs to return to or new theatrical projects to start working on—but Al had to try to revive his struggle to keep alive his fading career as a tunesmith, with no immediate hope of new activity on Tin Pan Alley, and with the wind pretty much knocked out of his sails. No small wonder he soon came appealing to Joan and me for us to help do something, anything, to try to get *Christy* out of the file drawer and off the ground and into a production. He was making an attempt at developing a supper-club or cabaret-style act out of his treasure chest of melody-drenched memories, and being knowledgeable in graphics and print because of my ad agency production background, I was able to help him design and type-set and have printed a handsome announcement flyer for his projected act. But even if the act took off, its appeal was going to be limited, and it wouldn't have been enough. He needed the shot in the arm that probably only a new show could provide. It may not have been common knowledge among his old acquaintances and friends, but soon afterward Al had been "reduced" to driving a cab during the last working year of his life. I think the choice was an honorable attempt to earn honest income, and truly an admirable effort on his part, but surely he and Celia must have felt the latter pursuit a measure of desperation, and beneath his dignity as an artist. I mention it here not in any gossipy way, but because the aura of desperation about Al (in my view of the story) at this time in our lives has a lot to do with what happened to *Christy* and the how and when and why.

In the spring of '75 (about a year after "Bordello"), Joan and I dropped in on a rather primitive but earnest production of one of our favorite musicals, *The Happy Time*, at what was then the *Bert Wheeler Theatre* in the *Hotel Dixie* in New York. I'd noticed (in some trade paper ad or announcement, I think) that a company named Octagon Productions had been reviving a few interesting musicals including *Anyone Can Whistle*, which I'd never seen and had wanted to catch in this revival, but missed out on again. Commending them in advance in my mind for their innovative taste in selecting such obscure old musicals for revival, I was prepared before actually attending a performance to like what they had done with their next production, *The Happy Time*, the first show of theirs I *did* get to see, and to make allowances for any imperfections that might exist in so informal a production. Joan, generally agreeing with my own taste, was prepared in advance to enjoy it and make allowances, too. And so it was that we were entertained by *The Happy Time* again as we expected to be, and were perhaps ready to pounce on the producer/managing director at Octagon about *Christy* without even verbalizing this unspoken plan to each other. Earlier that week I'd had my most recent in a series of desperate-sounding telephoned appeals from Al—couldn't we please do something about *Christy*? To me the plea had all the earmarks of meaning he didn't care how simple a production we could get going, as long as we could arrange *some* exposure for the show so that perhaps a more seasoned theatre pro with imagination and bucks would see it, like it, and pick it up and develop it into a major production for Broadway or elsewhere. So that maybe, I inferred, though Al didn't state it, he wouldn't have to continue driving a cab for the rest of his life. Any attempt that would offer him hope would be better than no attempt at all. This, once again, is *my* version of the story in the *Rashomon*-like scheme of things.

Bearing in mind Al's plea, Joan and I did wind up approaching the producer/manager of Octagon, Joseph Lillis, about *Christy*, on the very night we saw *The Happy Time* at the *Bert Wheeler*, and wonder of wonders, Joseph was interested, and asked to see a script and to hear a tape. He then called us in for a conference, introduced us to a director (also a designer) with whom he'd worked, Peter David Heth, started preparing a budget, and asked that we think about helping to raise money for the proposed production. We soon started talking script revisions and a possible time schedule.

Naturally Joan and I had also immediately gotten in touch with Al, and while he was pleased, incredulously he nevertheless sounded wary. Who was this charlatan, Joseph Lillis (the producer/manager of Octagon)?—he wanted to know. It seemed to Joan and me that whoever Lillis was, whatever his qualifications, and however primitive the production might have to be—here was our big chance to *get the show on* with minimal hassle, at minimal expense (Joseph could produce it as a non-union venture, with many of the people involved working for the experience and exposure only, with little or no salary or fee at all), and actually see if the show had potential. Joan and I already knew what Octagon had done with Ebb and Kander's *The Happy Time*, and by now we had also seen its interpretation of *I Had A Ball*, and the songs were pleasantly sung and the actors were professional enough, and we concluded that Lillis and Octagon could do a reasonable enough job with *Christy*, and if not, no real harm—on to a better production elsewhere next time around, if we could ever get it off the ground again. Lord knows, up to that point we had certainly tried to get *Christy* off the ground for several years and failed dismally.

I guess now, in retrospect, that there existed at least one so major a philosophical difference between us—(Joan and I were so much more attuned to risk-taking, and Al and Celia were so much more conservative in approach)—that seeing eye-to-eye on important decisions regarding *Christy* was an ambition devoutly to be wished for, but almost doomed in advance to fail.

This was the point at which I was starting to find Al maddeningly inflexible and negative in every aspect of attempting to make progress on finalizing arrangements for the proposed production. However, be those differences as they may, despite his objections and doubts, he still evidently thought well enough of the idea of having the production done at all, to try to help start drumming up financial support for it, even though he was still wary enough to expect accountability for every decision I would be making, and to question every creative suggestion the team of Lillis and his director would be coming up with.

The proposed budget was only, at maximum, in the high four-figure range, and we anticipated no trouble in being able to reach that goal, if necessary by enlisting the aid of friends and family (a foolish thing to do, we later learned in another project). The fact of the matter is that for *Christy*, Al and I jointly obtained a pledge from a patron of the arts from California named David Fasken who had been the leading backer of *Bordello*. He had been so taken with Al's music and talent that when Al and I jointly phoned Fasken from my apartment and explained to him the circumstances about the proposed *Christy* production and its very modest budget requirements, without even first getting something in writing he agreed on the phone for us to count him in on being the *sole* investor, an arrangement my dear wife was not entirely happy with because she'd had her heart set on crap-shooting a little, too. [By this time she had been working for fifteen years, and was justifiably becoming a wee bit smug about her financial "independence," and her entitlement to crap-shoot if she wished. In addition to that, she was proving once again, bless that big, oversized heart of hers, how much she actually believed in me and in *Christy*.]

It all sounds like a wonderful Judy/Mickey style scenario again, doesn't it? Only problem, and we didn't know it at the time, was that Al was probably suffering even that early from the brain tumor from which he died less than a year later. (Again, the latter is my supposition in the *Rashomon*-like unfolding of the developments.)

Since Al had never been the easiest person in the world to work with, and since he had already previously laid the groundwork for acting and sounding opinionated and stubborn on other occasions, I didn't give too much thought to the problem I was having with him about the proposed re-writes I had discussed with producer Joseph Lillis and our director, Peter David Heth. I assumed Al's unwillingness or inability to

BERT WHEELER THEATRE in the HOTEL DIXIE
250 West 43rd Street, N.Y.C. 221-9143

World Premiere October 14, 1975

JOSEPH LILLIS
(in association with JOAN SPIRO)

presents

CHRISTY

a darlin' musical about a daring deed
based on John M. Synge's
THE PLAYBOY OF THE WESTERN WORLD

Book & Lyrics by
BERNIE SPIRO

Music by
LAWRENCE J. BLANK

Musical Direction,
Vocal Arrangements
and Incidental Music by
ROBERT BILLIG

Entire Production Designed and Directed by
PETER DAVID HETH

Choreographed by: JACK ESTES
Master Carpenter: JOHN CONCANNON
Master Electrician: RAY DUVAL
Production Stage Mgr.: AMY SCHECTER

THE CAST

Christopher Mahon (Christy)	JIMI ELMER
Pegeen Flaherty	BETTE FORSYTH
Shawn Quin	BEA SWANSON
Michael James Flaherty	JOHN CANARY
Old Mahon	ALEXANDER SOKOLOFF
Jimmy Farrell	BRUCE LEVITT
Philly Cullen	BILL HEDGE
Sara Malone	MARTHA T. KEARNS
Susan Brady	LYNN KEARNEY
Maggie Tansey	MARIE GINNETTI
Honor Blake	BENE SACES LANDIS

PLACE: The West Coast of Ireland
Most of the action takes place in and around
a rough pot-house or tavern on the Mayo Coast.

TIME: Around the Turn of the Century

The *Christy* program

make changes at this point was simply an extension of his usual contrary behavior. But even before the problem of revisions of the score had a chance to become finally resolved, another confrontation between Al and me took place, with our respective wives understandably each taking the side of her own husband, and thus a feud began between Bernie and Joan against Al and Celia, or, if you wish, between Al and Celia against Bernie and Joan, which led to irreparable damage to the relationship and left us (Joan and me) holding the bag as far as commitment to Octagon and Joseph and Peter, etc., and without the score—for the feud continued with an ultimatum by Al forbidding me to use his score in that production! If Al had his druthers, he would have pulled out the words, too. [He and Celia threatened to do so, claiming copyright infringement, and insisting that my lyrics were inseparable from his music which had been copyrighted by their private music publishing firm.] Therefore, they stated, my lyrics no longer belonged to me. They then tried to keep the show from going on at all, and had I paid heed or not checked with a lawyer, I would have found myself not only scoreless, but showless as well. And the show penniless, inasmuch as they had also prevailed upon our California-based angel to pull out his money pledge, too, which he did. Again, all of the above is *my* interpretation of what happened, and if Joan were alive today it would be hers, too. Needless to say there are two sides to every story, and with Al deceased since 1976 there is only Celia left to relate *their* side. Briefly, Celia insists that our differences had nothing to do with Al's illness and that my motivation for the production was less involved with concern for Al's future and welfare than with my own self-aggrandizement, and that the reason for the firmness of their stand was simply that they would have nothing to do with so amateur a production.

My side again: I suppose we could have cancelled our agreement with Joseph without too much financial responsibility at that point, but because Joan and I had been involved from the beginning in developing the idea of the production with Joseph and his staff and friends, I must admit that by now Joan and I could taste and smell and salivate about the prospect of the production that I insist we had been motivated to seek out in the first place more for Al's sake than for our own.

The final confrontation that took place between us was immediately concerned with choice of musical director. Joseph Lillis had to bring one in on budget, and the budget was zero. Basically the budget for almost everything and everybody was zero, but we all were being promised a piece of the pie if by some miracle we were able succeed with this showcase and take it a step or two further. (Wasn't this style advance "workshop" production proving enormously successful with *A Chorus Line* that very year?)

Joseph knew a very young but qualified musician by the name of Larry Blank who by this early time in his fledgling career had already guest-conducted at *Goodtime Charley* on Broadway. Larry was free and able to take on the responsibility of *Christy* for a limited time, and he was willing to do it for the experience and for the opportunity of adding musical-directing of an original musical to his resumé. Overqualified to be working for so little, it's true, but grateful for the opportunity nevertheless. The final confrontation between Al and me had to do with Larry.

My judgment is that Al could and should not have been able to afford grandiosity at bargain-basement prices. What if anything he didn't like about Larry aside from his youth, I did not find out until recently when, in rehashing memories with Celia, she explained to me that Larry was using more contemporary chords during his one-time attempt to play Al's score so that Al might hear Larry's interpretation of it—cold. We were having what I'd thought was a pleasant "getting to know you and your score" introductory meeting between the principals (and their wives) at our apartment, a meeting which was cordial enough, and at which I thought Larry asked all the right questions and made all the right responses in as knowledgeable and respectful a manner as anyone could conceivably have wished. But evidently this young fella who after *Christy* was to go on to music-direct and conduct *Copperfield* and *Onward Victoria* on Broadway, and *Evita* and *Sugar Babies* and many others in Los Angeles and San Francisco soon thereafter and ever since, was in 1975, in Al and Celia's eyes, not good enough for the almost "informal" production we were planning for *Christy*. Joan and I thought it was sheer pigheadedness in Al at the time, but it did briefly stalemate us as Al followed with his "I forbid" dictum, till Larry came up with an idea which he didn't quite have the nerve to present to us, and so Joseph did the asking for him. What if Larry re-wrote the music?—would we, could we, consider forsaking Al's?

Here we were "X" number of weeks away from scheduled previews (I don't recall the precise details); we had already contracted for and left a deposit on the theatre rental for a particular time slot, and were well into other plans and preparation. Could the score be redone quickly enough? How would Bernie have the time to work up new lyrics quickly enough, considering that Bernie had his full-time ad agency job to contend with and had been writing lyrics and librettos only avocationally? Sure it would be a terrible slap in the face to Al, but didn't he deserve it, having been so stubborn? Wouldn't it serve him right? We had every question asked and every answer ready, and every justification in the world, we thought, for every decision we were making. Larry promised that I would have no or only minimal additional work to do on the lyrics. What he was undertaking was to use my lyrics precisely as written and compose new melodies and rhythms to accompany the words as deliberately different from Al's melodies and rhythms as he could make them sound.

He succeeded, in one respect anyhow. What never occurred to us was that it was important for the score to sound not just different rhythmically and melodically, but also as rich as Al's score, because the words the score was accompanying were so colorful and lush and poetic (as much in the tradition of John Millington Synge and the original *The Playboy of the Western World* as I had been able to fashion them), that *Christy* would not work well unless the music were on the same level. I do not fault Larry for not entirely succeeding; I think he did a remarkable job—all at breakneck speed—which turned out to be just fast enough to permit us to roughly adhere to the schedule we were locked into. But Larry was no Al, and the score, while ingenious (particularly considering how frantically it was done), was seldom more than mechanical and uninspired.

By no means do I attribute the show's final failure in that only production of *Christy* to date solely to its score being Larry's and not Al's. There were other reasons why it failed, a few of which unfortunately could not have been rectified in this production, which was skimpy and primitive and not thoroughly professional down the line. Not all of my lyrics were sparkling enough, and we had a second act book problem which I never could or did completely resolve. So even if we had gone into the production with Al's score rather than Larry's, it is not likely we would have gone on to a bigger and better production elsewhere. I doubt that we would have attracted much attention or praise with this showcase if Richard Rodgers himself had been the composer. It was, in the final analysis an amateurish production, and that cannot be denied. So—nothing lost—except a few thousand dollars of Joan's hard-earned money (*she* wound up being the sole backer) and a lot of blood, sweat and tears (which is the norm, and true of any show), *and* the friendship of Al and Celia, which was irreplaceable inasmuch as Al died soon afterward, and I never did make amends to him, and I sorely regret that. A year or so later Celia did seek peace with Joan and me in time for a memorial tribute she had arranged in Al's memory. But the ensuing relationship still remained somewhat strained and distant till beyond the time of Joan's death almost ten years later, and, in fact, until quite recently, when Celia and I had occasion to spend some time together and try to make peace in earnest. Our aspirations, Celia's and mine, for the future of *Christy* and for any other work I shared with Al remain constant and strong. Thus, hopefully, we have buried the hatchet for all time, and are working sensibly toward the same goal.

In attempting to heal old wounds I have pledged to Celia that if any further production of *Christy* should take place, the music we'd use would be Al's only, or if we need something musically that didn't exist in Al's catalog, we would at least use nothing from Larry Blank's score (the produced one). I have nothing against the latter, but understandably, Celia does.

I am indeed grateful to Al for the opportunity to work with so enormous a talent as his, and nothing would give me greater pleasure than to be instrumental in bringing back his music to being performed live again in one project or another, and thereby providing a long overdue living tribute to him.

[If I may digress momentarily, I have recently completed and am circulating among prospective producers an intimate revue for the stage in retrospective style also entitled *Of Rhyme and Reason*, consisting of songs and scenes I've collaborated on with five different composers, including a delicious selection of Al Frisch numbers, some of which have never been heard beyond the one-time presentation to the producer of the prospective project for which each was conceived, or during the actual creation of them in the music room of Al's and Celia's home in Orangeburg, New York. This may become another way of getting some of Al's music heard again.]

From our experience with *Christy*, Joan and I learned a lot about who is responsible for what in the theatre, and Joan herself learned much more about producing and management from Joseph. We held on and hung in there with the production for forty-five performances. We had ups and downs with Joseph, but wound up being great friends ever since. The young woman he was dating at the time also became a lasting friend through the years. The new composer, Larry Blank, likewise stayed in touch, as did the young musician, Robert Billig, who took over the music directorship responsibility in Larry's place. Once Larry donned the composer's role, he had to find someone else to replace himself with, to rehearse the singers and work out vocal arrangements and the like. He chose Bob, who, as Larry had before him, thought the opportunity a good one to "bring in" a new, original musical, no matter how modest it was going to be. Bob Billig has also gone on to be conductor and musical director of one distinguished production after another ever since, his two most recent long-term stints being the original New York productions of *Little Shop of Horrors* and *Les Miserables*.

Our male lead, Jimi Elmer, while inexperienced and a somewhat undisciplined actor at the time, nevertheless had extraordinary skills and qualities as both an actor and singer and was enormously winning in the title role, and became a lasting friend, one whose professional services we called upon later for various recordings and presentations on other projects. My son-in-law Ken had a friend, Bruce Corwin, who was a photographer at the time and took some wonderful publicity shots of *Christy* in action. Through an associate of his, Larry Solomon, we got to the prestigious independent radio station, WBAI, which offered to make its facilities available to us for a studio recording of the entire show in exchange for our granting them permission to air the recording of the complete production of *Christy*, dialog and all, at their discretion. They've aired it any number of times since. From that recording we later extracted the songs alone to use in an original cast record of the entire score. This record was produced and distributed by Bruce and Doris Yeko of Original Cast Records, and is still available at a few shops in New York. And there were two other major developments from the production of *Christy* which are also worthy of mention.

The first, to return momentarily to the personal subject of progress on my sexuality problem, was the vague indication to me of my arrival at a slightly new level of conscious awareness and possibly even acceptance of my homosexuality. I still wasn't sharing it with anyone and still not acting it out except in my same old closeted fashion. And I have no real proof of this because nothing actually happened . . . but—for the first time ever, I believe I was being made a play for, and it was by one of the male cast members of *Christy*, and I think back now to how it must have flattered the hell out of me, and to what a wonderful opportunity it would have been for me to finally have an affair (including the built-in understanding, I suppose, that I as the writer and husband of the associate producer, which was now Joan's title, could have been helpful in *his* going on to fortune and fame if the show ever got anywhere). I think back now to all my younger years of homosexual fantasies and desires (including the army and college and the frat), knowing full well that the urge in me was so strong that if anyone had come on to me I would have succumbed with the snap of a finger, I was that arousable and the need in me was that intense. Although, on second thought, it might have required a little seduction or coaxing by the other party; I obviously can't be sure. But no one ever came on. I think back to my over forty years of being far less than fulfilled in my sexual yearnings, and as I have said before I think back to the waste of energy and productivity and the guilt and the resentment over not having been able to be my natural self because of societal pressures. But all that while I was shielded from acting out the fantasies and blocked from coming to terms with the desire because no one came on to me. I think back in anger over having had to keep my true self a secret, and now I often wonder how I managed; but I'm sure that part of the reason I did manage was that no one "came on." This aspect of my own history makes me all the more dedicated to coming out all the way now, and to lending my voice to the cause of anti-discrimination against gays and the quest for openness about and acceptance of who we are *when we are young*. And by God, with the publishing of this book, I'm on my way to that goal of coming out all the way, and on my way to finding a solution to my becoming a more active voice in the gay community, and on my way to contributing more of my energies toward helping improve the image of gays and gayness in the eyes of the world and helping to get our voice heard.

But back to—let's call him "Jack"—in the cast of *Christy*. I think back to him and to the fact that for the first time ever I was conscious of someone actually coming on to me—and what did I do about it? Nothing. Absolutely nothing. During rehearsals he sat near me in the theatre a lot (when he wasn't on stage) and he made a habit of laughing at my lyrics a lot and of telling me how good he thought they were. And he was very, very attractive, and I don't know if I consciously suspected at the time that this was a "come-on," but I did definitely feel an electricity and tension between us. Thinking back to the situation now, with all I now know about men flirting with each other, boy, was it *ever* a case of coming on! I want to kick myself now for not having acted on it. But c'est la vie. I hear there are lots of wasted opportunities in these pursuits. I single out this situation with "Jack" simply to help me understand myself, and to help those readers who are interested understand how "perilously" close I came to having that first homosexual affair (I don't consider the few sleaze incidents counting for more than what they were, and they were not affairs). And yet I was still too naive or green to pick up the signals, signals that I may have started receiving from others as early on as when I was in the army or even before that, away from home for a couple of summers as a busboy in a Catskill hotel when I was 15 and 16, but signals I never recognized as such because I didn't know that other guys had those feelings, too. With the happening of *Christy*, and because we were now in the more liberated mid-70's, I became more aware that there were lots more of us out there. But in retrospect, I must have figured then, by the time *Christy* came around, that it was too late for me to do anything about my "closetedness" except to continue to fantasize behind closed bathroom doors. I now loved Joan more than ever, and with *Bordello* and *Christy* she and I were experiencing two successive years of such stimulating theatrical activity, in addition to our normal family and social and job activity, that we were true partners in life, living, working, enjoying and sharing. Our lives were as full as if we were starting a family all over again, and as a matter of fact it was at about this time (September, 1975) that our granddaughter was born. And so I chose to remain homosexually unfulfilled and not rock the boat, and to simply continue my normal role and relationship as a husband and family man.

The second major development that arose from the *Christy* production was that I invited a few agents to see it, among them Bertha Klausner, and she thought it was promising enough to invite me in turn to become a client of hers. And so after years of my having presented myself to one agent after another in search of someone who would represent and guide me in my avocational writing career, I was finally being recognized as at least having enough talent to be worth representing. Till then the answer had always been courteous but "too busy" to handle unknowns.

Bertha has been spectacular in the fourteen years I have been a client—in boosting my morale and encouraging me onward to new theatrical projects, in her continued support of me on old theatrical projects, and in her taking total charge of submitting this book to prospective publishers. She has been a true friend to me, and to Joan as well, and I love her dearly. As alluded to previously, because I was secure in her affection for me and therefore had no trouble in "coming out" to her as soon as I was sure this book was truly under way, it felt especially good to have done so with someone from my past who is senior to me, someone for whom I have respect and who still respects me no matter what or who I am.

What else can I say about the *Christy* that was actually produced? Joan and I gave it our all. We saw all but one of the 45 performances. We used our home only to sleep in for two months; we did a day's work, Joan at school, I in my office, then went straight to the theatre—first for auditions and rehearsals, then for performances every Tuesday through Friday. And we practically lived in the theatre all day Saturday and Sunday for two shows each weekend day. We welcomed friends and/or family and/or business associates at almost every performance. We tried publicity stunts and I used every promotion device I had learned in the advertising business or from having been a theatre devotee all those years, to try to stimulate box office sales. We even handed out flyers at Duffy Square. But our reviews were generally poor, and the fact of the matter was—and I never counted on this—there were not enough New Yorkers around terribly interested in Synge's rough and ready pub on the Mayo coast of Ireland or the quaint and earthy characters who inhabited it. And *Christy* seemed not to be the type of show tourists or tired businessmen flock to either. (I should have realized that in advance.) So the time finally arrived when, with even the cast growing restless because of small audiences, Joan and I faced up to failure, sadly posted the closing notice, cleaned up and cleaned out, and came home to our little den of iniquity on the Upper West Side, and tried to return to a normal way of life.

The lyrics I wrote for *Christy* fell into several categories. Joseph and Peter (producer and director) suggested I forsake three of the more poetic concepts and be more theatrical. I eliminated the first two printed here, so no audience has ever heard them, and the only music that ever accompanied them was Al's. First was the prologue opener, sung by a minstrel—"When the Penny Poets Sing"

> I'll sing you a song for a penny
> A song that is tender and rare
> Of a laddie so bold
> That his deed must be told
> When the penny poets sing
> At the August fair.
>
> Alas, a grave crime he committed,
> Then fled from the scene in despair.
> But a good woman's smile
> Gave him courage the while.
> So the penny poets sing
> At the August fair.
>
> Now it's heigh-ho,
> Back we go
> To a time when the world was young,
> When a tale told
> Couldn't unfold
> Till they set it in rhyme to be sung.
>
> And when we have come to an ending
> We'll know that it doesn't end there.
> Though his moment is gone,
> Sure, our hero lives on
> When the penny poets sing
> At the August fair.

The second "never-heard" number took place well into the first act, when our fugitive hero, Christy, describes to the young woman who has befriended him, Pegeen, what it is like to be on the run from the law. "It's a Lonesome Thing." It was eliminated from Lillis' production, but with Al's plaintive musical accompaniment to me it remains a never-performed rare jewel.

> It's a lonesome thing
> Passing through a town

When the house lights shine
As the night goes down . . .
With no home to call your own
It's a lonesome thing.

When you need a friend
But you find instead
Howling dogs behind,
Growling dogs ahead.
As you face the great unknown
It's a lonesome thing.

And you feel the stare of lovers
From the shadows in the night.
Almost everywhere the lovers
Waiting till you're out of sight.

It's a lonesome thing
As you travel on,
Feeling born alone
As the moon of dawn.
If your heart's not made of stone . . .
It's a lonesome thing.

Next (after the "Penny Poets" prologue), was the original opening number (as written with Al), "There's My Rainbow," obviously wrong for the spot because it was too lethargic and bloodless to follow the gentle "Penny Poets" already printed here.

In the revised version, with Larry Blank writing the music, I changed the lyric as follows, and gave it the title "Christy," and it was sung immediately after an opening speech in which Christy complains about his lot and his demanding father.

I've had enough of
Doing this for him,
Doing that for him.
I've had enough of
Being a mat for him to step on.
I've had enough of toil and sweat.
There must be something better.
So if my dreams are fancy free,
Well, who deserves them more than me?

Some day . . . a rainbow's gonna glisten
For Christy, Christy.
Some day . . . the world'll stop and listen
For Christy, Christy.
Some day this simple quiet feller
No one gives his due—
He'll come stormin' through,
Through the mud and mire,
Full of spit and fire.
Some day . . . the girls'll come a scorchin'
For Christy, Christy.
Some day . . . I'm gonna make my fortune and fame.

> Maybe I'm a sorry sight to look at
> But mark me just the same.
> Some day the world will know Christy,
> Christy is my name.

(He speaks to a finch flying by.)

Well, hello, bird. What early autumn breeze has brought the likes of you to these parts? You know, some day I'll be free like you are. Aye, free!

> Some day . . . there'll be a whole new vista
> For Christy, Christy.
> Some day . . . there'll be the title "Mister"
> For Christy, Christy.
> Maybe not today, tonight, tomorrow,
> But once I take my aim—
> Make way—the world will know Christy,
> Christy is my name.

Early in Act One there are three pivotal numbers, with music first by Al, then rewritten by Larry. In "Grain of the Salt of the Earth," the fugitive Christy cautiously enters a tavern on the Mayo coast, inhabited at the moment by three friendly but inquisitive people: The owner, Michael James, one of his cronies, Philly, and the former's high-spirited and attractive daughter, Pegeen.

MICHAEL JAMES (to Christy)
Why are you so concerned about whether the police show up in this place? Are you wanted, maybe? What was it you done, lad? Was it larceny?

CHRISTY
I'm slow at learnin'. A middling scholar only. What's larceny?

MICHAEL JAMES
Stealin' and robbin'.

CHRISTY (with a flash of family pride)
And I the son of an honest farmer? The saints forbid.

MICHAEL JAMES
If you're denying it so strong, it's larceny I'm thinkin' for sure. You don't have to say another word. I know exactly how it happened. (sings)

> Youth and temptation,
> Temptation and youth—
> They're hand-in-hand partners,
> 'Tis sad but the truth.
> Poor lad was but playin'
> A juvenile prank.
> A mask and a gun
> And some innocent fun at the bank.

CHRISTY
Oh, no, sir.

MICHAEL JAMES

If it's not stealin', it's maybe something big.

PHILLY

Ay! It's maybe something big. He's a wicked looking youth. Maybe he followed a young woman on a lonely night. (sings)

Lust and desire,
Desire and lust.
There's nary a feller
A maiden can trust.
He ravished, then left her
To weep in the grime.
I say that the bastard
Be hung for his dastardly crime.

Confess, boy!

CHRISTY

Oh, no, sir.

PHILLY

Say yes, boy.

CHRISTY

Not so, sir.

Indeed it's agreed
Since the day of my birth
You'll find no such fault
With this grain of the salt of the earth.

MICHAEL JAMES

Hmmm! He said he was the son of an honest farmer. Maybe the land was grabbed from his dad and he did what any self-respecting lad would do. (sings)

Eye for an eye
And a tooth for a tooth.
He fashioned revenge
With the flame of his youth,
Set fire to the landlord
He'd come to despise—
Then fanned with a bellows
To hasten the fellow's demise.

CHRISTY

Not I, sir. Not that.

PHILLY

Did you marry three wives then?

CHRISTY

I never married with one. (He looks shyly at Pegeen)

PHILLY

Did you strike golden guineas out of solder maybe?

CHRISTY

Not a sixpence or a farthing.

MICHAEL JAMES

Then what could it be?

PEGEEN

I know. (sings)

> If it ain't stealin'
> Or passion or gall,
> I'm thinkin' the lad did
> No ill deed at all . . .
> A poor orphaned traveler
> Who wouldn't know how
> To slit through the throat
> Of a screechin' old goat or a sow.

Confess, boy.

CHRISTY

Oh, no, Ma'am.

PEGEEN

Say yes, boy.

CHRISTY

Not so, Ma'am.

PEGEEN, MICHAEL JAMES, PHILLY

> Indeed it's agreed
> Since the day of his birth
> We'd find not a fault
> With this grain of the salt of the earth.

CHRISTY (offended)

That's not true, I tell ya. I maybe didn't commit the kind of storybook crimes you pictured me doin', but what I did do was terrible fearful enough. (Sheepishly) I killed my poor father, God rest his soul, Tuesday a week.

MICHAEL JAMES

(Leaning in with the others to breathlessly await the rest of Christy's explanation.)

Killed your father?

PEGEEN

Killed your father, is it? (They retreat.)

MICHAEL JAMES

You should have had good reason for doin' the like of that.

CHRISTY

And so I had. (sings)

Cranky and crusty,
A dirty old man—
He scolded and screamed
Till I upped and I ran.
He chased me and beat me.
I struck and I fled.

MICHAEL JAMES, PEGEEN, PHILLY

Poor frightened young lad
With a God-save-him-Dad that was dead.

MICHAEL JAMES

How shameless!

PEGEEN

How darin'!

CHRISTY

I'm blameless, I'm swearin'.
I'm swearin' . . .
(They have a brief confab.)
I'm swearin' . . .
(They start nodding affirmatively.)
I'm swearin'.

MICHAEL JAMES, PEGEEN, PHILLY

Indeed we concede
He has proven his worth.
Sure it wasn't his fault,
He's a grain of the salt . . .

CHRISTY

Sure it wasn't my fault.
I'm a grain of the salt . . .

ALL

Sure, it wasn't his (my) fault.
He's (I'm) a grain of the salt of the earth.

An interesting problem arose in the staging of the latter number when we first saw it in rehearsal and it didn't work quite as well as I'd imagined. The change of mind and change of heart by the others toward Christy near the end, wherein the group finally accepts him as being the gentle soul who had been abused, happened too suddenly, and was simply not believable enough. But with the added device of stopping the song for a brief confab—a collaborative idea born during a brief confab of our own between the director, music director and me—the number became believable, made sense, and worked like a charm.

Second of the pivotal numbers, and acknowledgement by Christy and Pegeen of their immediate interest in each other after his having been accepted by her father and his crony, and after Christy and Pegeen have been left alone for the night while Michael James and Philly go off to a cousin's wake: "Until the Likes of You"

CHRISTY

I've told my story nowhere till tonight, Pegeen. And it's foolish I was here to be talkin' freely maybe, but you're decent people, I'm thinkin', and yourself a kindly woman, and I wasn't fearin' you at all.

PEGEEN

You've said the like of that maybe in every cot and cabin where you've met a young girl on your way.

CHRISTY

I've said it nowhere till tonight, I tell ya. And I'm thinkin' now I know why, too. (He reaches out and gently turns her around to him and sings.)

All my words are still unsaid.
Who was I to say them to,
Knowing they should stay unsaid
Until the likes of you.

All the world was mine to see,
Yet my eyes enjoyed no view
Knowing there was naught to see
Until the likes of you.

Silently I waited,
Searching all the way,
Certain we were fated
To meet one special day.

All my life was meant to live,
Live with someone dear and true.
All my love was meant to give,
But still I wondered who
Until the likes of you.

(He kisses her gently.)

PEGEEN (backing away)

Well, aren't you the forward one!

CHRISTY

I'm sorry. I've no wish to be offendin' you.

PEGEEN

Let me be the judge of what it is I'm offended by.

CHRISTY (regaining his courage)

Well, then, would there be any offense if I was askin' are you single now?

PEGEEN

What would I want weddin' so young?

CHRISTY

So! We're alike. (He draws closer and she takes his hand.)

PEGEEN

Aye, we're alike. (sings)

All the world was mine to see
Yet my eyes enjoyed no view
Knowing there was naught to see
Until the likes of you.

Silently I waited
Searching all the way,
Certain we were fated
To meet one special day.

CHRISTY

All my life was meant to live,
Live with someone dear and true.

BOTH

All my love was meant to give,
But still I wondered who—
Until the likes of you.

In the third of what I consider the early pivotal numbers, Christy, now alone on stage after having been sought out by neighbor Widow Quin, who tries to get him to return home with her, looks over the comfortable bed Pegeen has fixed for him for the night, and begins to feel self-important for the first time. "Picture Me"

(He stretches and yawns and feels the quilt.)

Ah! That'll be fine sleeping.

(He surveys his new home.)

Is this yours, Christy Mahon? Is all this yours?

(He spots a looking glass on the wall, takes it and leans it against a chair and faces it and stares.)

Is this yourself? Is it the likes of you two fine women are fighting over?

(He pats his chin and tries to see his profile.)

And a handsome devil you are at that! (He sings)

Picture me
The picture of contentment!
Picture me
The center of the stage.
Just a tramp and hour ago.
Rub the lamp and what do you know?
Suddenly I'm quite the latest rage.

Picture me,
A sprout from out of nowhere

Flapping both my wings and fancy free!
Whatever it is I've got
It pleases the girls a lot.
Now, tell me, who am I to disagree?
Once a lowly thing,
Overnight a king—
Picture me.

Imagine, after all this time, being sought after and fussed about! Aye, I'm beginning to get the image more clearly now.

Picture this,
The grin that wins 'em over.
Picture these
The lips they'll soon have kissed.
Take a pup who's eager to please—
Scrub him up, get rid of his fleas.
How can any lassie pup resist?

Picture me,
Surpassing Casanova,
Lassie after lassie on my knee.
Whatever they love me for,
I have what it takes and more.
I question only how it came to be.
Once a simple clod,
Suddenly a god.
Picture me!

(He feels the mattress again.)

Ah! 'Tis a clean bed and soft indeed. 'Tis surely great luck I've won me in the end, all this, and being made potboy, too.

Picture me
The center of attraction.
Picture me
The lover in demand.
Take a lad who hadn't a pot—
Kill his dad and what've you got?
Quite the proudest potboy in the land.

Picture me
So shy and unassuming
Blooming like a merry cherry tree.
However it's taken place,
Perfection in form and face
Replaced the mortal man I used to be.
Yesterday a blah,
Now a lah-de-dah!
Picture me!

You know something, Christy Mahon? Weren't you a foolish fellow not to have killed your dad long years gone by?

Picture me!

Then there were three darkly comic numbers, the first two of which I added for the final production after confabs with director Peter David Heth who thought we needed more comedy. He was right. I learned recently that we've lost dear Peter to AIDS, and though I didn't ever get to know him too well, I'm indeed saddened by his passing. He was a sweet and talented man. I'm glad that there was evidently someone who did know him well enough to be instrumental in Peter's name having a place in the AIDS memorial quilt.

These next two, then ("darkly comic" numbers, as I call them) were never actually accompanied by Al's music, only Larry's. First, "Rumors" as sung by three friends of Pegeen who have come to get a glimpse of the daring young man they've already heard so much about. They are later joined by Widow Quin.

(Maggie knocks at the door and peers inside. The others wait anxiously.)

MAGGIE
Look at that! He's been sleepin' there all night.

SUSAN (Calling)
Pegeen! Pegeen!

(No answer. The girls turn away.)

SARA
Well, it's too bad if he's gone off now, never letting us set eyes on a man who killed his father—and we after rising early and destroying ourselves running fast on the hill. (sings)

I couldn't sleep a wink
Just waiting for the dawn to rise.

MAGGIE
I couldn't hardly wait
To see him with my own two eyes.

SUSAN
The stories they recite
Are almost too delightful to endure.

ALL THREE
Well, Mister, come ahead,
And prove to us instead—that you're . . .
More than a rumor!

SARA
They say he's only twenty.
They say he's murdered plenty.
And everywhere he's went he
Has killed along the way.
SUSAN and MAGGIE

Rumors . . . rumors . . . rumors a-plenty today.

MAGGIE

They say his voice is boomin'.
His strength is super human.
His shining eyes illumine
The gloom and dark of night.

SARA and SUSAN

Rumors . . . rumors . . . rumors are taking to flight.

ALL THREE

Where oh where
Are you, curiosity man?
Are you a marvel,
Not just catch-as-catch-can?

SUSAN

The man's so tall he towers.
They praise his virile powers.
Each maid that he deflowers
Keeps smiling for a year.

MAGGIE and SARA

Rumors . . . rumors . . . rumors are flying, I fear.

ALL THREE

But rumors . . . rumors . . . are oh, so romantic,
Oh, so romantic—
Oh, so romantic to hear.

(The Widow Quin enters, and snoops around.)

WIDOW

Christy! Christy! Where are you hiding, lad?

(Now the Girls sing "Rumors" again as Widow Quin sings "Come Out Wherever You Are" simultaneously.)

GIRLS	WIDOW
They say he's only twenty.	Come out in view
	Wherever you're hid,
They say he's murdered plenty.	And let this shrew
	Be making her bid
And everywhere he's went he	To comfort you
	Whatever you did.
Has killed along the way.	Come out wherever you are.

Rumors, rumors, rumors a-plenty today.

They say his voice is boomin'.	Come out, be bold,
	And dashing, my sweet.
His strength is super human.	My stew I'm told
	Is heaven to eat.
His shining eyes illumine	And you are cold

– 211 –

The gloom and dark of night. | And I am in heat.
Come out wherever you are.

Rumors, rumors, rumors are taking to flight.

Where oh where
Are you, curiosity man?
Are you a marvel,
Not just catch-as-catch-can?

The man's so tall he towers.

Come out, I pray,
Invisible friend,

They praise his virile powers.

I'll make it pay
For you in the end.

Each maid that he deflowers

You'll have your way;
I've naught to defend.

Keeps smiling for a year.
Rumors, rumors,

Come out wherever you are.
Come out, come out,
come out, come out,

Rumors are flying I fear.
But rumors, rumors

Come out wherever you are.
Come out, come out,
come out, come out,

Are oh, so romantic to hear.

Come out wherever you are.

Immediately afterward the Widow and Girls find Christy and excitedly ask him to share all the lurid details of his crime with them. "One Fell Swoop"

WIDOW
Come here and tell us your story before Pegeen returns.

CHRISTY (pleased but bashful)
It's a long story. You'd be destroyed listenin'.

WIDOW
Don't be letting on to be shy, a fine, gamey, treacherous lad the like of you. Was it in your house beyond you cracked his skull?

CHRISTY (still shy but flattered)
It was not. We were diggin' spuds in his cold stony devil's patch of a field.

WIDOW
Spare no details, lad.

CHRISTY (singing)
With one fell swoop I struck him,
With one great mighty blow,
With the blade of a spade
That I use for diggin' spuds.

SUSAN
Oh, my goodness. How terrifying!

CHRISTY
With one fell swoop it landed—

His big fat skull below.
As it fell I could tell
T'was a thud to end all thuds.

SARA

Must have sounded like an earthquake.

CHRISTY

I can see it, I remember,
How he stared in disbelief.
I can hear it, I remember,
What a feeling of relief!
(Girls in unison breathe a loud sigh)
With one fell swoop it happened,
With one great mighty blow,
And his head freely bled
Like a thick tomato soup,
And the daring deed was done
With one fell swoop.

MAGGIE

How did the fight start? What led you to it, Christy Mahon?

GIRLS (singing in unison, with interspersed nods from Christy)
Did he rant, rave and holler
That you did such a deed?

Did he scream so much it made your temper short?
Did he keep you in squalor
Like the pigs in their feed,
And with never any leave for joy or sport?

Were you too angry headed
Not to heed and obey?
Were you scheming then to leave him flat and cold?

CHRISTY

No, he wanted me wedded
With the Widow O'Shea
Who was rich but fat and forty five years old.

I can't marry her, says I. You do as I say, says he, or I'll flatten you out. You
will not if I can help it, says I. God have mercy on ya, says he, lifting the
spade. Or on your own, says I, grabbing it back.
With one fell swoop came freedom
To make my way at last.
What to do? Where to go—
As I kissed the corpse goodbye.

With one fell swoop—excitement.
My heart beat extra fast,
Disinterred, like a bird
That has just learned how to fly.

I can hear it, I remember,
How he screamed before he dropped.
I can feel it, I remember—
How my pulse and his both—stopped.

With one fell swoop it happened.
I left my sordid past,
The remains of his brains
Lying limply in a group.
And to think I did it all . . .

GIRLS
And to think he did it all . . .

ALL
And to think he (I) did it all . . .
With one fell swoop.

The third of the darkly comic numbers, "Great Company," was included in the original version of *Christy* with music by Al, then re-written by Larry, and for the first time in this transition from one composer to another Larry didn't precisely match my lyrics. No problem, of course. I simply adjusted the lyrics to match the rhythm and meter of his music, and presto!—the revised "Great Company." The latter is the version set down here, though incidentally this number was deleted during previews, and was therefore not included in the original cast recording. I have a piano version of it somewhere among a collection of a couple of dozen or so practice tapes. But no matter—here it is as rewritten for the production before discarding.

WIDOW (to Christy)
Didn't you hear me saying at the fall of night that the two of us should be great company?

CHRISTY
I'll have no want of company the likes of you when all sorts here is giving me all I need or all I ask.

WIDOW
But Christy, it's only you and me that's the murderers in these parts, remember? I've destroyed my man as you've destroyed your dad, so I am your like, and it's for that I'm taking a fancy to you. And I, with my little houseen above, where there'd be me to tend you, and none to ask were you a murderer or what at all. Can't you see we're not like all the others, me and you? (sings)

Me and you should be great company,
Great company, lad.
We're the two who killed one husband an'
One dirty old dad.
We'd be wise to harmonize
Together arm in arm
Free from guilt for blood we've spilt.
We really meant no harm.
Night by night by firelight we'll sigh,

—214—

Telling tales of lurid days gone by.
You and me, great company,
Great company, we two,
If you don't strangle me
Before I poison you.

CHRISTY

It's maybe the truth you're sayin', but what would I be doin' if I left Pegeen?

WIDOW

I've many nice jobs for you, and let you not forget we'd be together, and
there's joy in that by itself.

CHRISTY (now playing along with her)
Aye. It's true enough our interests are the same.
(he sings and she retorts.)

CHRISTY	WIDOW
You and me	
Should be great company	I'm a sinister villain.
	You're a villainous knave.
I'm like you	
And you're a lot like me	Sure, we've proven our skill in
	Sending men to the grave.
Night by night by firelight	
We'll reminisce of sin	And the havoc we've wrought . . .
Till some day we find a way	
To do each other in	What a marvelous thought!
We'd be great together,	
What a pair!	We're a treacherous twosome
	Who are never afraid.
Spreading strife	
And sorrow everywhere	We are equally gruesome
	With a pick or a spade.

BOTH
You and me, great company,
Great company, it's true,
If you don't butcher me
Before we poison,
Strangle, smother,
Slay each other . . .
And murder me before I slaughter you.

For a change of pace, here's a sample of transforming Synge's poetic language
into a ballad for musical theatre. Its title, "The Heart's a Wonder," reminds me that
after I finished writing my version of *Playboy* I learned that there had been an earlier
musical based on the Synge play, and that that one, coincidentally, was called not

Christy but *The Heart's A Wonder*. Actually, the phrase was invented not by me or the author of the other musical, but by John Millington Synge himself.

PEGEEN

And what is it I have, Christy Mahon, to make me fitting entertainment for the like of you, who has such poet's talking and such bravery of heart?

CHRISTY

Isn't there the light of seven heavens in your heart alone that will be my lamp from this day on?

PEGEEN

Isn't it you that put it there? (she sings)
Dark's the night,
Yet the heart's a wonder . . .
Lovelight will light
Every step of our way.

CHRISTY

Faint, your word,
Yet the heart's a wonder . . .
Speak, and I hear
Wondrous melodies play.

PEGEEN

Flowers now grow
Where no seeds have been sown.
Rainbows appear from the blue.
I was lonely before,
But I'm lonely no more.
A miracle came, and it's you.

BOTH

Brave, our dream,
Yet the heart's a wonder,
Bringing your love
On this wonderful day,
Bringing your love
On this wonderful day.

The rest of *Christy*'s lyrics are on its original cast record, and in print in a manuscript in the archives of the Library for the Performing Arts at Lincoln Center, New York, and who knows, the show itself has modest enough production values for it to be possible for there to be another mounting of *Christy* some day—so I need not subject my readers to more "ersatz Irish" for the moment. I think the *Christy* lyric samples I've selected to be printed here and some of the anecdotes involved with the production of the show speak for themselves in making it obvious why *Christy* has been and probably is always going to be my favorite. And so for here and now (if not for my lifetime)—goodnight, sweet prince.

FOURTEEN

70's miscellany: "Picasso" and resumption with Saul, barely scratching a few surfaces like "Skin of Our Teeth," "17th Doll," and "Climate of Eden," and the oddball "Amateur Sinner."

"The time for dreams is over / When you've heard what love's about / And you've got to try it out / Or else you'll die."

AFTER JOAN AND I MOVED TO MANHATTAN IN 1970, one of the first things I did on one of my first leisurely days was to stroll a few blocks over to West End Avenue and 98th Street to the apartment building where I remembered Saul Honigman had lived, to look at the directory downstairs in the lobby to see if his name was still listed. Thus would I obviously determine whether or not he still lived there. After all, even though at the time I had my hands full with two other composers—Al Frisch and Karl Blumenkranz—and live projects with them to reckon with, wouldn't it be nice, I mused, (always thinking geographically) to have a partner who lived just a few blocks away? In case Saul Honigman's name escapes my readers' memories, Saul was the first composer with whom I'd collaborated at the B.M.I. Musical Theatre Workshop eight years or so previously, where and when we never really had the chance to do any memorable work together.

Anyhow, Saul's name was not in the directory in that lobby that day, so I assumed that he had moved and "that was that," though I also recall checking the phone book once, to see if I'd remembered the address accurately; and when I didn't readily spot the name in the phone book, I shrugged my shoulders with a kind of "so be it" finality, and never really expected to have contact with Saul again. Wrong. Very wrong. And I'm so glad.

Some five years later Saul was the one who made the move to reunite us. He'd caught my name in a newspaper advertisement listing me as librettist and lyricist of *Christy*, decided to look me up, and with his wife he attended one of the performances of *Christy* in Fall '75. Thus finally *he* re-established the contact between us as he sought *me* out. Where did he now live? Same place. Why didn't I see his name in the directory in the lobby? I found later I had looked in the lobby of the wrong building, not remembering the house number, mistakenly thinking his was the one on the corner, instead of the one *next to* the corner building. Why didn't I find his name in the phone book? I don't know. It was there all the time, as it still is, and I can only guess that my search must therefore have been careless or half-hearted. Anyhow, here we now were, reunited in 1975, except that I was still busy with *Christy* and its aftermath, and not ready to settle down to work with another new (re-discovered) collaborator. So we just kept in touch for a couple of years . . . until I was ready.

During those couple of years Joan and I had a shot at producing at a summer stock theatre, and hopefully for all time got the Judy-Mickey syndrome out of our systems. Our venture took place in the absolutely breathtakingly beautiful small-town-America locale of Milford, Pennsylvania, and the reason we wound up in a far afield venture like that in the first place is that my dear Joan was so sympathetic toward me and my plight of a constant merry-go-round of jobs in advertising production and the constant state of turmoil I was in, that she was ready to do anything to help get me out of what we assumed was a never-ending vicious circle and trap.

She was now earning enough for us to take a little chance. What we didn't allow for was that theatrical producing can be just as hazardous in its own way to one's mental health and feeling of stability, if not more so, than the toll-taking advertising industry. In advertising, at least, I was still getting paid, whereas when Joan and I worked in theatrical production together that summer, not only was there loss of new income, but loss of old savings, as well. (Nobody else was staking us, though our original intention was to be partners in it with old friend Arthur Altman.)

That experience is too painful to this day for me to recreate in its entirety—suffice it to say that the shows Joan produced (with assists from Joseph Lillis and me) in repertory during the summer of '76 at Milford included such well-known titles as *Wonderful Town*, *Carnival*, and *Babes in Arms*. And we managed to sneak in a reprise of *Christy*, too, only to prove that the subject matter of the latter was even less welcome in small-town America than it had been in New York City the year before.

My first writing project with Saul, after a suitable period of inactivity and mourning and smarting from the failure of the Delaware Valley Music Theatre, Milford, Pennsylvania, was a show called *A Nickel for Picasso*. Saul had been persistent enough in his phone calls after he "rediscovered" me to finally pin me down to resuming work with him on the score (music and lyrics only) for an existing small biographical Depression-years family drama of the same name written by a professional acquaintance of his, Elliott Caplin, who happened to be the brother of famed cartoonist and satirist Al Capp. Actually, this project was a good warm-up exercise for Saul and me, because we did not have to give too much thought to discovering or developing a book or a play. It was already there. We could concentrate from the beginning on what we both did best, music and lyrics. The new project gave us a chance to explore how we worked best together, and to become more attuned to each other's style. It was almost as if the earlier experience we'd had of briefly collaborating fifteen years or so before in the B.M.I. Workshop had never existed.

We capped *Picasso* with a too-ambitious "reading" of it at the Dramatists Guild for an audience of invited guests only, many of whom were contacts of Elliott Caplin's. But *Picasso*, despite its amiable, sincere and touching subject matter, proved to be too much of a "downer" for musicalizing, even though Saul and I surely gave it our best shot. And we may have been too undiscriminating in our selection of work for presentation that night at the Dramatists Guild, for only some of our material sounded really impressive—certainly not all of it. And despite the earnest efforts of four dedicated performers, tedium had to be setting in with all those words, and with no action with which to relieve them, and with no variety in musical arrangement with which to accompany them.

Elliott Caplin had his "straight" (non-musical) version of *A Nickel for Picasso* performed several years later in a showcase production, but none of us (including many submissions in our behalf by my agent Bertha Klausner to regional and other prestigious theatre groups) could ever move *Picasso* another inch closer to a production of our musical version, or get a soul out there in the theatre world even remotely interested in it. So *A Nickel for Picasso* remains little more than a latter-day exercise for Saul and me, but it surely must be included in my lyrics in this book, for among the following samples are some I'm rather proud of, as well as others that bear repeating for special reasons which we'll get into as we reach each of them.

First was the opening number, "Home," which does what openers are supposed to do, in that it tells you what this is going to be about. In this respect it was adequate. But talk about heavy-handedness and lack of imagination! Whew!

The stage is dark. A spot illuminates MARK, a young man of seventeen, who begins to sing.

Home, I remember home
When I was a boy,
Then, ever wondering when
Life would be a joy.
Love, never was there love
Showing in my father's face.
Did he think it was out of place . . .

At . . . home? I remember home,
Being very poor.
How, someone tell me now,
How could we endure?
Love, never was there love
Showing in my mother's eyes.
Did she think it was compromising?

Did he know of love?
Did she know of love?
Did they ever love each other
Once before they gave me their . . .

Home? . . . I remember hope
Entering the room.
Hope, time and time again
Turning into gloom.
She, anger in her voice,
He with just a silent stare.
This is where I was home.

(Spotlight on Mark fades as another picks up his father, PHILIP, who now sings.)

Home, I remember home.
I remember her.
Cold, both of us were cold.—
This is how we were.
Once maybe there was love
Promised with a wedding ring.
All too soon came the end of Spring-time.

Sons, bright and shiny sons,
Something to be proud.
Then—I remember when—
Suddenly a cloud.
Sons mean you have to work,

Mean that there are mouths to feed.
You keep working but not succeeding.

Once my life explored
Worlds of poet's words.
Now I was responsible
For other lives that chained me to . . .

Home, dreary is the home
When you have to stay.
Dawn, suddenly the dawn.
There's another way.
Try working on the road
Traveling till I'm free again.
Maybe then I'll come home.

There was also another chorus for Mama Martha, but it was all so dreary that I'd rather skip the rest and proceed instead to Martha's first solo, which pretty much tells you where she's coming from. It's called "Nice Is," and she sings it in complaint to Eddie, her husband's brother, when he asks her what's wrong with being nice to people you like. "First make a living," she says. "First put some food on the table." She sings.

Nice is for people with a steady income.
Nice is for people who can pay their way.
Nice is you never have to tell the butcher:
"Oops, I'm sorry.
I forgot my pocketbook today."

Nice is for people who can eat a snack out.
Nice is a movie every month or two.
Nice is not coming home to find a blackout.
"Oh, my goodness!
My electric bill was overdue."

For ne'er-do-wells it isn't.
For phony swells it isn't.
For living hells it isn't.
So I think twice—before I'm nice.

Nice is you never have to beg for credit.
Nice is when worry doesn't turn you gray.
Nice is the nights you don't stay up and dread it—
Soon it's morning!
How can I begin another day?

After the opener we revert in flashback to ten years earlier when young Mark was only seven, and when he was both impressed and influenced by his loving and beloved Uncle Eddie. When Mark expresses an interest in drawing, Eddie, ever the bigshot, waves a dollar bill at the boy (a lot of money in those days) and offers to buy him art supplies. "We'll select a box of water colors for you, and later on when you've mastered them you'll learn to use oils like the old masters." "I Knew Him When"

MARK

Uncle Eddie, did you know the old masters?

EDDIE

They lived centuries ago.

(Then to redeem himself, still the braggart.)

However, I know the young old masters. Not intimately, but you could say
we are friendly.

MARK

You know almost everybody in the world, don't you?

EDDIE

Yes indeed, Mark. My interests are wide and varied. (sings)

When I was just a youth
I used to catch Babe Ruth.
Now that's the honest truth.
I knew him when.
Perhaps you've also heard
I once adverturered
With Admiral Richard Byrd.
I knew him when.

Charles Lindbergh took me flying once.
I've sparred with Maxie Baer,
But of all of these celebrities
There's no one to compare . . .

To one more name I vow
Some twenty years from now
Who'll make the world say "wow"
And cheer and then . . .
I'll look at you with pride
And standing by your side,
I'll boast a bonafide
"I knew him when!"

Our family tree's been budding
At least a hundred years
With teachers, painters, writers—
And other bright careers.
Our family tree's been budding,
Yet never burst in bloom—
But there's a spark we see in Mark
That makes us all assume:
Give him light, give him air—
Give him plenty, yes, plenty of room . . .

When you're a great success,
A household word, no less,
I shall of course profess:

"I knew him when."
When you have reached your prime,
And climbed your highest climb—
Who knew it all the time?—
I knew him when.

Picasso is a friend of mine.
I'm buddies with Matisse
And an also-ran named Paul Cezanne
Is on my mantelpiece.

But there's a place for you
For all my friends to view—
And when you're up there, too,
I'll boast again:
"You see that genius there?
Well, don't forget from where
He got that certain flair.
I knew him when."

MARK

Gee, Uncle Eddie. Let's go down to art supply store now.

EDDIE

I tell you, Mark, I want to spend a little time with your Aunt Esther. An artist
should select his own tools. Why don't you go to the store yourself? I'll join
you there. All right?

MARK

All right, Uncle Eddie. But come soon.

EDDIE

Of course, Mark. And don't forget . . .
Old Titian was before my time
And Rembrandt's long since gone,
But it's a cinch he and Da Vinci
Still live on and on . . .

Because of fools like me
Who all but guarantee
That once upon their knee
They held these men.
And as I say of you—
"A genius through and through,
And best of all, I knew—
I knew him when."

With an uncle like that, was it any wonder Mark grew up to be as successful as Al
Capp? But with an uncle like that, was it also any wonder that young Mark had an
accident when he went off to the art supply store by himself, because he was too
young be traveling by himself, and because Uncle Eddie was too interested in immediate pleasures of the flesh to accompany the kid downtown? It was on that trip that
the kid had the accident which deformed him.

Here is the first act closing number, "Things Will Be All Right," sung by Philip, the ineffectual father, in which he practices in advance, while alone, what he is going to say to his son upon confronting him for the first time since the amputation . . . trying first to convince *himself* that they'll be able to survive.

Things will be all right, my boy.
Things will be all right.
Look beyond the dark, my boy.
Soon you'll see the light.
Nothing stays all wrong for long.
That's my point of view.
Even in that age-old song
Gray skies turn to blue.

Draw yourself a face, my boy.
If it has a frown,
Wait until tomorrow, boy—
Turn it upside down . . .
See the frown become a smile,
Presto, overnight!
Just like that in just a while
Things will be all right.

Why, I know from my own experience! How many times have I been down?
But could they count me out?

You hear a click
Inside your head.
It happens quick.
It starts to spread.
It's in your heart.
It's in your veins.
That's when you start
To break the chains.

You wake from sleep.
You spring from bed.
You breathe in deep
To forge ahead.
Your juices flow;
You drain the dregs.
You charge with both
Your arms and . . .

I'm sorry, son. So sorry. But just you wait. I promise. I'll help, I'll . . .

Things will be all right, my boy.
Things will be all right.
Have a bit more faith, my boy.
Soon you'll see the light.
Somewhere there's a rainbow, son,
Somewhere out of sight.
Take my hand; I'll help you find it.

Things will be all right.
Just you wait and see—I promise—
Things will be . . .

All wrong!

"What Is an Artist?" is an interesting "book" number which takes place early in Act Two between 17-year-old Mark and Mama Martha, which I think successfully depicts the kind of confrontation many kids go through. Barbara Hartman, though a bit young for the role at the time, did a splendid job of conveying the bitter despair of a typical Depression years Mama in presenting this and her other numbers at the "reading" at the Dramatists Guild.

MARK

I'm going to study to be an artist. I want to leave high school and go to art school.

MARTHA

An artist? Why should you want to be an artist?

MARK

Mama!

MARTHA

"Mama!" is no answer to my question. (sings)

What is an artist,
Tell me what's an artist?
Who can afford it
But a man of means?
What is an art school?
Tell me, what's an art school?
What will you learn from it?
Money you earn from it
Won't buy you beans.

What is an artist?
Better be a doctor.
Doctors make livings
And they're in demand.
What is an artist?
You could be a druggist.
They're in such short supply.
They're in a business I
Can understand.

A dentist, yes.
A lawyer, yes.
A grocery store man even.
Your second cousin Steven
Is in that line
And doing fine.

What is an artist

With his paints and brushes?
Even a genius,
Could you tell he's smart?
What is an artist
With his rags and canvas?
Starving for years till you've
Made it inside the Louvre
Only would serve to prove
You can't eat art.

I'm not supposed to discuss my son's future? Mothers are only supposed to cook and make beds and tell lies to the world about when you're going to pay your bills?

MARK

We're not talking about the world. We're not even talking about you. We're talking about what I hate, school—and what I want to do with my life.

MARTHA

The only thing in the world that's important to me is what you do with your life. That's why I don't want you to throw it away.

I still say no.
You must not go.
It's worse than a musician.
Why not a politician?
You might go far
Like F.D.R.

What is an artist
As he begs for handouts?
Such a decision
Never make in haste.
What is an artist?
Even all the standouts
Wind up on drinking jags,
Nibbling from garbage bags,
Living in filth and rags.
It's such a waste.

Don't ruin your life, Mark!

It's such a waste.

But when he arrives, he disappoints Mark for the first time ever by addressing him no longer as a child and his favorite nephew, but as a grown man. "The Time for Dreams Is Over."

EDDIE

You had a good head on your shoulders—even then, Mark. You should have known that nobody talks to . . . God. Christ, how could you have swallowed crap like that? All right, so it was a white lie. But we grow up, Mark, we develop our brains. And what we accepted as children, we learn to reject as adults. (He sings)

The time for dreams is over
When you end your love affair
With your favorite teddy bear
And nursery rhyme.

The time for dreams is over
When you pass the candy store
And ignore its open door
And save your dime.

When your feet are oh so firmly on the ground
That your ears don't even hear the happy sound
Of the merry-go-round.

The time for dreams is over
When your golden rainbow day
Isn't half as far away
As once it seemed,
And you start to live
The dreams you've dreamed.

Take me—when I left here I made up my mind this world wasn't for dreamers. Dreams are for kids, and invalids, and failures. Snap out of it. You're almost a grown man.

The time for dreams is over
When you've heard what love's about
And you've got to try it out
Or else you'll die.

When you wake up in the morning all aglow.
When you feel that you can conquer any foe.
When the juices all flow.

The time for dreams is over
When you kiss the kid goodbye
With as bright a gleaming eye
As ever gleamed,
And the man fulfills
The dreams the boy has dreamed.

Next, a confrontation between Mark's parents, Martha and Philip, over letting Mark go out on his own. "Your House, My House"

MARTHA

You'll only be making the boy another promise you can't keep. Is that fair?

PHILIP

I'll keep the promise this time. He's got great talent. We owe him a chance.

MARTHA

We owe him? Who'll wind up paying?

PHILIP

Martha, I told you I'll be responsible. My God, it's like talking to a brick wall. (he sings)

Your house, my house,
My life, yours.
Separate, distant,
Ceilings, floors.
Your road, my road
Singly tread.
Your house, my house—
Joined by a thin
And fragile thread.

MARTHA

Your house, my house,
My life, yours.
Separate, distant,
Windows, doors.
Your tears, my tears
Singly spent.
Your house, my house,
Fertile with seeds
Of discontent.

PHILIP

Built with walls of silence,
Spaces that divide.

MARTHA

Room for standing face to face
But never side by side.

PHILIP

Your house, my house,
My life, yours.
Separate, distant
Far off shores.

MARTHA

Your dreams, my dreams,
Singly spun.

BOTH

What does it take
To make them one?
What does it take
To make them one?

And for a little show, we had a big emotional whopper of an ending which despite its length I'll leave intact for the record of it upon these pages. It's that much of a "unit." Also, it's what the play is about, and it's why it works well as a musical even though the tone of the show is generally down. "Mama Will Find a Way"

MARTHA (alone on stage)

Mark, my boy . . . you won't be home for a long time. So if I make a little sacrifice here and there, you won't even know about it. And what's more important now is that you should finish school without having to worry. Right? (she sings)

> What does it matter . . .
> Things looking gloomy?
> Mama will find a way.
> Wasn't she born for,
> Doesn't she always—
> Manage to save the day?
>
> Never you mind
> The strength in her arms is waning.
> Never you mind
> The hole in her purse.
> Is she complaining?
>
> Tell her she has to,
> Somehow she'll do it.
> Mama will find a way.
> Even if trouble
> Is making her old and gray.
>
> Ready to suffer,
> Rising above it.
> Doesn't she live it?
> Doesn't she love it?
> Leave it to Mama . . .
> Mama will find a way.

(The doorbell rings. An unidentified man enters. She leads him to the refrigerator in semi-darkness. He takes out money and hands it to her, then as he wheels the refrigerator off and replaces it with an icebox, she speaks to him, then sings to herself.)

You'll see. It's as good a new. Just like I told you on the phone. I wouldn't part with it for the world, except who needs such a big fancy one, when there's nobody home but me myself, and I—eat like a bird.

> Nice is to keep the new refrigerator.
> Nice is not selling it for half the price.
> Nice is just trying to remember later
> While it lasted
> It was nice just trying to be nice.
>
> For heartache pills it isn't.
> For art school bills it isn't.
> For empty tills it isn't,
> So I think twice before I'm nice . . .
> But don't worry, Mark. This is my concern and I can handle it.
> Give her a problem,

Give her a headache.
Mama will find a way.
Even if "nice is"
Is saved for another day.

Miracle worker,
Mender and healer,
Even the expert
Wheeler and dealer . . .
Leave it to Mama—
Mama will find a way.

(Lights dim on Martha and come up on MARK—narrating to audience.)

MARK

I wrote to my father and thanked him for paying the balance on my tuition. The letter came back marked "no forwarding address." It wasn't till I came home for Christmas that I found out what had really happened. And when I knew the truth I stood in the middle of the kitchen and I cried.

(MARTHA re-enters carrying two big paper grocery bags and the kitchen is illuminated.)

MARK

That's how you got the money for my rent and tuition, isn't it?

MARTHA

(Beginning to unpack groceries and his suitcase.)

Who needed it? Believe me, it's better this way. More compact.

(They sing simultaneously, with the music slowly picking up in volume and tempo.)

MARK	MARTHA
Who else finds the way?	What does it matter,
It's got to be Mama.	Things looking gloomy?
	Mama will find a way.
Who else saves the day?	Wasn't she born for,
It's got to be Mama.	Doesn't she always
	Manage to save the day?
Who else	Never you mind
Can a family count on	The strength in her arms
When it's down and out?	Is waning.
Is there any doubt	Never you mind
	The hole in her purse.
Who we couldn't do without?	Is she complaining?

BOTH

Tell her she has to.
Somehow she'll do it.
Mama will find a way.
Even if trouble
Is making her old and gray.

MARK   MARTHA

Who else follows through?
It's got to be Mama.
Who knows what to do
When you're in trouble
Or feeling blue?
Mama. Mama. Mama. Mama.

Ready to suffer,
Rising above it.
Doesn't she live it?
Doesn't she love it?

Leave it to Mama.
Mama will find a way.
Mama will find a way.

Mama will find a way.

CURTAIN.

Between *Picasso* in the late 70's and the first rumblings of the next major effort (my last and latest show to be produced, *The Shop on Main Street*, which germinated in late '79 but didn't materialize into production till late '85) lay one other complete new musical, *Mother Shanghai*. But just prior to or just after those two major efforts, *Shop* and Shanghai, there were also passing flings at other new projects, which I'd spend anywhere from two to six weeks on, doing outlines and taking stabs at a lyric or two, just to keep the creative juices flowing, and just to see if the projects were workable or not, before going to the trouble of inquiring about the rights. Into the latter category briefly fell *The Skin of Our Teeth*, *Summer of the Seventeenth Doll*, and *The Climate of Eden*. The fact that I abandoned them doesn't mean they're not workable; nor does it mean that someone else may not do them some day, nor that I might not go back to them myself. But for now, here are a few "chicken scratchings" among the aborted Spiro attempts in the late 70's based on the above-named properties. First, a general theme song for *Skin of Our Teeth*—"Sixes and Sevens"

It's the middle of August and freezing—
Now try explaining that;—
With animals coughing and sneezing
And the dog curled up like a cat.
His paws got all stuck to the sidewalk
When last he went out for a chat.
Well, hey, diddle, diddle,
If you couldn't piddle,
You, too, would be mad as a hat-ter
Or daft as a bat.

In fact . . .

The whole world's at sixes and sevens.
It's slowly going mad.
I quiver and tremble with every new minute.
What terrible fate will be lurking within it?

The whole world's at war with the heavens.
Our future's looking bad.
Catastrophe threatens and chaos abounds
With freakish phenomena making the rounds.
It sounds like the end and it's worse than it sounds.
Oh, what are we to do?

The whole world's at sixes and sevens
And I'm at half-past two.

Next, a proposed title song for *Teeth*, recorded here because it simply comes with the territory.

Famine, fire and flood
Can't devour us,
Poverty or plague
Overpower us.
We survive, alive,
By the skin of our teeth.

Though the years have
Hocussed and pocussed us,
Bankrupt, ice-aged,
Seven-year-locust'd us,
We've pulled through like new
By the skin of our teeth.

And that's the way it's always been
Throughout our history.
And that's the way it's always gonna,
Always gonna be.

Though the world's
Ablaze with hostility,
Through our spirit's
Invincibility
We'll unseat defeat
By the skin of our teeth . . .

By the epidermis on our molars
Coming on strong in tux and bowlers,
Hanging in to win
By the skin of our teeth.

I'm aware now (I wasn't then) that Leonard Bernstein, Betty Comden and Adolph Green made an attempt at *The Skin of Our Teeth* too, possibly around the same time, and I conclude they found it as puzzling as I, and I sincerely hope they didn't spend too much more wasted time on it than I did. And I do humbly apologize if by accident I have infringed upon territory of theirs that is still viable. It's sometimes hard to know if you've run that risk.

The sweet first Australian play I'd ever seen, *Summer of the Seventeenth Doll*, by Ray Lawler, which may have had some of the same earthy quality which first attracted me to *Playboy*, provided inspiration for my next attempt at creating a new musical. The opening number, with an eye (as it ought to have) toward establishing time and place and characters and a little of what the play is about, especially when we're dealing with foreign situations and people and places, is called—what else?—"Down Under"

(A split stage consists of the verandah of Olive's house with Olive and Pearl frozen in rockers, and a sugar cane field with Roo and Barney also frozen in position in work clothes, with cane cutting equipment. Movement starts on both sides simultaneously as the men begin to work and sing.)

MEN
There's a place down south
Where the women stay
Down under, down under,
While I'm here up north
Working seven lonely months a year.

WOMEN
There's a place up north
Where the men earn pay
Down under, down under,
While we wait down south
For the day they reappear.

BOTH (Facing each other)
Say, Baby! How I miss you, Baby!
What I'd give to . . .

WOMEN
Have you here with me . . .

MEN
Be back there with you . . . now.

BOTH
But my heart must wait,
As it always waits
Down under, down under,
For that great, great day
It can leap and say hello . . .

And make up for those seven months
Apart—in five sheer heaven months
Together—till it's time again to go.

MEN
It's the cane season, the cane season.
And that's the time we've got to bust our backs.

WOMEN
It's the cane season, and good reason
To sit at home and knit and just relax.

MEN
Cause by the day the layoff comes
We've got to have some dough—
Enough for us to show the girls a time.

WOMEN
Cause by the day the layoff comes
With lover back in tow . . .

I've got to gleam and glow and primp and prime.

ALL
And there isn't no denying
That the layoff time is coming,
That the layoff time is coming, coming soon.

I can feel it drawing nearer,
I can hear it sounding clearer—
I can see it in the color of the moon.

It's coming. Layoff's coming.
I can see it in the color of the moon.

But meanwhile all that we can do is wait . . .

Then when we—
Reunite again we
Are as close as . . .
Two could ever be
Say you'll never be-long
To another but me.

And my heart must wait
As it always waits
Down under, down under,
Till that great, great day
It can leap and say hello,

And make up for those seven months
Apart—in five sheer heaven months

MEN
Together—till it's time for us . . .

WOMEN
Together—till it's time for them . . .

ALL
Together—till it's time again to go.

As might be sung by the two women, Olive and Pearl, about the two men, Roo and Barney, the next number is called "A Coupla Kings"

Kings, a coupla kings.
Y'know it's been to
When they walk into a room.

All others nigh
Would suffer by comparison—
The way they stagger you,
Swank and swagger you,
All their rank in bloom.

They're kings, a coupla kings,
The rest are peasants;

That's how their presence comes through.

What's new, your majesties,
Ooh, your majesties,
Any old thing we can do?—
Like pull impossible strings
To ease the burdens life brings
And please a coupla kings like you.

Though we're mere
Young maids in waiting,
Still unskilled
In courtly sating,
Ask and we
Will brew your royal tea
Quite simply, sirs,
To prove our loyalty,
Even brew a little royal pot
Of royal hotcha cha-cha choc-o-lat—

In other words,
More simply put,
Wait hand in glove
And hand and foot
At beck and call
To give our all
To you . . . and England . . .

For kings, our coupla kings
With dedication
We give your station its due.

Command, your majesties,
And, your majesties,
We'll be awaiting our cue
To pull impossible strings
And ease the burdens life brings
And please a coupla kings—like you!

"Other Girls," sung by Olive to Pearl, defends Olive's style of being only a part-time lover to her man.

Other girls
Have legal papers
Sealed and signed
With golden rings.

Then they find
A world of headaches . . .
Popping pills
For all the ills
That marriage brings.

Other girls

Have homes and babies.
Lots of bills
And lots of fights.

With "I do"—
So many problems.
Stifling tears
Through years and years
Of sleepless nights.

What I have
Is joy in waiting.
Peace and bliss
Anticipating.

Other girls
All right and proper
All too soon
Grow bored and cold.

Other girls
Don't know they've blown it,
But me—I own it.
It's mine to hold.
All the love
That never lasts for other girls
Is mine to keep and have and hold.

PEARL

Yeah, I suppose so. But nobody would say exactly that yours is a decent way
of living. You know what I mean?

OLIVE

Wouldn't they? I would. Decency—depends on the people who are doing it.

Let them go ahead
And get it in writing—
The other girls.
Writing never struck me
Especially exciting—
Like other girls.

Let 'em be secure and sure
And decent and dry.
Bet they haven't had it—
And loved it as recent as I—have . . .
Other girls
All right and proper
All too soon
Grow bored and cold.

Other girls
Don't know they've blown it,
But me—I own it.

It's mine to hold.
All the love
That never lasts for other girls
Is mine to keep and have and hold.

In the late 70's I also toyed briefly with a noble failure by Moss Hart called *The Climate of Eden*. First I came up with lyrics for a title theme song. Then I gave up, not in despair, but evidently distracted by another project. Till now no one has ever seen this lyric, and it's incomplete. But I submit it here—more to keep the idea alive and conscious than for any other reason.

Savages, savages,
With civilized existences,
Savages traveling
Crazy airplane distances.
Savages, savages—
People from the cities, they.

Savages, savages,
With clocks and guns insanity,
Savaging, ravaging,
Battering humanity.
Come with me, come with me,
I have found an alternate way.

Here am I
In the Climate of Eden.
If you try
You can enter it, too.

Here you'll find
As you leave all your shadows behind
Peace of mind
And perennial springtime.

Come explore
In the Climate of Eden.
Filled with awe
As two children we'll be.

Take my hand
And together a wonderland
Will be ours to discover,
Dear lover, you'll see.

Lost in time
In a world of unending time
As you wander the wonderful
Innocent, wonderful
Climate of Eden with me.

In the midst of all of the preceding, dear agent Bertha Klausner was not content with my not having a major project on the drawing board, and drummed one up for me by introducing me to two new clients of hers, a writer named Aubrey Wisberg and a composer named Cecil Bentz. Aubrey needed a composer and lyricist for a musical version of a play he had written called *The Amateur Sinner*. Cecil was chosen first as the composer, I next as the lyricist. I did a few rather interesting lyrics in a short time, and got one very good number out of the collaboration with Cecil. But he and I were too mismatched in the very basic area of taste, and Aubrey didn't exude a great deal of confidence in either of us, so we abandoned *Sinner* before too long and left Aubrey to his own devices. I no longer have a copy of Aubrey's play, and frankly don't remember too many of the details of its whimsical and complex plot. But I do at least recall that it took place in France, involved a grape harvest, that its hero's name was Syballe, and that prominent in the cast was a mythical-type creature named Pippe, who I believe was half-man and half-animal. I simply could not exclude these four lyrics from this book. Two of them in particular are rather extreme for me, a good indication, I think, of the extreme subject matter.

First was an opening production number called "High Time," sung and danced at various intervals throughout the scene at the Baudemont Vineyard by characters who avail themselves of wine from casks, then burst into song, interspersed with dialogue vignettes.

> It's high time.
> Time for joy and jubilation,
> High time.
>
> It's high time.
> Join me in a wee libation.
> High time.
>
> If—we've—
> No good reason
> To drink, except to escape,
> Don't—grieve—
> It's grape crop season.
> Let's celebrate the squeezin'
> And glorify the grape.
>
> It's high time,
> Time for wild and wicked frolic.
> High time.
>
> It's high time.
> If the content's alcoholic,
> Here's mud-in-your-eye-time.
>
> It's kiss inhibitions goodbye.
> It's soar to your star in the sky.
> It's gen'rally girl and her guy
> And high, high time.

The next number was called "To Know Me Is To Love Me," and consists of a farcical confrontation between the vineyard owner, Baudemont, and the hero, Syballe. I'd seldom written farce before. I still don't know if this one works or not.

> BAUDEMONT
> My watch! My watch!

The scoundrel stole my watch!
Disgorge it, sir, or you shall face arrest.

It strains belief
I've let a common thief
Get closer to my coat than is my vest.

He dared intrude,
And begged for wine and food.
He might as well have kicked me in the crotch!

That's how it hurt
To offer him my shirt,
While, blast his soul, the bastard stole my watch.

    SYBALLE
You wrongfully accuse me.
There's been no crime.
You batter me and bruise me.
An angel I'm.

You speak too harshly of me.
I've oft been told
To know me is to love me . . .
I'm good as gold.

A deeply philosophical and darkly brooding puzzling gut-wrencher, for which I have no plot-wise explanation, is next sung by Syballe in Scene Three. Because it would not have been at all in my nature to invent so many things to complain about, I assume the content of the following lyrics must have been based quite literally on the text of Aubrey's play. "The Miserable Clowns"

I am sickened by cities
And I'm saddened by towns,
By the clamor of committees
And of bureaucrats' frowns.
I am weary of sharing
The bland hand-me-downs
Of the miserable clowns.

I'm revolted by vultures
And their victims of prey
In the civilized cultures
We contend with today.
With the scowls they are wearing
From their jowls to their crowns
They are miserable clowns.

To breathe of the air
With no pressure or care;
To room with my heart's own desire . . .
Is this really too much to aspire to?—
To be what I want,
When I want to and where?

I'm incensed with the mores
Of the peasant who toils
And the intellect's forays
Through society's spoils,
And of words I keep hearing
When they're all proper nouns,
And of skies that are clearing
While humanity drowns,
And of rainbows appearing
Ha!—In all shades of browns!

(He makes a "fuck you" sign, his left hand slapping the bend in his right arm.)

The miserable clowns!

The last lyric from this project and surely the most impressive of the four exercises was a romantic ballad in which Syballe explains to Pippe (the half-animal creature he comes upon), what "A Woman Is." Cecil Bentz, the composer, arranged for a demo recording of this number, and coincidentally the singer's voice sounded so much like cabaret artist Bobby Short that all I could think of was that Bobby should be recording this one of these days.

Neither Cecil nor I have yet presented the song to him, so its resurrection for these pages has inspired me to give such a venture a priority one place on my "to do" list as soon as this book is completed. May I suggest that the reader imagine this number being performed with several appropriate accompanying hand-gestures, along with also imagining how the song might sound being performed by Bobby Short.

A woman is . . .
Now, let me see.
A woman is
Like you and me,
Except we're he
And she's a she—
A woman is.

A woman is
A man but changed.
In special ways
She's rearranged,
With more of these
And less of this—
A woman is.

A curve or two
In places you
By instinct come to know—
Till soon your eyes
Can recognize them
Passing to and fro,
Everywhere you go.

And then it's "Vive
La Diference"—
Your eyes perceive,
Your body wants
And needs to hold
And to enfold
And follow through
With everything
A woman is,
A woman is,
A woman is to you.

FIFTEEN

"Mother Shanghai."

"How fast ripples spread/When you throw one pebble in the sea./How fast leaves are shed/When autumn falls upon the tree."

ALTHOUGH I RECENTLY STARTED CIRCULATING *MOTHER SHANGHAI,* librettos and scores for musicals sometimes decorate producers' offices for five to ten years before any action takes place.

When Bertha Klausner first suggested I think about this project over eleven years ago, she mistakenly advised me that the source material, a famous melodrama of the late 20's, *The Shanghai Gesture,* by John Colton, was now in public domain. I read the play, loved it, and went to work on it as a musical immediately. Karl Blumenkranz was also available, and he and I hadn't collaborated in a long time, and coincidentally he had recently asked me, "How about a new project together?", and in reply I asked him if he would consider this one. He, too, was most taken with the material, and it turned out to be the major project he and I had fewest problems with and finished in the shortest length of time. It consumed us, and we had a ball with it. Our wives, too, loved the work we were doing in the formative stages, and their encouragement gave us all the momentum we needed. *This* was going to be *it.* Commercial as all get out. No rights problem; in public domain (ha!)—and truly inspired work on it from the word "go." As we probably should have guessed, this scenario was too good to be true. The bubble burst as soon as we started showing our work around and learned that *someone else* had picked up an *option* to the rights, rights incidentally which were not only *not* in public domain, but were under the control of one Sheldon Abend of American Play Co., our old friend who had handled the rights to *Johnny Belinda.*

Well, we thought, at least we had a sympathetic ear in the person of Shelly, and so we explained our predicament to him and he amiably agreed to listen to what we had created. But this time around Shelly did not feel as kindly toward our work as when we performed *Belinda* for him, and evidently this time around Shelly was being offered compensation by others early on (which had not been true with *Belinda* until the later stages). And so this time around Shelly suggested to us that we cease and desist pursuing a production and forget about our *Mother Shanghai* altogether. That's hard to do when you've lived with creating a new show for almost a year, as Karl and I had done. But we seemingly had no choice, and so reluctantly we put our work away in a file cabinet and let it accumulate dust for eight years or so. From time to time we did check in with Shelly to try to determine if there were any changes in the rights situation, only to learn that there seemed to be lots of interest in reviving *The Shanghai Gesture* in one form or other by a number of other theatre people, and in fact they were lining up one after another to take an option on the property year after year, for which Sheldon Abend was presumably receiving annual compensation. We couldn't break in.

Then after a brief discussion some three years ago about our failure to move *Mother Shanghai* along, Karl and I finally came to the conclusion that we should no

"Only Sunshine" from *Mother Shanghai*, music by Karl Blumenkranz

longer stand still with it, and that something, anything, should be done. Our next step was a risky one. It meant investing some money in the project, in order to have a good demo recording made, so that we could then hopefully finally win Shelly over to our side, so that he would permit us to start showing our work around for a brief time when and if the then current option ran out. Lots of "ifs" and "whens" in that one. But risks are almost invariably an essential. And strangely enough, this strategy was logical, particularly since no one else was evidently making enough headway toward getting another production going of someone else's adaptation of *The Shanghai Gesture*. And so we gambled and spent the money and made the demo, which everybody else who heard it thought was a good one, but which still did not impress Shelly Abend much. Or maybe the presumably big bucks he was presumably earning from other people's options was simply impressing him more. The bottom line is that *Gesture* is still out on option to someone else this very day.

I have my probably very valid ideas as to why no one who has optioned the rights to the original play to date has yet been able to do anything successful with their proposed version of the show, and therefore lets the option drop after it runs its course. These are ideas I cannot discuss here, because I would then be giving an advantage to my competitors for the rights, and though I may not always be as wise as I'd like to think I am, I am never quite that suicidal.

At this moment the fact is that Karl and I with Bertha Klausner's help have been showing our work around discreetly (not saturating the market with it), always with candor about the rights problem, in the hope that one day we will find a reputable producer (with clout) interested enough in our work to latch onto the rights himself in our behalf. We're obviously not in a position to spend big bucks for it ourselves, and even if we were, it would be foolish for us to do so without having a producer first.

Well, that's where we are now: Several producers are actually considering our *Mother Shanghai* for a tryout production, and as I understand the specifics of the rights question at the moment, we could not possibly latch onto them till the present option runs out, so we've got to keep all of this movement fairly low key still. If we are preempted by another writer or producer, we could wind up in another *Belinda* situation in which we could offer our work to be used in collaboration. (God, I hope not.) Our work is of course copyrighted even though we did not have the rights to adapt the original *Gesture*. Once we had unwittingly done the adaptation we at least had to protect ourselves, and to ascertain that no one would plagiarize our version, even though we were not free to take our version as far as we hoped we could. Complicated? Na-ah-hh! This, too, is show biz.

Meanwhile, there's no problem with my including herein some lyrics now, for they *are* copyrighted and are therefore protected, and *Of Rhyme and Reason* is after all, a collection of *my* work, and the collection would not be complete without representative entries from one of the major projects I created. I'll use the continuity dialog as sparingly as possible, editing most of the lyrics down to one or two verses. (Some of them go on for pages in the original text.) Please, ladies and gentlemen, accept my "Humble Invitations."

(Sung to the audience by CAESAR-HAWKINS, secretary and companion to Mother Shanghai.)

Humble invitations
We extend you.

We befriend you.
Come along with me.

Back through generations
Seven decades,
Seven decades
Far across the sea.

The evil delights
Of Shanghai nights
Laughingly thumbed their nose.
In opium flights
They reached new heights
While morals reached new lows.

Humble invitations—
Come receive them
As we weave them
Through the web of years.
The stage is set.
Reality now disappears.

(A gong sounds. He calls out and exits.)

Yes, Madame. I come to you.

(Lights come up upon Mother Shanghai's sitting room where she is reading aloud invitations she has just written—to a number of Shanghai notables—to attend dinner at her place that night (New Year's). Then Hawkins enters and she hands him the invitations to distribute, and she sings.)

Humble invitations . . .
Each hand-written,
Planned and written
All with loving care.

First negotiations
Must be Charteris,
Sir Guy Charteris.
He's the one to snare.

The others will fly
To join Sir Guy
Wondering why he's here—
A mystery I
Shall by and by
Make absolutely clear.

Humble invitations
Hand delivered,
And delivered
Person'ly to please
To seek none less
Than positive RSVP's.

HAWKINS

Feather in your cap if you lure Sir Guy to your brothel—number one man in the richest British firm in China.

MOTHER

Feather indeed! He'll come, I tell you.
Humble invitations,
Hand delivered,
And delivered
Person'ly to please

BOTH

To seek none less
Than positive RSVP's.

The musical number continues, and next includes Hawkins making the rounds about town actually dispatching the invitations; most of the crucial characters are introduced in this manner, as music and lyrics are interwoven through the scene.

Later that day Mother Shanghai reckons with memories at Cherry Mountain with the panoramic view of "Plum Blossoms" overwhelming her at this most religious time, when they say one must make good feeling with the gods and pay one's debts. "But," she says, "I don't believe in gods and I owe no debts, and all I can think of now is tonight and the New Year's dinner I'm giving, when others will pay their debts to me."

And she sings:

Plum blossoms, plum blossoms,
Dancing in the air,
Dancing everywhere within view . . .
Where were you then,
Where were you when I needed you?

Plum blossoms, plum blossoms,
Bubbling like champagne,
Born to entertain with a flair . . .
Where were you then,
Where were you when I used to care?

You laugh, you sing,
As if to comfort me,
To set me free from bitter tears.
Too sweet, too sugary
Too late your song
To ease my long and lonely years.

Plum blossoms, plum blossoms
Slanting in the breeze,
Chanting in Chinese on your own . . .
Where were you then,
Where were you when I was alone?

Do you remember I visited once when I was a lovely young Manchu princess? Do you remember when the young princess left her native mountains and ran away to Shanghai to marry a handsome young blue-eyed Englishman and have many sons by him?

> I stole my father's money,
> I stole ten bags of gold
> To give them to my lover
> So he could buy our place in the world.

> He took my father's money.
> He took my father's gold,
> But threw me to the junkmen
> As helpless as the day I was born.

> Then they bid for me
> On an auction plate
> In an ugly rotting Blood Town shed.
> On the China Sea,
> On a junk of grimy girls
> Too soon I learned
> The worst that men can do.

Chained under a battened hatch in a floating catchball for the filth the land spewed out!

> How the coolies screeched
> And the gangmen yelled
> As the junks came sliding in from sea!

> And for every girl
> There were forty men a night
> To have their way
> And leave us doomed to die!

> Shrieking whips when I was stubborn
> I survived.
> Hut dung thrust inside my nostrils
> I survived.
> Stinging leeches in my eardrums
> I survived.
> Sulphur burned upon my body
> I survived.
> The soles of my feet cut open,
> And pebbles sewn inside
> So I'd never run away—
> Even pebbles I survived!
> I survived!

> Hate helped me.
> Black gods helped me.
> Hell and the will
> Of the devil helped me—
> Helped me to be free again,
> Be here again—to see again . . .

(She catches her breath and suddenly changes her mood from introspective to one of appreciation of the enchantment of the view.)

> Plum blossoms, plum blossoms,
> Dancing in the air,
> Dancing everywhere within view.
> Where were you then?
> Where were you when I needed you?

> Plum blossoms, plum blossoms,
> Slanting in the breeze,
> Beckoning to please and atone—
> Where were you then?
> Where were you when I was alone?
> Where were you then?
> Where were you when I was alone?

Later that evening after Charteris arrives at Mother Shanghai's establishment, he quickly becomes enamored of her. The scene and number: "Two Wicked People"

MOTHER
So tonight you wish us to dip into the darkness, eh?

CHARTERIS
Yes, tonight we shall be two wicked people, afraid of nothing.

MOTHER
Shanghai's great English hero! Shanghai's great Chinese whore!
(She cups her hand to her ear.)

> I hear a note of danger,
> Of deep impending doom
> If we pursue . . . this rendezvous.

CHARTERIS
I'll chance the note of danger.
I'll chance the dance of doom
To be with you . . . to be with you.

(he sings)

> Tonight I'll risk your Chinese spells
> And let you pit your wolves against my hogs.
> Tonight I'll risk my Saxon soul
> As you unleash your wildcats at my dogs,
> And open up a hornet's nest
> And put our passions to the test and see . . .
> My locusts here, your spiders there—
> Oh, what a motley evil pair are we to be.

> Shall we start all our insects
> Swarming, stinging?—
> Start all our wild beasts
> Growling, snarling?—

Pitting of wicked woman and man
Befitting this wicked night we plan?

A night of danger,
Tonight with you.
A night of stranger-than-fiction
Fantasies to pursue.
A night of sounding
Of strange alarms.
A clash of East and West
Sequestering in our arms.

A vast inferno,
A witches' brew.
A night when demons shall dream
Which terrible dream comes true.
Unmask our Satans,
Perhaps to see
With wicked people
Like you and me—
A night less danger-fraught
Than ever thought to be—
When two wicked people find love.

But Mother Shangai has not really asked her dinner guests there for a party, or Charteris there for love. She has for years been engineering an elaborate plan of revenge, and this dinner party is the first step in its fulfillment. Before a roomful of horrified continental guests, she has a slave girl brought in, and announces that she is about to auction the slave off to the flesh junks. "The Auction" (interspersed with bids).

MOTHER

These merry men have come to bid for her. She is setting sail for the open seas, and you, my dear dinner guests, are here to tell her bon voyage.

(She urges the bidding on in song, first from among her guests, then directed to the Junkmen.)

What am I bid tonight?
What am I bid tonight
For young virgin flesh at our disposal?
This is a prize I sell.
What am I bid, pray tell?
Let us hear a generous proposal
Or the Junkmen will take her for their own
To the very bowels of life she's never known.

She will earn her weight in gold for you,
Doing carnal feats untold for you.
What a chance for you—within your reach
For a girl who's yours to train and teach!
And what's more, she's not Chinese!
Oh, no! She's English . . . all English!

No bids? Then the Junkmen shall have their chance.

What am I bid, Wang Ti?
What am I bid, Chang Po,
For young virgin flesh at our disposal?
What am I bid, Shu Ki?
Five hundred tael? Oh, no!
We must have a worthier proposal.
Shall we start with a thousand, maybe two
For the lovely loving bride I offer you?

Did I hear two? Not enough!

She is worth at least a thousand more.
Do I hear a three—do I hear a four?
There is not a yellow man alive
Who for pure white flesh wouldn't offer five.
For a thrill you've never known . . .

Four?

Oh no! I'm selling, not giving!

Think of her kiss upon your mouth.
Think of her breasts against your chest.
Think of a night of pure delight,
The skin so white
Performing every rite you like the best.

Do with her everything you will.
Do with her everything you dare.
Lingering lips and fingertips
To guide your trips
Through eager hips to her eclipse of golden hair.

What am I bid, Wang Ti?
Five?

What am I bid, Chang Po?
Six?

At last now, a generous proposal.

Think of the prize in store.
What am I bid once more?
Pure and fresh, this flesh at our disposal!

Ten and sold!

She is sold for a final bid of ten
To my friend Chang Po, the worthiest of men.

Next, in a continuation of the scene of "The Auction," and in preparation for an emotionally devastating Act One climax, in "Hello, Mr. Blue Eyes" Mother Shanghai exposes Charteris for the opportunist he was years ago.

CHARTERIS

Call back that monstrosity of yours, and have the slave girl put into proper clothes at once.

MOTHER

You will buy her for yourself? Ah, that makes me jealous. Remember—you have pledge with *me* after dinner.

CHARTERIS

Do what I say or there'll be the finish here tonight of a Chinese brothel—and a very troublesome Chinese woman.

MOTHER

And also the finish of a British merchant who must now chew what he has bitten off. Now let all social Shanghai look its last at you. I think a Chinese woman helped you once, my friend.

CHARTERIS

Who are you, you painted—yellow—jezebel?

MOTHER

I was a princess of Tung Kow. My father had 10,000 camels and 5,000 horses and many boxes of gold. Now my name is Mother Shanghai; my trade is flesh. And now I, too, have many boxes of gold because I keep the largest brothel in the world. Damned funny, isn't it? You know me now? Look at me. Tell me who I am. Quickly, the little name you used to call me as your lover!

CHARTERIS

You, that Manchu girl! Oh, God, no!

MOTHER

Hello, Mr. Blue Eyes—
Do you remember Miss Pink?
Weren't we once on the brink
Of something beautiful,
Something wonderful—
Our day of love?

Hello, Mr. Blue Eyes.
Do you remember the vow?
Where are the promises now
Of something beautiful,
Something wonderful,
Our day of love?

To think that we should meet again,
Invoking ghosts inside,
Inviting hearts to beat again
When long ago they died.

Farewell, Mr. Blue Eyes.
Who can recapture a sigh
After the bitter goodbye

To something beautiful,
Something wonderful,
Our day of love?

Not you, not I, never again.
Not you, not I, never again.

Early in Act Two, Mother Shanghai finds her kindly secretary and companion, Caesar-Hawkins, appalled and frantic over the tumultuous goings on of the evening up to that point, giving us a chance for our only semblance of a "pop"-type ballad, "Only Sunshine." And it is always sensible to have at least one potential commercial entry incorporated into the score if one can, if only to be able to refute critics who skeptically ask: "Yeah, but what do you remember well enough to hum on your way out?"

MOTHER
Don't worry so, Mr. Caesar-Hawkins. Perhaps I should not have asked you to mix up in my events. Perhaps you are too gentle.

HAWKINS
Perhaps so.

MOTHER
Let me see . . . what is it you do for me to relax my tensions? This time, shall I do it for you?

Shall I read you a poem
And speak of pleasant things,
Predicting your future brings
Only sunshine?

Shall I sit at your bedside
And tell a joke or two,
Avowing in store for you—
Only sunshine?

Shall I say look away
From clouds overhead?
In time you will find
Skies of blue instead.

Shall I rub at your temples
And knead your shoulder blades
Till all of your mis'ry fades
And cares depart
Leaving sunshine, only sunshine
Shining in your heart?

HAWKINS
May I soothe you now as you have soothed me?

Shall I read you a poem
And open windows wide
Ans welcome the warmth inside

Of the sunshine?

Shall I sit at your bedside
And brew some tea for two
And dawdle as lovers do
In the sunshine?

And relax, turn our backs
On all matters of state,
And find peace of mind
While we hibernate?

Shall I tell you a secret?
I'm glad there's you and me.

MOTHER
Without you I'd never see
The night depart . . .

BOTH
Leaving sunshine, only sunshine
Shining in your heart.

Mother Shanghai is not through with dragging Charteris down, not by a long shot. The next number is interwoven through the expanse of an entire scene in which Mother Shanghai "comes out" all the way to the man who "done her wrong." While the reminiscences of twenty years before are being acted out by a pair of dancers on the opposite side of the stage, Mother Shanghai and Charteris re-live in lyrics and dialog (as if going through a photograph album) in "Funny Pictures" whatever details of their relationship the audience has not previously become familar with.

MOTHER
What's in my mind? Only funny pictures. Look over there, twenty years ago, Charteris. Perhaps you can see them, too.

I see a man with a banjo
Who played "Annie Rooney"
A bit out of tune.
I see his eyes in the moonlight,
And still hear his promise,
His promise, the moon.

Conjure up the funny pictures:
Two young lovers, we.
Our dream house by the sea.
The life of love to be.
Conjure up the funny pictures:
Young man on the rise
Who told a few white lies sweet and low.

I see a man with ambition
Who needed a proper
And English young bride.
I see a man who was greedy,

Who needed a mistress
Or two on the side.

Conjure up the funny pictures:
On your wedding day
You kissed me on your way,
But bade me please to stay.
Conjure up the funny pictures:
I, to wait my turn,
To sit alone and yearn for you so.

    BOTH
Funny pictures, funny pictures
Spinning round the brain
Are all that now remain, all I know.
Funny pictures, funny pictures
Flashing through the mind
Of two we left behind long ago.

(They now do a bit of thrust and parrying in dialog, he, justifying himself,
then admitting he never had any intention of marrying her.)

    MOTHER
Why did you suddenly hate me so much you sent me to Blood Town?

    CHARTERIS
My wife was in a delicate condition. If you'd been intelligent we could have
gone on as always. But you wanted all or nothing.

She was expecting a baby,
And you were a nuisance
And terror and fright.
I was afraid she would see you
As you kept returning
To spy in the night.

Conjure up the funny pictures:
I, without lament,
To Blood Town had you sent
To ponder and repent.
Conjure up the funny pictures:
You, to bullies' sticks
And vicious whips and kicks, screaming "No!"
But even the bullies and hags of Blood Town wouldn't stop you from
    coming.
I see a woman with vengeance,
With hate and the devil's own
Look in her eye.
I hear her banging at windows
Until, I remember,
I prayed you would die.

Conjure up the funny pictures:
Every bullies' kick

And screaming whip and stick
Just made your skin more thick!
Conjure up the funny pictures:
Still each night you came
To plead in pain and shame of your woe.

    BOTH

Funny pictures, funny pictures
Spinning round the brain
Are all that now remain, all we know.
Funny pictures, funny pictures
Flashing through the mind
Of two we left behind long ago.

(Further parry and thrusting in dialog, during which Mother reveals that she gave birth to a daughter by Charteris (he never knew) and that and in order to insure that her child would have a proper upbringing, she switched her own infant with the one his wife had given birth to around the same time. This tricky plot turn is also repeated and expanded upon in the accompanying lyrics.)

    MOTHER

It is *my* daughter who is in your home. In that cage, at the front entrance to my house—there is *your* daughter, Charteris. Yours with your wife. The blonde white English girl I sold tonight. I mixed up these two infants—yours and hers—yours and mine—an exchange I made one night—long, long ago—now, you see?

    CHARTERIS

No, I do not see!

    MOTHER

Well, my Lord, I came to see you just one more time—the night before you sold me to the Junks—after the many window bangings that harried you so much, Charteris.

I see my journey from Blood Town.
Strapped to my back
Was a child three days old—
Stumbling through mud, rain and darkness,
Creeping and crawling
And falling and cold.

Conjure up the funny pictures:
You asleep in bed.
Your wife inside lay dead.
I seized your child and fled.
Conjure up the funny pictures:
Praying as I flew
The switching of the two would not show.

I see a girl raised in Blood Town,
So happy and carefree

And gentle and pure . . .
Pigs, rats and lice crawling round her,
Graces and airs
That were bred in manure.

Conjure up the funny pictures:
There, my friend is she
To ridicule and be
Exposed for all to see.
Conjure up the funny pictures:
See your own first born
Be spit and shit upon . . . cheerio!

I put your daughter just where you put me, you see. Dirt for dirt, hunger for
hunger, cold for cold, blows for blows, English for Manchu. And there she hangs,
my blue eyed god, as you hung me, twenty years ago tonight, before drunken,
brutal, brawling mobs of the Chinese New Year, to advertise a brothel!

Cheerio to funny pictures
Spinning round the brain.
At last they bring no pain. Let them go.
Funny pictures, funny pictures
Flashing through the mind
Of two we left behind long ago.

(The New Year's revelers whoop it up around the cage as Charteris dazedly
mutters "no—no—no" and Mother Shanghai takes his arm and leads him out
as lights dim into blackout.)

The sad but tranquil denouement—Mother Shanghai alone with her daughter's body,
reconciling herself to the tragedy that has befallen them: "One Pebble in the Sea"

MOTHER
Poor little Poppy! I first missed the way, not you. Then—how fast—the sins came.

How fast ripples spread
When you throw one pebble in the sea.
How fast leaves are shed
When autumn falls upon the tree.

How funny, too, this cruel jest
That finds me so alone—
For now that you've returned to nest,
How suddenly you've flown.

How deep sorrows grow
When one tear lodges in the eye.
How soon one hello
Becomes an evermore goodbye.

Oh, well.

We know what's ahead,
For Fate has written it must be . . .

How fast ripples spread
When you throw one pebble in the sea . . .

CURTAIN

SIXTEEN

The 80's, "The Shop on Main Street," and its production.

"This is the way the world is run now, / Special laws for Jews,
Marching off in twos, / Obeying dont's and do's."

I didn't do much creative work in the 80's that didn't deal with The Shop on Main Street or the beginnings of this book. But for all intents and purposes that's because "The Shop on Main Street" was begun at the beginning of the decade, and has stayed with me in one form or another till the present.

Earlier I mentioned that the seed for musicalizing *The Shop on Main Street* first came to be in 1979—February, 1979, to be exact. A seed is always necessary. It's where you start from, and why. At the start of *Shop* it was my turn, I thought, to get involved with a big one—and an "important" one—and I went looking for inspiration. My father had died in early '77, which contributed a new note of sobriety to my life. Soon afterward (late '77), I was able to stop smoking after 40 years of being hooked, which contributed to the removal of some of the smoke screen I had set up between me and the rest of the world, and between me and my emotions. Along with this achievement, too, came an unexpected level of maturity.

My job situation was temporarily at its most sane in the history I had of insane professional allegiances in which I'd always thought I was selling my soul to the devil. The management of the new agency I joined in late '77 was ostensibly going to treat me like a human being. That, too, gave me an additional sense of security and maturity. And in mid-'78 my darling Joan had to go through her first bout with open heart surgery. I accompanied her to Houston, Texas, where she was operated on successfully by Dr. Denton Cooley, and I remained with her every moment I was permitted to, even sleeping in her room in the hospital, and then through all the post-op care, and for that, too, I reached for and found new strength. Thus, having faced emotional and psychological trauma for about a year-and-a-half and having come through with flying colors, I was ready to face new challenges creatively.

Sexually I had long since put my secret yearnings to rest, in the sense that there was no overt acting out of my desires except for my private routine in the john (seldom at home) with magazines. Thus I was largely removed from feelings of profound guilt during that time frame. I was ready to make my creative mark. But what was to be the subject of my still unborn new project?

I asked Joan to join me for a two-week immersion in nightly movie-going to catch up on revivals of some famous foreign films we had never seen. The neighborhoods we'd lived in in Brooklyn seldom showed foreign films; our Manhattan life to date (nine years at that point) had been involved with exposing ourselves to a few series of operas for the first time, and keeping in touch with current theatre and revivals, and current films. Seldom was there time to devour the prestigious foreign oldies at double-feature revival houses like the *Thalia*, the *Carnegie Hall Cinema* and the *Cinema Village*—all of which served up, usually with English sub-titles, a different delectable double-feature every night or every other night. At that time in the recent past there had been a trend toward new Broadway musicals being based on foreign films, a trend which led me to this exploration of the idea myself. And indeed the broad spectrum of the source seemed fertile enough for me to find something special—to my particular liking—to provide the inspiration for my next project for adaptation for the musical theatre.

And, as planned, I did indeed find the right subject during that two-week immersion period in February '79—in spades—in *The Shop on Main Street*, the brilliant black and white Czech film that had won the Oscar as best foreign film of the year in 1965. It "talked" to me in a far more seductive manner than any other film came close to; and for a non-musical with a basically sombre theme, it practically sang for me right there on the screen. When, several weeks after I saw it for the first time at the *Thalia*, like a signal from a higher power, the film also appeared at a special evening's cultural activity at a nearby synagogue, I *knew* it had become a calling in life for me, and in fact, from that second viewing on, *The Shop* became an obsession with me. Since Joan was with me all the way as it charmed us with its humor and hominess, and devastated us with its tragedy; it became like a mid-life child to us, draining our time and attention through the last five-and-a-half years of Joan's life. We were willing and loving, and captivated by it, and I guess it also felt good to have a "baby" again, especially when this time it involved no diaper-changing.

Having learned a lesson from two of the other major projects I'd been involved in, I wasn't going anywhere this time without the certainty of rights availability in writing. My agent, Bertha Klausner, tried to help me get information about the rights by making inquiries herself about them from Dilia, the agency (then behind the Iron Curtain) that handled these matters in Czechoslovakia, and Doubleday, whom we learned had published an English translation of the Czech novel on which the film was based. Both Dilia's and Doubleday's replies were inconclusive, and so it was only as a last resort that I phoned the film's director, Jan Kadar, whom Bertha had met once, and who was now working in Los Angeles, and whose phone number she was able to obtain. Kadar in turn advised me that the owner of the rights would be the author of the original story, one Ladislav Grosman, who was now a resident and citizen of Tel Aviv, Israel, and whose mailing address he had mislaid, but whose phone number he was able to pass along.

[A brief digression to describe how the fickle finger of fate was at work on this one. On the phone Kadar sounded in especially bad shape physically; he apologized and attributed his difficulty in breathing to a sore throat. We read in the *Times* several months later that he had died of lung cancer. I'd managed to establish contact by phone just in the nick of time.]

Making any contact at all by now seemed to have become so complicated, that I impulsively decided to simplify matters from that point on as much as possible, and equally impulsively I picked up the phone that next Sunday and tried direct dialing

Mr. Grosman, the author, in Israel (direct dialing Tel Aviv was new then). I was both surprised and delighted that he, himself, answered a moment later, in broken English, but with enough comprehension to repeat his address for me so that I could write him the letter of proposal I proposed, and explain in more detail in the letter to perhaps at least partially satisfy his incredulity, the whys and wherefores of musical adaptation for the theatre in general (a field he knew relatively little about), and specifically the why and wherefore of my being interested in *his* baby, *The Shop on Main Street*. It wasn't easy to convince him that I would treat his work with affection and respect. He didn't know me from Adam, and my phone call was from out of the blue. It wasn't easy to convince him that it would not ruin the memory or durability or quality of his work of art if my project failed. It was not easy to convince him, period.

We corresponded for almost a year, during which time he suffered a heart attack, and therefore for a few months he could not give serious thought to much of anything except his recuperation. But with persistence in my behalf at Thanksgiving-time, 1979, Bertha Klausner, who was visiting her family in Israel, met with Ladislav and presented my case to him, and returned home with a tentative verbal agreement by him for me to begin work on the project. And then, in early April, 1980, while Dr. Grosman [I didn't learn about his doctorate till then] and his wife were holidaying in London and visiting with their son who was completing his Masters degree at the Guild Hall School of Music there, Joan and I met with Ladislav and Edith, and their son and future daughter-in-law, and spent the better part of two days together (Good Friday and Easter Sunday) getting to know each other reasonably well on "neutral" ground, discussing the project in depth. And we returned with a signed agreement, after having left a rough draft of an early script with him, and after having played for them a rough audio tape of some of the songs Saul and I had already written and informally recorded.

I haven't mentioned till now that I thought Saul Honigman had the right quality and feeling for the subject matter, and so early on in my interest in the property I asked Saul to be the composer, and he and I (the geographically perfect collaborators) at long last were taking long-term advantage of our proximity to each other.

Being the creative talent he was, Ladislav Grosman was fascinated by the process of conversion and adaptation, and I was glad to let him be involved in the development. But I pretty much had carte blanche, as long as I retained the integrity of the original. Ladislav had actually seen one American musical (*Chicago*) on a visit to the U.S. several years before, and had of course seen Israeli productions in Hebrew of a few others, and he evidently knew well enough that he didn't know enough about the breed to try to influence me. So long as he was convinced that I understood his characters and situations totally, he was convinced that I would do his baby no harm. And in the long run our mutual conviction proved to be valid. The musical *Shop* finally did get off the ground in a miniaturized showcase production in December, 1985, and January, 1986, and was respectable but generally unsuccessful, suffering mainly, we think, from mutilation and miniaturization in trying to keep costs down. But the original film still towers over most, without its reputation having suffered one iota, and time has proven that my musical version did not affect its status as a classic. It's one of the few foreign films of its decade, or even era, to be converted to videotape; and is regarded in some circles as being one of the ten greatest films of all time. To me—for many reasons—it is the *single* greatest, and always will be.

So many strange and wonderful things happened in the pursuit of a production for *Shop* that I hardly know where and how to begin to describe them. First and foremost, Joan and I met dear lifelong friends in Ladislav Grosman, his wife, Edith, and their son, Jiri, and daughter-in-law, Helga. They have been a pleasure to know, and get to know well, and to spend happy and sad times with. Tragically, Ladislav died suddenly in January of 1981. Tragically, Joan died after surgery for recurring heart-valve problems, in September, 1985. In both cases, each family consoled the other. And in between we met and spent pleasant times with other members of each other's families, opening up our spare rooms for each other, and getting to understand each other's backgrounds and cultures as strangers seldom can and do. We now look upon each other as *meshpoche* (family), and though we no longer have the tie of the pursuit of that production of *Shop* to bind us, those of us who are left, particularly Edith and I, have the shared memories that will always insure depth of feeling, no matter how infrequently we now see each other. In fact, if I had not decided to follow my heart's true sexuality for the first time in my life, it might have become a natural consequence for Edith and me to become more than just friends; we were and are that fond of each other. I know my homosexuality will come as a great surprise to her when she learns of it, and I *am* planning to tell her about it during our next visit with each other, be it here in New York or in Toronto where she now makes her home.

Another plus result of Joan's and my involvement with *Shop*: Joan and I met and/or became acquainted with, by phone or correspondence or in personal meetings, a number of old friends of the Grosman clan. They were an interesting society of refugees and expatriates, this group of Czech Jews who had suffered through but survived the Holocaust, and then became scattered world-wide. Some had emigrated soon after the war, to the U.S., Canada, England, France, Switzerland, Israel, etc. Others picked up their lives in Czechoslovakia and rebuilt them, only to have their freedom threatened again in 1968 when Russia invaded. Ladislav and Edith Grosman and their teenage son Jiri fell into the latter category, and in '68 fled to Israel where some members of Edith's family had migrated earlier. Yet, scattered as they were, these old comrades kept in touch with each other through the years, and so it was my pleasure and Joan's to meet and be welcomed by, to dine with or correspond with, or be phoning, the Schermers of Toronto, and director Voytech Jasny of West Germany, and Edith's sisters and brother-in-law in Tel Aviv, and Ladislav's cousins in Troy, Michigan, Bernie and Emery Klein and their charming wives, the late director Jan Kadar in California, George and Alice Braun in Riverdale, New York, Ladislav's cousins, the Bramson family, in Mt. Kisco, New York, Ladislav's old friend, Arnost Lustig, when he was teaching in the southwest U.S.; and Ruth Kaminska, daughter of Ida Kaminska who starred in the film, and her friend, the late actor Karel Latowicz, and famed film directors Milos Forman and Ivan Passer, and American author Alan Levy who reversed the trend and settled in 1967 in Prague, soon to have to flee to Vienna to insure his and his family's safety and independence. And best of all, Ladislav and Edith's good friends, the warm, wonderful couple from Brooklyn, Bianca and Fred Baar. Joan and I learned almost as much about the Holocaust and the spirit of survival and bravery of a people from our contact with this group of new acquaintances as we ever would have known had we lived through those times ourselves, and I thank them all for welcoming us into their "inner circle" and making us feel at home with them. It has been a privilege and an honor.

And yet another plus: My dear wife Joan and my dear agent Bertha became loving friends because of *Shop* also. Joan was a teacher for almost ten months a year, but a full-time assistant to Bertha that first summer after the completion of the first draft of *The Shop On Main Street*, working exclusively on informing producers and directors and money-people about the existence of the show, and trying to enlist interest in it. With innocent grandiosity and optimism, Joan and I were sure we had something so extraordinary here that the producers would have to fight over who would bring this new musical to the world, for fear of not losing out on it. But I guess that really happens only in the movies!

Anyhow, *Shop* evidently did not strike New York theatrical producers as being as commercial as Joan and Saul and Bertha and I thought it would. It was the element of tragedy that most of them found risky, and spending big bucks on that risky a project was unheard of, particularly if the writers didn't have track records to speak of. Yet Joan and I couldn't reconcile that evaluation with the fact that *Carousel* and *West Side Story* and *Fiddler on the Roof*, and many other commercially and artistically successful musicals had elements of darkness or sadness or tragedy, and yet were readily accepted by the public. Therefore, for about two years, Joan and I proceeded with our grand plans, firmly believing that somewhere there was a producer out there who would take a chance. And so we reached them all, one by one. After all, didn't we have on our side that this was an important property, one that had been given an important award and that had achieved a modest amount of international fame? And we had the rights to it! Didn't that count for something? Obviously not enough.

The Shop on Main Street may well have shown up on the desks of more producers, theatrical attorneys, agents, directors, choreographers, Jewish businessmen and philanthropists and investors than any show in history—that's how well Joan did her work. And I must say that once sold on the project, she stayed sold, even more staunchly and longer than I. There was a point (in late '84 or early '85) at which I was ready to give up. The pursuit of a production was taking too much out of us and away from our family and friends. But it was Joan who talked me into giving the pursuit a "little" longer try, and it was during those next few months that we got the offer from Jewish Rep and decided to accept their production as a last resort. Several years earlier in the disappointment sweepstakes, for the express purpose of launching *The Shop on Main Street*, Joan resorted to registering herself as producer (still hoping to enlist the participation of more seasoned producers), and getting incorporated (she did so under the name of Tanrydoon Productions, Ltd., the name having been borrowed from her favorite old novel *Islandia*, roughly meaning "super-hospitality" from one friend to another as expressed in keeping a special place in each other's homes for each other). She hired a lawyer and general manager and whoever else she was told she needed in order to get S.E.C. clearance, a prospectus, Attorney General approval for raising money, and the works.

From that point on, for about three years, she and I juggled our paying careers with our non-paying careers on a daily basis (I assisted her in her theatrical management and producing efforts), meeting ever more prospective backers and professional theatre people with whom we would associate, and upon whom we called for assistance (paid and unpaid) in one way or another. Therein lies one more plus of the whole undertaking . . . our relationship with the wonderful professional people with whom we worked or associated over the last three years or two years or one year or several months (as each individual case may be) before the show actually went into its tryout production. These people included performers, our general manager Ralph Roseman of Theatre Now, Bill Herman of the accounting firm of Lutz and Carr, our attorney Robert Youdelman, our P.R. firm, Chen Sam, followed by our ongoing publicist, Dolph Browning, the fine seasoned agent Robert Lantz who had represented Ladislav Grosman on earlier efforts, our talented director Fran Soeder and our talented musical director Norman Weiss, the wonderfully talented people who helped us through several different and difficult major attempts at backers' auditions—Joe King and Naomi Riseman and Lynn Nickerson and Martha Schlamme, and other artists too numerous to name—and the management and staff at the Jewish Repertory Theatre on East 14th Street where the production was performed, and the limited partners who invested in this early production, thereby showing their ultimate faith in us and *Shop* as well. And our supportive families. Joan would have wanted me to thank all on her behalf and my own—and I do.

Joan died just after she had made one grand effort those last six months to raise money for what was then being referred to as a workshop production of *The Shop on Main Street*. A cousin of mine, Larry Landsman, with the assistance of his fiance, Alyson, videotaped Joan doing her spiel about investing, and then edited the video together with some scenes from the film *The Shop on Main Street*, along with audio of three songs from the show, and Joan used this 31-minute video as a sales tool in trying to develop new and additional financial interest in the show. It worked only minimally, but it was a great idea. During the last couple of months while she was showing the videotape around, her health began to fail seriously, but not before we had made final arrangements with Jewish Rep for *Shop* to fit into their second or third repertory season slot. Her surgery was performed again in Houston, again by Dr. Cooley, and because it had been so successful the first time, we were optimistic. Fool that I was, I couldn't and didn't conceive of coming back from Houston without her.

Right on schedule, *Shop* went into rehearsal about two months after Joan died, five-and-a-half-years after I'd started working on it. As I said before, it was like a mid-life baby for Joan and me. It has not been easy for me to re-live all this now by writing it down. Perhaps part of the reason for my surge into homosexuality was to escape from the tragedy of Joan's death and the enormous void I felt immediately afterward, and, to a certain extent, have been living with ever since. Even with all the effort that had gone into the show (particularly by Joan in those endless afternoons after coming home from a rough day in school to man the telephone for three productive hours before I returned from the office), I was ready to let it all go down the drain after I lost her. I truly no longer cared as much about the future of the show. More for the sake of the other people who had tried and were still trying so hard to help, and to simply tie things up neatly and let it go at that, I did finally give my approval to our going ahead with the commitment for the Jewish Rep production.

Unfortunately some ugly backstage arguments and confrontations took place while we were still in rehearsal and previews. Mostly they concerned Fran Soeder's making unauthorized deletions and substitutions which I as author should have had the right to approve. I let the alterations happen, not in an approving sense at all, but by refraining from being the fly in the ointment that would have closed the show before it opened. (That's how confrontational the differences were.) I owed the memory of Joan enough love and respect to let *Shop* go on peacefully, mutilated as it was, and then quietly withdraw. I only wish Fran Soeder had felt that he, too, owed Joan that kind of love and respect (and he did owe her at least that and a lot more), for then he might have acted more out of generosity to her memory and spirit than from his own arrogance and insecurity. I longed to record in writing the detailed history of his

"Mark Me Tomorrow" from *The Shop on Main Street*, music by Saul Honigman

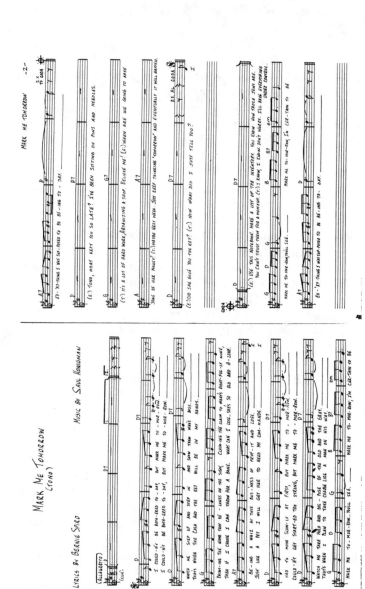

unprofessional attitude and conduct while artistically in charge of our production. Had Joan still been alive, he wouldn't have dared to even try to get away with the usurping of power that he engineered in those last weeks; in total disregard for the moral and ethical standards that should prevail in any business situation, he took advantage of a tragedy—the death of the producer, Joan—and had his own way entirely, despite the strong objections of the author and composer. I was planning to send the story about him, as a warning to other writers, to the Dramatists Guild, in the hope that the Guild would publish it. But my attempts at recounting and reliving the details of the actual events were so painful that I escaped as soon as I could, removed myself at least temporarily from the atmosphere and memory of the production and the quest for its fulfillment, and went on with the rest of my life.

In more than a few instances *Shop* was turned down by prospective producers because it was too big. That's a laugh today, what with size and expense being almost a prerequisite for insuring getting a production going (if you can get it produced in London first) rather than killing its chances. For example *Cats* and *Starlight Express* and *Phantom* and *Les Mis*—all so big and unique tech-wise that their theatres themselves had to be and were partly reconstructed before the shows could be accommodated.

Shop was big because I was trying to re-create a whole town and time, and as I first wrote the adaptation it required physical size and space. Also, what the hell, I was writing this big because I envisioned it as a possible successor to *Fiddler* on the Broadway stage in the hearts of Jewish theatregoers from New York—they with their theatre parties can be a unique animal, sometimes almost single-handedly responsible for the success of a show. Anyhow, because *Shop* was not going to be skimpy, I thought it was entirely within the realm of practicability to give it the following opening scene and musical number, "Triangle in the Square," which it actually had in the show's first, second and third drafts. But it had to be replaced with something far more simple when the mini-production actually took place, because of size, space and cost limitations.

(WORKMEN settle on or around the base of the frame of wooden pyramid under construction in the town square, in Sabinov, Czechoslovakia, June 1942. They sing)

High above the chestnut trees
Rises this isosceles
Triangle in the square.
Here amidst the street and shops
Flirting with the chimney tops—
Our triangle in the square.

What is it here for?
What does it stand for?
What is it doing in the middle of the square?
Why do we need it?
What do we feed it?
What is it brewing in the middle of the square?

Don't ask how it came to be
Or wherefore.
Word was spread the frame to be
Goes here—and therefore . . .

Saw the wood and sand it down.
Pass it up and hand it down.
Busily we've banded in mid-air
To see the job complete,
A tow'ring fifty feet (high!)
Of triangle in the square.

(The men are visited by Guardist Commander Marcus Kolkosky. The foreman calls the men to attention.)

MARCUS

At ease. I'm going up to the landing to wave at the crowd. Let the men take ten. (He starts his climb.)

(Underscoring and choreographed movement continue as Tono Britko enters, pulling a wagon with his dog Cognac in it, and looks over the work project as he is addressed by an older statesman, Kuchar, also an observer.)

KUCHAR

Hey, Tono . . . keeping an eye on our Tower of Babel, I see.

TONO

I've never seen such a waste of good lumber in my life.

KUCHAR

Tell me, how are you doing? I know there isn't much work for carpenters in town.

TONO

I get by with odd jobs. But my wife keeps complaining.

KUCHAR

Why not ask for work on the pyramid from your brother-in-law? There he is waving up there. Go on and smile at him. Maybe you'll win him over.

TONO

Who—Marcus? Never. He refused me once. "I've got better, cheaper carpenters than you," he said. He can go to hell.

KUCHAR

Give him time.

TONO

All the time he needs. Meanwhile, whenever I get the chance I come to see what's going on. So far they haven't passed any law against looking, have they?

I like being there
Wherever there's wood,
To breathe in the air
Wherever there's wood.
And always for me
It touches the heart.
Imagine a tree
Becoming a cradle or cart.

I picture the fun
Wherever there's wood
Of work being done
As proper men should.
I even enjoy
Just making repairs
Like mending a toy
Or fixing a table and chairs.

And from the smell and the sight
I feel the sun and its light.
I know the world is all right
Wherever there's wood.
And from the sound and the feel
I sense a fence or a wheel.
It all seems honest and real
Wherever there's wood.

These hands of mine ache
With nothing to make,
But give them a chance
To work as they should—
They practically dance
A polka all over the wood.

That is why I come by
Looking up in the sky
Where this pyramid stands.
Always questioning why
Aren't I climbing high
With some wood in my hands.
But I know deep inside
If I swallowed my pride
And I worked on that crate
With each ounce of my sweat
I would be more in debt
To a man that I hate.

KUCHAR
You mean he doesn't fill you with awe
Like no one else you ever saw?

TONO
For ten heller I'd burn down the pyramid, and him along with it.

KUCHAR
Good idea. But Shh! No so loud.

TONO
You know I only half mean it. The other half? . . .

I've busted my back,
Got drunk on shellac,

And splintered and bled
As much as I should.
Thank God when I'm dead
I'll still be surrounded by wood—
For God, it feels good
Wherever there's wood.

KUCHAR

Wherever except here. That much seems clear, Tono.

TONO

The damned thing confounds me. What do *you* think it really is?

KUCHAR

I can only guess, like you.
A new observatory
For viewing outer space;
It could be.
Perhaps the crowning glory
For all the master race;
It could be.

To please the German nation
And minimize their threat—
With deep appreciation
For not invading yet—
Instead of occupation,
This new erector set
Half the world can see . . .
It could be.

(Several workmen walk over and join in.)

KUCHAR

It could be, it could be, who knows?
But up, up, up it goes and grows—and . . .

(THE WORKMEN sing, joined at intervals in counter-point by Tono with his "Wood" theme and Kuchar with his "It Could Be" theme, and choregraphed.)

High above the chestnut trees
Rises this isosceles
Triangle in the square.
Here amidst the street and shops
Flirting with the chimney tops—
Our triangle in the square.

Don't ask how it came to be
Or wherefore.
Word was spread the frame to be
Goes here, and therefore . . .

Saw the wood and sand it down,

Pass it up and hand it down.
Busily we've banded in mid-air
To see the job complete,
A towering fifty feet (high!)
Of triangle in the square . . .
Of triangle in the square . . .
Of triangle in the square.

Overblown as it may be, "Triangle in the Square" had the right color and texture for the town and its people. But more than likely we'll never know how well or badly it worked. By the way, the dog in that proposed opener was for real. One of the first changes I made in adapting from the novel (and film) was to eliminate Tono's dog. But our director Fran Soeder wanted Cognac reinstated. In fact, in order to placate Fran, I even built up the dog's part a bit, and Cognac was still included in the cast during the first few weeks of the mini production's rehearsal, and into the third performance of previews, as I recall. But we had to terminate the poor animal's employment in order to preserve an aura of sanity for Gregg Edelman, our fine leading man, to perform in, for having a dog in the cast (especially in such a small production) was too awesome a responsibility. During rehearsals Saul and I were even asked, obviously before Cognac's dismissal, to write some new music and lyrics for Tono for when he was alone with the dog early in the show after the opening scene. We did, and the new work was quite good, but it, too, had to be eliminated when Cognac was. Several different attempts at a Number Two number were scrapped, notably several variations of "You Make Do," a song Saul and I spent many, many hours and days on. It was supposed to have summed up the futile relationship between Tono, the carpenter, and his nagging wife, and I think in its final re-write form it was quite acceptable and worthwhile, but Fran asked us to scrap it. Our first number in the show *as produced* was the title song, "The Shop on Main Street," which takes place when Tono Britko and wife Eveline are visited unexpectedly by Eveline's sister, Rose, and her husband, uniformed Marcus Kolkosky, the guardist commander who came to inspect the pyramid in the discarded opener "Triangle in the Square."

MARCUS

There are big things in store for you, Tono. I've made you Aryanizer of old Lautman's shop. Now maybe you'll be glad I'm your brother-in-law. (He flings a document at him.)

TONO (reading it aloud))

It is hereby decreed the Dry Goods shop of widow Lautman at 52 Main Street, is transferred to Antonin Britko.

EVELINE

Tono!

MARCUS

Heil Hitler! Now you're a rich store proprietor. Your carpentry days are over. (Sings, while during this entire scene they all do a good bit of drinking to celebrate.)

A bright new note,
A brand new song.
Come sing along.

Come sing along.
A glad refrain
About the shop on Main Street.

MARCUS, EVELINE and ROSE
A brand new job,
A nice old shop.
Come fill the cup
And never stop
With French champagne
To toast the shop on Main Street.

MARCUS
It may have been
A bit run down
But look, it's in
The heart of town.

ROSE
Location-wise,
No reason to complain . . .

MARCUS and ROSE
And mark my words,
You'll live in style.
A bank account
To make you smile . . .

MARCUS
You heart will sing
And like a king you'll reign . . .

MARCUS, EVELINE and ROSE
When you begin
Your future in
The shop on Main.

MARCUS
Why so pensive, Tono? You're the reason for the celebration.

TONO
There's plenty of people have grown fat on aryanization, but I've a feeling it
might make me sick.

MARCUS
What's to be sick about? The Widow Lautman is too old to take care of the
shop. You'll save it from going under.

ROSE (popping a sardine into Tono's mouth)
Come on now, try this in the meantime, and start getting used to living like
the rich.

Rich, rich, rich,
You are going to be rich

And you'll learn to see
The difference money makes.

    EVELINE
Rich, rich, rich,
We'll be elegant and rich,
Wearing fancy clothes
And eating fancy cakes.

    MARCUS
Drink, drink, drink
To your hour of success
And the family united once again.

    EVELINE
Think, think, think
Of the riches we'll possess
From the moment Tono steps inside and then . . .
Suddenly a tingling down his spine
As he repeats: "This shop is mine."

    TONO
This shop is mine?

    MARCUS, EVELINE and ROSE
This shop is mine!

For those who doubt
As well they might
Well, here it is
In black and white
That Tono Britko
Evermore shall reign
With pride and love
As master of
The shop on Main.

I've condensed the above scene, but retained as much of its guts as space will allow. Saul's bright and infectious European-flavored music was just right for keeping the action dominant, and for moving a complex scene briskly along. The number and scene worked well, although it is difficult to erase from my mind the brilliant scene from the Czech film which inspired it. Again in a condensed version, I next offer you the lyrics and skeleton of the scene of the next number, "Chatter of An Old, Old Woman," which takes place in Mrs. Lautman's shop the following morning when Tono tries to take over the business.

    TONO
Here, read this.

    MRS. LAUTMAN
I'm sorry. I don't see very well. Explain what it's about.

    TONO
I've been made Aryan Controller of your shop.

MRS. LAUTMAN

Oh, buttons. Bone or wood? We have a very large selection.

TONO

Look, Mrs. Lautman—you're Jewish, right? And I'm an Aryan. Jewish shops are finished. Kaput. It's the law now. From now on this shop belongs to me. It says so right here.

MRS. LAUTMAN

Mmm. Interesting. You're from Taxes and Excise?

TONO

Not Excise. Aryanize.

MRS. LAUTMAN

I'll get the file out in a minute. (She goes scurrying off to look for some papers while continuing to talk.) How old would the young gentleman be now? Not forty yet, I'd guess. Oh, dear, what did I do with them? I've got two daughters myself, you know, Clarica and Pirica—and my poor dead husband, Heinrich . . . well, well, what is past is past . . . what did the young gentleman say his name was?

TONO

Britko. Tono Britko.

MRS. LAUTMAN

Brisket?

TONO

Britko. With a "ko."

MRS. LAUTMAN

I was right what I thought the minute I saw you. Such a fine young gentleman. But you have to be patient with me. (sings)

Please forgive the chatter
Of an old, old woman.
Sometimes I don't hear well anymore
Even though my memory is clear
Of many things I used to hear before.

Now and then I chatter
Like an old, old woman
When I'm having trouble with my sight.
Then I turn to pictures of the past.
They mean much more than words in black and white.

TONO

This is now, Mrs. Lautman, not the past.

MRS. LAUTMAN

Oh, the past.

Well, I like to sit and talk

About my wedding,
My handsome bridegroom
With lovelight beaming,
And the music I still hear
Like kettles whistling,
And Sabbath singing . . .
Or am I dreaming?

I suppose I chatter
Like and old, old woman.
Also I'm forgetful and confused.
Did I ask if you could stay for tea?

TONO

No, but about this . . .

MRS. LAUTMAN

I've been so busy you would be amused.

But don't think that I'm complaining
Or I worry
That growing old means growing lonely, too.

TONO

That's not what was on my mind.

MRS. LAUTMAN

No, not while all the chatter
Of an old, old woman
Is listened to by someone nice . . . like you.

TONO

Listen is right. You don't let me get in a word.

MRS. LAUTMAN

Would you believe, Mr. Brisket . . .

TONO

Britko. With a "ko."

MRS. LAUTMAN

. . . there are certain times of day I still hear my children playing? They're all grown up now and far, far away. But even so, I hear them.

And I see my papa smile
And Mama crying
With Rabbi saying
The wedding blessing,
And I feel my husband's
Ring upon my finger,
His arms around me,
His eyes caressing.

Look at these photographs. That's my younger brother Joseph before he went to America and sent for my children. "You're a widow," he told me. "I can provide for their future better than you can," he said. Ah, me . . . he was right.

But don't think it's only memories that matter.

> TONO
>
> God forbid!

> MRS. LAUTMAN
>
> Oh, no. I've got a million things to do.

> TONO
>
> So I've noticed.

> MRS. LAUTMAN
>
> While in between the chatter
> Of an old, old woman . . .

> TONO
>
> Mrs. Lautman, I . . .

> MRS. LAUTMAN
>
> Sha!
>
> I listen to a fine young man like you.

> TONO
>
> I give up!

(Music tag.)

Tono is convinced by Kuchar (his and Mrs. Lautman's mutual friend) to let her think that he's a shop assistant, for she knows nothing about aryanization and probably doesn't even know there's a war on. In a complete departure from anything else in the show rhythmically, but thoroughly in keeping with the plot and situation, for "Mark Me Tomorrow" Saul composed a musical accompaniment that is wonderfully ironic and resolute and melodically enhances everything the lyric is saying, and seems to be the most seamless, effortless piece of work we've ever done together, even though it is over and done with in hardly more than a moment, and doesn't often come to mind when we select our favorites. It takes place on Tono's way home after his first day in the shop. He's talking to himself, trying to reassure himself that he's not being won over by the old woman.

> TONO
>
> What the devil? How did I let them twist things around like that—so that I'm working for her? And I'm even fool enough to go along with it. How stupid can I be? Don't answer that question. (sings)

I couldn't be bothered today,
> But mark me tomorrow.
> Watch me step up and step in
> And show them who's boss.
> Painting the name
> That belongs on the sign,

Claiming the claim
To what's rightfully mine.
Being a whiz
At this business of profit and loss.

I had to move slowly at first
But mark me tomorrow.
Watch me take hold
And dispose of the old and the gray.
Mark me tomorrow—you'll see.
Mark me tomorrow; I'm certain to be
Everything I was supposed to be being today.

(He arrives home.)

EVELINE

Tono, what kept you so late? I've been sitting on pins and needles.

TONO

It's a lot of hard work, Aryanizing a shop, believe me. But the way I look at it, the shop is like a cow. A cow's got to have hay to produce; a shop's got to have money. If you put money into a shop, the gold'll come streaming in like milk from a good milker.

EVELINE

All right, but when are we going to get some of it?

TONO

Maybe next week. Maybe next month. But just keep thinking "tomorrow" and soon enough it will happen.

EVELINE

Did she give you the key?

TONO

Now, what did I just tell you?

I couldn't be bothered today,
But mark me tomorrow.
That's when the cash and the key
Will be in my hands.
Then if I choose
I can throw her a bone.
What can I lose?
She's so old and alone.
Just like a pet,
I will get her to heed my commands.

I couldn't get started too strong,
But mark me tomorrow.
That's when I plan to take charge
Like a man on his way.
Mark me tomorrow, you'll see.
Mark me tomorrow,

I'm certain to be
Everything I was supposed to be being today.

EVELINE

Use this notebook. Make a list of the inventory. You know how those Jews are. You can't trust them for a moment.

TONO

I know. I know. Don't worry. I'll have everything under control.
Mark me tomorrow, you'll see.
Mark me tomorrow; I'm certain to be
Everything I was supposed to be being today!

The following morning is the Jewish Sabbath but Tono doesn't care, and wants to open the shop. He and Mrs. Lautman have their first opportunity for domesticity with each other in the scene and musical number "Someone to Do For"

TONO

We've got to hurry and open the shop. There's a lot of people in from the country. We could do good business.

MRS. LAUTMAN

I know exactly how you feel. I just had breakfast, but there's plenty left for you.

(He glances about as she arranges a table setting.)

TONO

You've got too much furniture for such a small space. Also, it could use a new veneer. In a week I could have everything as good as new.

MRS. LAUTMAN

I'm not rich, but there's sure to be something of Heinrich's that you could use. Shirts. A suit. An umbrella. A hat. We'll see about it soon. Come eat.

TONO

No breakfast, Mrs. Lautman. It's time to open the shop.

MRS. LAUTMAN

The shop? Whatever are you thinking of? I've never opened on Shabbas in my life. Now don't refuse. I know very well you haven't had any breakfast. And here's some gefilte fish left over from last night, if you feel like a taste.

(She scurries off to her bedroom, going to a closet to remove some of Heinrich's clothes. A spot remains on Tono as he eats, then surveys the land.)

TONO

So this is gefilte fish, eh? Hmm. Not bad. (sings)

So I'll wait . . .
For another week or two
To be rich.
What's my hurry?

MRS. LAUTMAN

It's so nice . . .

Hearing someone else's voice
Even though . . .
He talks softly.

TONO
What a mess . . .
Every piece of wood is scratched
And like her . . .
It's old fashioned.

MRS. LAUTMAN
He should fit . . .
Into all of Heinrich's clothes
Even though . . .
He looks thinner.

TONO
I'll let her keep the running
Of the business to herself
As long as I get my share.

MRS. LAUTMAN
I'll use him just to carry
Or to reach the highest shelf,
But otherwise who needs him there?

TONO
Poor woman doesn't even know
She's lucky that it's me.

MRS. LAUTMAN
Poor nebbish doesn't even know
How lucky one can be.

TONO
But she will soon enough, when I make this place look like new.

MRS. LAUTMAN
But he will soon enough, when I put some meat on his bones.

(She sings while removing and smoothing out some of Heinrich's clothes.)

Someone to do for,
I've someone to do for.
Such a good feeling—
The power of healing
Is someone to do for.

Someone to share with—
How strange!
A real human being
For touching and seeing;
It's nice for a change.

Someone to care for,

To please and prepare for,
And aren't I lucky
He's perfectly happy to be
My someone to do for
Who also has someone,
His someone to do for . . . in me.

(Lights dim on her and intensify on Tono who is seen examining the furniture.)

TONO

Well, it'll take a little longer than I expected—but—
Someone to do for,
I've someone to do for.
Such a good feeling,
The power of healing
Is someone to do for.

Someone who tells me . . .
I can.
My own human being
Who sits there agreeing
That I am a man.

Someone to stay with,
To help pass the day with,
And aren't I lucky
She's perfectly happy to be
My someone to do for
Who also has someone,
Her someone to do for . . . in me.

(She returns holding Heinrich's coat and hat.)

MRS. LAUTMAN

Here, try these on.

TONO (getting into the coat.)

I'll bring my tools Monday. I was wrong. You have enough repair work here
to keep me busy for months.

MRS. LAUTMAN

Now the hat. Try on the hat.

TONO (looking into mirror to adjust it)

Imagine that . . . a perfect fit. I look like Charlie Chaplin.
(They turn away from each other; he sings.)

Someone to care for . . .

MRS. LAUTMAN

To please and prepare for . . .

BOTH

And aren't I lucky
She's (he's) perfectly happy to be

My someone to do for
Who also has someone,
Her (his) someone to do for . . . in me.

(Lights fade as they slowly turn toward each other.)

In *The New York Times* review of the production, the lyrics for the above number were singled out as being banal, and the reviewer even quoted a phrase or two, and was careless enough to *mis*quote. This less than fair judgment, and an historical inaccuracy about the Holocaust in another review in a holier-than-thou assessment, should give you an idea of my general opinion of reviews and critics.

The next number is stagey and artificial, compared to some of the naturalistic material from *Shop* reprinted so far. But as far as I'm concerned it's a fine example of what can be done in musical theatre to make a whole town come to life in one brief scene of song and dialog. It's called "Noon Sunday Promenade." Again, Saul's music provided superb accompaniment for the words.

By the way, even though this number and scene were completely removed from the mini-production at Jewish Rep (by Fran Soeder) and without Saul's or my agreement for him to do so, it worked wonderfully well as staged by Fran and our expert choreographer, Janet Watson, for it *was* thoroughly staged and rehearsed before being dropped! It's primarily an ensemble number with leading cast and chorus members taking turns at lyrics and interspersed dialog. The dialog and description of accompanying action are eliminated from this reprinting.

All set to begin
Is the noon Sunday promenade.
Just settling in
Is the band in the square.
Come follow the throng
To the noon Sunday promenade.
Come follow the song
Through the noon Sunday air.

Now leaving behind
The organ's peal
All having made peace with God—
Everyone—
All over the town
Joins in neighborly, leisurely
Sun-radiant fun at the noon promenade—
Noon promenade.

Alms for the poor,
Alms for the blind,
Midst your procession of legs.
Is there a heart?
Is there an ear
To hear what the beggarman begs for?

Fine gentlemen dressed
With a touch of gentility,
Fine women caressed

By their silken chemise.
Fine weather suggesting
That all is tranquility.
God doing his best
And his utmost to please.

Come echo the mood
Of oom-pa-pah!
Come follow the leader's nod!
Everyone—
All over the town
Finding gentle, romantical
Sun-radiant fun
At the noon promenade—
Noon promenade.

Have some ice cream,
Chocolate ice cream.
Or sherbet in rum or lime.
Come have your fill
While it is still
Hours till dinner time.

Some ready to fight
At the noon Sunday promenade.
Some shedding some light
On the news of the day.
None ready for war
At the noon Sunday promenade.
All practicing peace
In their own special way.

How comforting, guards
In uniform
Upholding the calm facade.
Everyone—
All over the town
Echos affable, sociable
Sun-radiant fun
At the noon promenade,
Noon promenade.

Come see your image
In charcoal and whites
Blossom in front of your eyes.
Sit for your portrait
And take in the sights.
You're in for a lovely surprise.

I make *everybody* beautiful!

A small bouquet,
Dear sir, I pray,
To warm the lady's heart . . .

A simple spray
Of buds today
Tonight will play their part.

Youth having its fling
Would appear irrepressible.
Thank goodness that Spring
Now is ending at last.
All over the town
Girls are all too accessible.
All over the town
Boys are learning too fast.

Sky-high in the square
The frame that grows
Looms bigger than life, and odd—
Isn't it?
All over the town
We have happy-go-lucky and
Sun-radiant fun
At the noon promenade—
Noon promenade!

Next was a bright and comic number to open Act Two, "Market Day." Like almost every other number, this, too, went through its quota of rewrites before the final version herewith. This last version was "Market Day" at its best, and is an interesting example of exigencies caused by actual production being responsible for improvement. We had reshaped and rewritten "Market Day" at almost the last minute in order to have pity on our leading lady, the wonderful Lilia Skala, and turn a song full of rapid fire lyrics and movement over to the care of the much younger and more energetic and equally wonderful male lead, Gregg Edelman. As I condense the lyric for including the scene and lyric herewith, I'll refer to all the various customers as "CUSTOMER." For these purposes it doesn't matter which customer is delivering the line. But I must also add a disappointing postscript and advise that this number and scene were among the material totally removed from the final production by Fran Soeder without my knowledge and against my will.

CUSTOMERS (in rapid fire)
Who are you? . . . Where's Mrs. Lautman? . . . Do you have any rickrack? . .
Why aren't you open early for Market Day?

TONO
We *are* open. For an hour already. I—uh—had to go to the toilet, so I locked the door for five minutes. She'll be back right away. Be patient. Look around.

CUSTOMER
You're her new assistant?

TONO
Oh, no. I own the place. She still takes care of the shop. I have other work— inside.

CUSTOMER

Do you have rickrack or don't you?

TONO

Oh, sure. Gallons. Just wait. Mrs. Lautman will show you where. "Now that I've got somebody to mind the store," she said to me, "I can go shopping like everybody else on Market Day." So off she went. But she'll be back any minute, I promise. (To himself) Just my luck. Not a single customer all morning, and now three at one time.

CUSTOMERS

That's the way on Market Day. That's the way on Market Day.
Curtain rings?
Tinsel strings?
Show me where is rickrack.

TONO

What the hell is rickrack?

CUSTOMERS

Such a nice assortment you have out
And on display,
I could spend a week or two
If you would let me stay.

TONO

Mrs. Lautman would say better you should buy something early and get home in time to make supper for your husband.

CUSTOMERS

I need snaps.
I need straps.
Show me where are pompoms.

TONO

What about the rickrack?

CUSTOMERS

Finally a thing or two that's new
I'm glad to say.

TONO

Maybe for a change you'll buy from us
This Market Day.

CUSTOMER

Where did you get the extra stock from this week?

TONO

You won't believe it. It was here all the time. In boxes on the top shelves for maybe ten years already.

On Saturday was Shabbas.
I took down twenty stacks.

CUSTOMER
You mustn't work on Shabbas.
My, no!

TONO
I know.
I did it to relax.

CUSTOMERS
God bless him!

I need crepe.
Mending tape.
Show me where are zippers.

TONO
What about the pompoms?

CUSTOMERS
All a body needs
From bugle beads
To pine sachet,
Everything with bows, a few with lace
Nestle-ing in rows ail through the place,
Brimming to the top at Lautman's shop
On Market Day.

TONO
Let me remind you, it's all marked down today.

CUSTOMER
Oh, how much are these?

TONO
One crown forty.

CUSTOMERS
You call that cheap?
What is she getting for kerchiefs?
Three crowns.
Offer two.
I can do better at Rubin's.
So what else is new?
Such an old fashioned assortment.
Some nerve, asking three.
What are they getting at Rubin's?
Who knows? Let's go see.

TONO
Just a minute. Where are you going? The best bargain is always here.

(Mrs. Lautman returns and sets down a parcel. All eyes are upon her.)

CUSTOMERS

Finally you're here, Rosalie. What kept you so long? How much for these kerchiefs?

MRS. LAUTMAN

Not a thread out of place . . . friend or family only one price, three crowns . . . not a heller less.

CUSTOMERS

I wonder if this one was always so yellow . . . Don't believe everything you see.

A-one she says, so old
They're barely worth a single crown.
By now the whites are yellow
And the yellows a golden brown.

So bargain, haggle all you want
And hondle all you may.
In just a week it falls apart
No matter what you pay.

Yes, that's the way on Market Day.
That's the way on Market Day.

Oh, I forgot, I also need a sampler. Have you got, Rosalie?

MRS. LAUTMAN

Tono—a box of samplers I need. Up there, like a good boy.

(She starts putting boxes away; he starts to climb a ladder for the samplers, and the customers start to leave—all at the same time.)

CUSTOMERS

My, it's late.
I can't wait.

TONO

Let me find the samplers.

CUSTOMER

Never mind the samplers.

TONO

How about a set
Of "Home Sweet Home" and "Let Us Pray"?

CUSTOMERS

Only if they come in pink and blue . . .
Maybe in a week you'll have some new . . .
Maybe in a week some rickrack, too . . .

ALL

On Market Day!

For the last lyric to be included here I've chosen "Who Are They to Me?," Tono's "eleven o'clock" number. It takes place inside the shop the following morning, while he is very drunk, and not able to cope with the blare of the loudspeakers outside in the town square which is calling up the Jews alphabetically (for transporting to concentration camps), instructing them to weigh in and line up in twos, and which warns that anyone harboring Jews will be punished.

Who are they to me?
Who are they to me?
Berman, Rabbi Blau and Nathan Bloomberg,
Who are they to me?
Who am I to care?
Who am I to care,
Care how they will fare, and when and how
And where they're going to be?

Who am I to cry?
Better say goodbye.
Danko and your mama, Mrs. Elias—
See, my eyes are dry.
Better turn away,
Turn away and say
They are only neighbors,
Only neighbors I may never see.

This is the way the world is run now—
Special laws for Jews,
Marching off in twos,
Obeying don'ts and do's.

This is the way to get things done now—
Quicker than a wink,
Not much time to think—
Except, I think,
I think, I think . . .
I think I need another drink.
(He drains the bottle.)
Who are they to me?
Who are they to me,
Erzika, the girl, and Katz, the barber,
Who are they to me?
Why should I complain?
Why should I despair,
Pitying a kid and some old . . . yid . . .
Who cut a little hair?

Let them go on with their lives
Long as they leave me be.
I have the right to my life . . .
Weren't we all born free?
Weren't we? Weren't we? Weren't we?
(sound of names reverberating.)
God damn Berman, Blau and Bloomberg!
God damn Goldberg, Greenberg, Grosman!

God damn Kuchar, Katz and Lautman!
Who are they to me?

[One brief digression about the use of the word "yid." I, the lyricist, was in the minority about the advisability of its use. Why, I wonder? Didn't Aryans, regardless of their sympathies, use the word in those days? Don't they occasionally still use it today? Tono, the poor carpenter, was trying to express himself in a moment of crisis. He was reaching for words that would come naturally to him, words he was brought up to use.

Why should writers be afraid to acknowledge that such prejudice existed, and be censored from putting such a word into the mouths of fictional characters they are creating, even sympathetic characters? Don't the best-intentioned of us in this ostensibly more enlightened age still secretly harbor a trace of prejudice here and there? Yet everybody was against me on that one, and so I acquiesced, and when the scene was performed, another line was substituted for the "yid" line. Yet, if there is ever another production of this version of *Shop*, or if it is ever published, as long as I am still its author, the line will read as it does above, "yid" included.]

What will happen with *The Shop on Main Street* in the future? Possibly nothing. But once again, if there are any would-be producers out there for cable, video, refilming in English this time, or restaging the play, the Grosmans and I are all ears, and you may contact us through the publisher of this book, or my ever-persevering agent, Bertha Klausner. If any of my readers wants to see and hear what the Jewish Rep mini-production looked and sounded like, there's a videotape of it in the archives of the Theatre on Videotape Department at the New York Library for the Performing Arts at Lincoln Center. I was having it shown just recently in fact, trying to get feedback from several new friends as to whether or not it paid to go any further with the show. To reiterate: I first created and imagined and wrote *Shop* as a large musical. Due to failure to raise enough money after over five years of effort, and mistakenly being unwilling after all that effort to just let the show lie or drop it altogether, I short-sightedly permitted *Shop* to be produced as not only a small musical, but as one that would almost inevitably become decimated and mutilated in the shrinking. Recently I've also written a small non-musical dramatic adaptation of *Shop*, and submitted it to a number of regional theatres, and judging from the lack of interest so far, it may simply be true, though I still doubt it, that *Shop* doesn't work "small" on the stage, in whatever version. But it should, because it's an intimate story, and so I must grant that maybe I haven't yet found the right key.

Perhaps I should settle for the likelihood that there's no future for *Shop* at all. Or perhaps with more distancing of time I'll be able to look back at the project more objectively one of these days, find some new ideas, and set off on still another new version. But for now, having explored it all I can for the moment, I shall permit the memory of it rest in peace as I envision it ever so gently drifting in space, hovering somewhere near the quiet graves of Ladislav Grosman and my darling Joan.

SEVENTEEN

The rest of the 80's; where we are and who we are
today and what about tomorrow?

A mixed bag of parodies and odds and ends from "How are
things at Bertha Klausner's?/Is it still a little crowded there?" to
"Don't sway those hips at me/Or pinch my tiddy-oh!/Or porn-o
my video./People will say we're in love."

THE SHOP ON MAIN STREET was so consuming that I didn't have time (or inspiration) during the 80's for any other major writing projects. Bearing in mind that famous lyricists such as Sammy Cahn also write parodies because they enjoy doing so and meet with responsive audiences, I too have been keeping my lyric hand having fun from time to time with things like "The Singalong with Bertha Klausner Happy Birthday Songbook" (for her 80th Birthday celebration nine years ago), with printed copies for all the invited guests to join in, on a half-dozen or so parodies such as (to the tune of "Glocca Morra"):

> How are things at Bertha Klausner's?
> Is it still a little crowded there?
> Do the readers still make quiet trips
> Through manuscripts
> That pile up everywhere?
>
> How are things at Bertha Klausner's?
> Does the joy of working fill the air?
> Busy fingers walking miles and miles
> Through index files,
> And telephones that ring
> clinching business deals
> Over home-cooked meals?
>
> So I ask her other clients
> And each former employee
> And most anyone she might invite to tea . . .
> How are things at Bertha Klausner's Agency?

Or—having established the format above—"The Singalong with Ruth and Bernard Happy 25th Anniversary Songbook"—for cousins Ruth and Bernard. To the tune of "Hello Dolly:"

> Hello, Ruthie,
> And Hello, Bernie.
> It's so nice to see you
> breeze through twenty-five.
>
> Though you're some pounds thicker

Still the sparks flicker,
So in truth, by George,
By Bern, by Ruth,
You're still alive.

And one thing's sure, Bernie—
If you still journey
To Lovers' Lane with Ruth but once a year—then—

She's still *your* Ruthie.
Honest, who could ask for more, Ruthie?
Twenty five more and you may score again.

Or—to help celebrate a special occasion for Gerie Gore, wife of the president of Chester Gore Company (the last ad agency I worked at full-time), a remarkable, diminutive, close-cropped gray-haired woman who performed devotedly and expertly year after year as Administrative Vice President, an office which included such diverse chores and tapped such diverse skills and expertise as "Key operator" repair of the copy machines, office carpentry, advice and instruction on golf and golf equipment, writing memos at the drop of a hat which she highlighted decoratively with colored magic marker pens and readily signed with her trademark "GG,"—the following lyric which I wrote fittingly enough to the tune of "Gigi" by Frederick Loewe, with an accompanying piece of actual "Gigi" sheet music doctored up to include Gerie's photo on the cover, and my lyrics instead of Alan Jay Lerner's matching Loewe's notes on the inside. It would also help to be advised that Chester Gore Co. was also known as C.G.C.

G.G.,
Our very own key operator,
Also veep administrator.
What a pair!
G.G.,
Our very energetic young gray mare.

G.G.,
Who with a burst of versatility
And ready knack
Can prove
With a screwdriver or ir'n
She's crack-erjack!

Oh, G.G.,
The girl with twice the same initial,
Making doub-le-ly official
She's got clout—
Oh, G.G.,
With pretty colors striping
All she's typing out.

After the day's first memorandum
Come a dozen more in tandem
From the G.G.
C.G.C. couldn't do without.

With my new sexual liberation I've also engaged in some flirtatious writing, and, again partly to keep the required mental gymnastics in motion, and partly for the fun of being "naughty" and/or romantic at an atypically naughty and romantic age, I've also come up with a few outrageous verses such as the following. I urge my readers to bear in mind that what most responsible gay men actually do sexually in this day of the terrible scourge of AIDS is much safer than what we may allude to. "People Will Say We're in Love"

> Don't sway those hips at me
> Or pinch my tiddy-oh!
> Don't porn-o my video.
> People will say we're in love
>
> Don't lick those lips at me
> Or eye my "ratio."
> They'll guess—it's fellatio.
> People will say we're in love.
>
> Use no—erecting things,
> Things to insert, push or shove.
> Sweetheart—they're suspecting things.
> People will say—
> What the hell—let them say—
> People will say we're in love.

And to celebrate the wedding of new friends Fred and Phyllis, who decided to make it legal after a five-year live-in tryout—to "Love and Marriage"

> Fred and Phyllis,
> Fred and Phyllis . . .
> With their five-year-plan head start to thrill us
> Now shall never falter.
> At last they've made it to the altar.
>
> Fred and Phyllis,
> Fred and Phyllis . . .
> Love in blossom like an amaryllis,
> Stronger by the hour
> But sweeter still than any flower.
>
> Try, try, try to separate 'em.
> Wow, would they learn ya!
> Try, try, try to separate 'em . . .
> God, you'd get a "hernya."
>
> Fred and Phyllis,
> Fred and Phyllis . . .
> With their song of love to "whip-poor-will" us
> Sing so well together
> That love's sweet song
> A lifetime long
> Will ring out strong and clear . . . forever.

Also to keep the thought processes active, I've started writing greeting card verses again—to people who were never on my receiving list before, the most recent being my two sons-in-law and my granddaughter. To my amazement I received a poem in return recently from Son-in-Law Number One. It was good, too! I never knew he had it in him.

I'm sure there'll be another project coming up soon of book and lyrics for a musical, though I don't know yet what it is likely to be. There are about a half-dozen candidates I've given some thought to. I have the desire to keep working, but possibly no longer the compulsion. We'll see. I think half the fun of working through past years was in sharing the work with Joan when it was "hot off the typewriter." This indeed is another day. No more Joan with whom to have instant replay And for that matter no more typewriter. It's amazing that at 65 I could have adapted so readily to the word processor I purchased when I was just about finishing chapter two of this book. I'm an old hand at it now, and I wouldn't go back to typing if my life depended on it.

As I mentioned before, after the first draft of this book, I put together a small, intimate musical revue consisting of favorite miscellaneous songs and scenes from miscellaneous projects included herein. That also helped me take inventory. Now that that phase is over, there are lots of other little details in my life that I'd like to get in order before starting on another major writing project. But probably the writing project, whatever it turns out to be, will win out in the end, and the details will remain on the "I'll do it tomorrow" list.

But this one, this book, has certainly been the big project I've had to get off my chest and out of the way first, in order to help me re-structure my life and career, and see where and who I am. And in order for me to start dealing with the catharsis of my coming out to the world, even though so far it's been mostly just by word-processor. This book, therefore, by enabling me to make a statement about myself professionally and personally, all of me, loud and clear, for the first time in my life, is the first step in the rest of my life. And I find that I like me as I am, and I very much like being able to say this openly after a lifetime of seeing myself and my lust as abhorrent. To any of my readers who are dubious about themselves, I highly recommend the feeling of self-pride in gayness and the ability to be open about it. For your sake, whoever and wherever you are, I hope you don't have to wait till you're 65 to reach a similar state of self-acceptance. It was much too long in coming.